# OTITIS MEDIA
## and Child Development

# Otitis Media
# And
# Child Development

Edited By
James F. Kavanagh, Ph.D.

York Press / Parkton, Maryland

This book was manufactured in the United States of America. Typography by Brushwood Graphics Studio, Baltimore, Maryland. Printing and binding by Maple Press, York, Pennsylvania. Cover design by Joseph Dieter, Jr.

Proceedings of a conference on otitis media and child development in a series titled *Communicating by Language* sponsored by National Institute of Child Health and Human Development, National Institutes of Health.

Library of Congress Catalog Card Number 86-50578
ISBN 0-912752-12-2

# Contents

# Foreword

The research programs of the National Institute of Child Health and Human Development (NICHD) are shaped around the concept that events in the early phases of the life cycle are critical in child development. There are exceptional opportunities during that time to prevent disabilities that may affect children later in their lives, even into adulthood.

One condition that presents this opportunity is otitis media. Although otitis media is one of the most common childhood ailments, especially during the first three years of life, its treatment remains one of the most controversial issues in pediatrics today. The effect of otitis media, with or without effusion, in infancy and early childhood on learning and cognitive development in later life is also the topic of some debate.

The conference reported in the pages of this volume addressed these issues from a multidisciplinary perspective. I wish to thank the conferees, leaders from diverse disciplines, who participated in the conference and prepared chapters for this book. I especially appreciate their advice regarding research that is needed to help resolve some of the controversies regarding otitis media, its treatment, and its effect on learning.

*Duane Alexander, M.D.*
*Director*
*National Institute of Child*
*Health and Human Development*

# Preface

Since it was established in 1962, the National Institute of Child Health and Human Development (NICHD), one of the twelve component Institutes of the National Institutes of Health, has supported fundamental biological and behavioral research to better understand the processes of normal child development and the factors that may interfere with or delay this process. One aspect of child development which has received special attention from the NICHD focuses on the mechanisms whereby children acquire and develop the ability to communicate, learn to speak, use language, master reading skills, and acquire knowledge.

For more than two decades, the conference series "Communicating by Language" has been an integral part of the NICHD's research effort. Through these meetings and resultant publications, the Institute has attempted to determine existing and potential directions of study and to identify the roles which various disciplines can and do play in expanding that knowledge, both independently and jointly. (Publications in this conference series are listed at the end of the Preface.)

With its child development orientation, the NICHD naturally and appropriately became interested in otitis media (OM), and its possible relationship to subsequent development. Otitis media is one of the most common diseases of childhood and one of the most frequent reasons for a young child to require medical attention. Most children with otitis media with effusion (fluid in the middle ear, i.e., behind the ear drum) have some degree of conductive hearing loss. This mild to moderate loss is frequently temporary because the otitis media usually is of short duration. It is well established that an uncorrected severe hearing loss in infancy will adversely affect a child's development of speech, language, reading, cognitive skills and academic achievement. However, one of the most controversial issues in pediatrics today concerns not only the treatment of otitis media, but also the consequences of OM and the resultant, usually temporary, hearing loss on later child development.

Many years ago I had a personal and very traumatic experience with my daughter's otitis media, her subsequent hearing loss, and speech/language disability. This experience prompted a long-standing interest in the problem and a desire to hold a meeting to exchange information about otitis media and its possible consequences with representatives of various disciplines related to the problem. That scientific exchange took place at the National Institutes of Health in Bethesda, Maryland, on September 29–October 2, 1985. This book, the product of the meeting, provides a deeper understanding of this disease and the role it may play in child development, and should help the NICHD and the scientific community identify and plan new research as well as provide clinicians and parents with practical directions.

I wish to thank all of the participants for their generous contributions of time and expertise during the conference and in the preparation of their chapters for this book.

Mrs. Etta Kidwell deserves special credit for her invaluable help during the preparation for the conference and the subsequent publication.

Finally, I wish to express appreciation to my wife, Kitty, who provided support throughout all phases of this project and who shared with me the deep concern for our young child and her otitis media.

*James F. Kavanagh, Ph.D.*

# Publications in the "Communicating By Language" Series

David B. Gray and James F. Kavanagh (eds.). 1985. *Biobehavioral Measures of Dyslexia*. Parkton, MD: York Press.

Grace H. Yeni-Komshian, James F. Kavanagh, and Charles A. Ferguson (eds.). 1980. *Child Phonology*. Volume I: Production. Volume II: Perception. New York: Academic Press.

James F. Kavanagh and Richard L. Venezky (eds.). 1980. *Orthography, Reading, and Dyslexia*. Baltimore, MD: University Park Press.

James F. Kavanagh and Winifred Strange (eds.). 1978. *Speech and Language in the Laboratory, School, and Clinic*. Cambridge, MA: MIT Press.

James F. Kavanagh and James E. Cutting (eds.). 1975. *The Role of Speech in Language*. Cambridge, MA: MIT Press.

James F. Kavanagh and Ignatius G. Mattingly (eds.). 1972. *Language by Ear and by Eye: The Relationships between Speech and Reading*. Cambridge, MA: MIT Press.

James F. Kavanagh (ed.). 1968. *The Reading Process*. Washington, D.C.: Government Printing Office. (0-324-414)

Arthur S. House (ed.). 1967. *The Speech Process*. Washington, D.C.: Government Printing Office.

Frank Smith and George A. Miller (eds.). 1966. *The Genesis of Language: A Psycholinguistic Approach*. Cambridge, MA: MIT Press.

# Participants

**Duane Alexander, M.D.**
National Institute of Child
 Health and Human
 Development
National Institutes of Health
Bethesda, MD 20892

**LaVonne Bergstrom, M.D.**
Division of Head and Neck
 Surgery
University of California
Los Angeles, CA 90024

**Fred H. Bess, Ph.D.**
Division of Hearing and Speech
 Sciences
Vanderbilt University Medical
 School
Nashville, TN 37212

**Julia M. Davis, Ph.D.**
Department of Speech
 Pathology and Audiology
University of Iowa
Iowa City, IA 52242

**Peter D. Eimas, Ph.D.**
Department of Psychology
Brown University
Providence, RI 02912

**Lynne Feagans, Ph.D.**
Department of Individual and
 Family Studies
The Pennsylvania State
 University
University Park, PA 16802

**Heidi Feldman, M.D., Ph.D.**
Child Development Unit
Children's Hospital of Pittsburgh
Pittsburgh, PA 15213

**Sandy Friel-Patti, Ph.D.**
Callier Center for
 Communication Disorders
University of Texas at Dallas
Dallas, TX 75235

**Rochel Gelman, Ph.D.**
Department of Psychology
University of Pennsylvania
Philadelphia, PA 19104

**G. Scott Giebink, M.D.**
Department of Pediatrics
University of Minnesota
Minneapolis, MN 55455

**James J. Jenkins, Ph.D.**
Department of Psychology
University of South Florida
Tampa, FL 33620

**Jerome Kagan, Ph.D.**
Department of Psychology
Harvard University
Cambridge, MA 02138

**James F. Kavanagh, Ph.D.**
Center for Research for Mothers
 and Children
National Institute of Child
 Health and Human
 Development
National Institutes of Health
Bethesda, MD 20892

**Jerome O. Klein, M.D.**
Department of Pediatrics
Boston University
School of Medicine
Brookline, MA 02146

**Alan Leviton, M.D**
Department of Neurology
Children's Hospital Medical
   Center
Boston, MA 02115

**Noel D. Matkin, Ph.D.**
Department of Speech and
   Hearing Sciences
University of Arizona
Tucson, AZ 85718

**Paula Menyuk, Ed.D.**
Applied Psycholinguistics
   Program
Boston University
Boston, MA 02215

**Frederick C. Robbins, M.D.**
President, Institute of Medicine
National Academy of Sciences
Washington, DC 20418

**Peter C. Scheidt, M.D.**
Center for Research for Mothers
   and Children
National Institute of Child
   Health and Human
   Development
National Institutes of Health
Bethesda, MD 20892

**Paul Shurin, M.D.**
Department of Pediatrics
Cleveland Metropolitan General
   Hospital
Cleveland, OH 44109

**Winifred Strange, Ph.D.**
Department of Communicology
University of South Florida
Tampa, FL 33620

**N. Wendell Todd, M.D.**
Department of Surgery
   (Otolaryngology)
Emory University Clinic
Atlanta, GA 30322

**Sumner J. Yaffe, M.D.**
Center for Research for Mothers
   and Children
National Institute of Child
   Health and Human
   Development
National Institutes of Health
Bethesda, MD 20892

**Peter W. Zinkus, Ph.D.**
Child Psychologist
LeBonheur Children's Medical
   Center
Memphis, TN 38103

# Common Terminology for Conditions of the Middle Ear

*Peter C. Scheidt* and *James F. Kavanagh*

The terminology of middle ear disease has evolved substantially over the past two decades and some have found it confusing and overlapping. Since many terms referring to various conditions of the middle ear are used in this book, and some readers may not be familiar with them, this short section is included to provide a description and common usage of these terms. The terms are presented roughly in order of their evolution as we understand it. Since authors were not constrained to use specific definitions, some variation in usage of these terms may be seen in the following chapters.

*OTITIS MEDIA:*   Narrowly defined, *otitis media* is the presence of inflammation in the middle ear cavity. Prior to widespread use of techniques to examine for fluid in the middle ear, such as pneumatic otoscopy, clinicians considered *otitis media* synonymous with the lay term "ear infection." When unqualified, the term still generally refers to infection of the middle ear space. However, current approaches to the diagnosis of middle ear disease in medical settings dictate the need to be more specific as in the following terms.

*ACUTE OTITIS MEDIA:*   This term is currently and more specifically used by clinicians to indicate an active inflammation and/or infection of the middle ear space of recent onset or resurgence. Bulging of the tympanic membrane and/or evidence of pus behind the tympanic membrane (red, yellow or white discoloration indicating effusion with purulent fluid) or purulent [pus] discharge through a perforation indicate the presence of *acute otitis media*. The condition usually results from infection of fluid within the middle ear space which in turn develops as a result of eustachian tube dysfunction. By definition and as actually observed, *acute otitis media* is not a static condition but develops over a relatively short period of time and either resolves (spontaneously or with treatment) or progresses to various other conditions of the middle ear such as otitis media with effusion or chronic otitis media.

SEROUS OTITIS MEDIA: Fluid in the middle ear space without obvious infection has for many years been referred to as *serous otitis media*. More recently some researchers and specialists working with middle ear disease have termed this condition "otitis media with effusion" as described below. However, many clinicians still use *serous otitis media* as defined above or more specifically indicating the presence of a thin watery and clear fluid which is seen relatively early in the process of eustachian tube obstruction.

SUPPURATIVE OTITIS MEDIA: This term and the term purulent otitis media are generally synonymous with acute otitis media implying the presence of acute infection with inflammation of surrounding tissue and the presence of fluid which is unquestionably purulent. In practice, a diagnosis of acute *suppurative otitis media* is usually based on the observation of the same finding described with acute otitis media above.

CHRONIC OTITIS MEDIA: In this condition, infection of the middle ear with production of purulent fluid persists beyond the period of time usually associated with acute otitis media either with or without the administration of antibiotics. Furthermore, *chronic otitis media* differs from the acute infection by the presence of relatively little pain compared to the frequent agony of an acutely bulging drum, by the presence of different organisms, usually staphylococcus or pseudomonas species rather than *S. pneumoniae* or *H. influenzae* common in acute otitis media, and by exhibiting chronic purulent or mucoid drainage through a persistent perforation of the tympanic membrane. *Chronic otitis media*, which in recent years is seen infrequently, generally represents an unfortunate consequence of either inadequate treatment or failure of an acute infection to resolve spontaneously.

SECRETORY OTITIS MEDIA: This term, also synonymous with mucoid otitis media, refers to a condition of the middle ear space which contains a thick glue-like fluid. The term, which is largely replaced by otitis media with effusion, was used more frequently a decade ago than at present. Based on animal models and clinical observations, *secretory otitis media* occurs either following acute infection or, in the absence of preceding infection, when an effusion of the middle ear persists for a period of several weeks or longer. The thick glue-like nature of the fluid seems to be caused by a chronic inflammatory response and by mucus production in the epithelial lining of the middle ear space.

OTITIS MEDIA WITH EFFUSION: The presence of fluid and infection in the middle ear space is usually based on the appearance and mobility of the tympanic membrane. Often, considerable uncertainty remains as to the content of the fluid and the presence or absence of infectious agents. Indeed, reports of pathogenic organisms cultured from serous fluid heretofore thought to be infection-free have added to this uncertainty. To allow for this uncertainty in the actual composition of the middle ear fluid and whether or not infection is present, the term *otitis media with effusion* was introduced in the later 1970s.[1] This term refers to the presence of fluid in the middle ear space in the absence of unequivocal signs of acute infection. As a substitute for the terms serous and secretory otitis media, the term *otitis media with effusion* avoids specifying either of these distinctions and is limited to the observation that fluid of a non-specific nature is present in the middle ear space.

*PERSISTENT OTITIS MEDIA WITH EFFUSION:* Following the onset of acute otitis media, fluid may persist in the middle ear space for varying periods of time. In approximately 40 percent of children, fluid will persist for more than two weeks and approximately 10 percent will retain fluid for three or more months after an acute infection. Whether heralded by a specific infection or nonspecific upper respiratory congestion or discovered as an isolated finding, this unresolved condition, when documented by repeated examinations, is referred to as *persistent otitis media with effusion.*

*RECURRENT OTITIS MEDIA:* When infections of the middle ear occur repetitively such as four to five times, over a defined period of six months or a year, the condition is referred to as *recurrent otitis media.* A clear distinction between recurrent, separate episodes of otitis media and persistent otitis media with effusion should be made. Both conditions are manifestations of underlying and persistent eustachian tube malfunction. However, the clinical management of these two conditions may be quite different.

---

[1]Bluestone, C. D.: Eustachian Tube Dysfunction, in Wiet, R. J., Coulthard, S. W. (eds.). *Proceedings of the Second National Conference on Otitis Media.* Columbus, OH: Ross Laboratories, 1979, pp. 50–58.

# The Role of Hearing in Early Child Development

# 1

# The Role of Hearing in Language Development

*Noel D. Matkin*

The role of normal hearing in the early acquisition of a verbal language system can be discussed from several viewpoints ranging from a theoretical consideration of the evolution of the human auditory mechanism to auditory deprivation studies of animals to a review of language studies with young children having either normal or disordered hearing. It is widely accepted that the rapid and seemingly effortless acquisition by the young child of the intricate system of symbols called verbal language requires an intact peripheral and central auditory system. Developmentally, the reception and subsequent comprehension of oral language is a fundamental prerequisite to the verbal expression of language or speech. In this context, hearing as a sensory modality is uniquely suited for the task of verbal language reception in that, like vision, it is a distance sense but, unlike vision, which is restricted to line of sight, hearing serves in a omnidirectional manner. At some basic level, hearing is the one sense that keeps us in touch with our environment at all times, even in our sleep (Myklebust 1960). Analysis of the acoustic spectrum of speech relative to sensitivity of the human auditory mechanism reveals that in an optimal listening environment various components of conversational speech are easily detected by the human listener with normal hearing. In sharp contrast, perception of various speech elements through vision is quite limited even in an optimal communicative situation. Phylogenetically, there is controversy as to whether the auditory mechanism evolved to receive the human speech signal or whether the speech mechanism evolved to produce a signal that would be maximally audible. Despite this controversy, it is of interest that the segment of speech that provides most of the intelligibility (80 percent) falls in the frequency region of 500-4000 Hz. It is within this frequency region that the human auditory system is most sensitive.

Traditionally, the first year of life has been referred to as the prelinguistic period and the infant viewed as a passive language learner. Yet, there is a growing body of research literature in the area of auditory speech perception indicating that the acquisition of auditory processing skills begins soon after birth and proceeds rapidly during the first 12 months of life. Which of these skills are prerequisites and which are merely precursors to both language comprehension and use is subject to debate. In addition, the emergence of language is closely related to fundamental cognitive abilities that also develop in the first year.

Development of speech-language production has received far more attention than has study of the auditory comprehension of language. Thus, the transition from differentiated babbling to the emergence of the first word, typically between 10 and 13 months, is often cited as the beginning of the linguistic period. Yet, auditory comprehension is a major process in the use of speech and it is generally believed that it develops earlier and more quickly than production. The premise that comprehension always precedes production is an oversimplification, however. It is documented that children occasionally will produce utterances that they do not appear to comprehend. As noted by Dale (1976), comprehension exceeds production in many instances, is simultaneous in others, and occasionally follows in yet others. Nevertheless, it appears that the two functions— comprehension and expression—mutually reinforce each other during the early developmental stages.

It should be noted that language acquisition is far more complex than simple imitation. Instead it appears that children formulate hypotheses relative to the rules governing the semantics, syntax and phonology of their native language and then proceed to test these hypotheses based on verbal language heard in the environment. Primary caregivers, usually mothers, intuitively understand the importance of hearing. They constantly talk to their children during daily activities. Further, they modify their speech by using shorter and less complex sentences, less diverse vocabulary, fewer verbs and function words delivered at a slower rate and with more repetitions. Such simplification in child-directed talk facilitates language development first by aiding auditory comprehension, then by providing positive feedback, and finally by encouraging active participation during conversations. In this context, a birth order effect may be present. A recent study suggests that the presence of older siblings in some communication situations may change the mother-child interaction due to frequent interruptions of the younger child and a reduction in his/her turns as speaker (Wellen 1984). Nevertheless, the typical child has a spoken vocabulary of 50 or so words by 18 or 20 months when he/she begins to string words together. The emergence of the two word stage also has been referred to by some authors as the beginning of true language.

Studies of normal language acquisition have revealed that the preschool years are characterized by a rapid growth relative to form, content and use (Bloom and Lahey 1978). Thus, despite a good deal of variability among children, the typical child of kindergarten age not only comprehends but uses an extensive lexicon in a variety of simple and complex syntactical structures with good intelligibility even to an unfamiliar listener. It is for this reason that the preschool years are considered as the critical or optimal language learning period (Lenneberg 1967).

It is important to keep in mind that the milestones of language acquisition are normally interlocked with other milestones, particularly in the area of motor, cognitive, and social/emotional development. Thus, language comprehension and production is best viewed in the context of the whole child. However, the importance of normal hearing to development can not be overstated. As succinctly described by Ramsdell (1960), there are three psychological levels of hearing: the symbolic level, the signal-warning level, and the primitive or affective level. At the symbolic level, audibility of speech is a prerequisite to detection, recognition, storage, and use of verbal language.

As noted by Ventry (1980), research on the role of hearing in language and learning is not a simple matter. Investigators can not manipulate experimentally or limit the auditory experiences of the developing child. This type of cause-and-effect research design must be performed with laboratory animals. However, generalization of findings from animal studies to the human condition must be viewed with caution (Webster and Webster 1977).

As an alternative approach, the crucial role of hearing in oral language development can be inferred by considering the language delay documented among children with bilateral hearing loss. There are a number of threats, however, to internal validity in such comparative research. The major threat relates to subject selection since normal-hearing and hearing-impaired samples should be similar on all subject variables except for the presence or absence of hearing loss.

Unfortunately, the bulk of available language literature focuses upon children with severe and profound sensorineural hearing loss. Further, there are very few longitudinal studies in which changes are monitored in subjects over time. In numerous instances, the language data reported are suspect in that nonstandardized instruments or tests with questionable reliability were employed. Finally, because random selection of subjects usually has not been feasible,

5

there is a major threat to external validity or the ability to generalize research findings.

There are a limited number of research studies, usually doctoral dissertations, in which samples were carefully chosen and a number of primary variables were controlled. A review of these investigations suggests that a systematic relationship exists between the degree of hearing loss and both primary and secondary language development. Such a relationship should not be surprising when the information displayed in Figure 1 is considered. The three curves plotted on an audiogram indicate intensity levels exceeded by normal conversational speech 90 percent, 50 percent, and 10 percent of the time as a function of frequency (Olsen 1984).

The information from an unpublished doctoral dissertation completed by Watson (1975) at Northwestern University highlights the effects of varying degrees of bilateral sensorineural hearing loss on receptive language development, including vocabulary knowledge and reading comprehension.

As indicated in Table I, it can be seen that progressively greater deficits are encountered, in terms of both receptive vocabulary development and reading skills, when one compares normal development with the performance of two groups of hard-of-hearing children, i.e., those having a high frequency hearing loss (HH-HF) and those having a relatively flat audiometric configuration (HH-F) with a group of youngsters who, having a hearing loss of 90 dB or greater, were classified as deaf for educational purposes. This study was based upon a selected sample of 48 children between the ages of 8 and 14 years, who were characterized by relatively early identification of hearing loss, normal intelligence, and absence of additional handicapping conditions. The increasing impact of the hearing impairment is clearly evident. Note that the hard-of-hearing children at age 11, having a moderate flat loss, are approximately 3 years delayed in both receptive oral language and reading skills.

In a study by Wohlner (1975), children ages four through seven were categorized as having either mild or moderate bilateral sensorineural hearing impairments and were compared in terms of expressive rather than receptive language development. Based on a systematic analysis of a speech sample while using a developmental sentence scoring procedure, Wohlner found that children classified as having mild hearing impairments manifested delays of at least two years in expressive oral language by age seven. In contrast, those children with moderate hearing impairments at age seven scored below the norms for normal-hearing four-year-old youngsters. It is of interest that, syntactically and semantically, the mild hearing loss group formulated correct sentences about 70 percent of the time as compared to normal-hearing children, who were correct approxi-

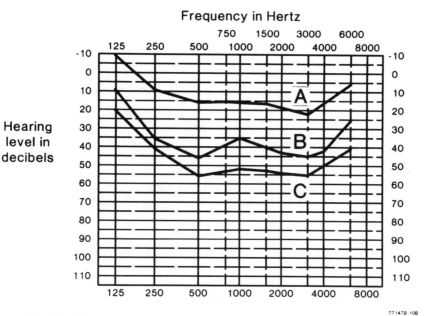

Figure 1. Plot of speech spectrum on an audiogram with speech sounds exceeding curve
A ninety percent of the time, curve B fifty percent of the time and curve C only
ten percent of the time (Olsen 1984 derived from Pascoe 1980).

mately 90 percent of the time. In addition, the moderate hearing loss group generated correct sentences only 50 percent of the time, a performance much like a typical two-year-old with normal hearing. Skinner (1978) has delineated eight problem areas associated with language acquisition when hearing is impaired. Her central theme is that lack of consistency in auditory input leads to confusion relative to semantics, syntax, and the emotional content of speech.

Davis (1974) reported an investigation in which two groups of hard-of-hearing children were compared with normal-hearing children in their knowledge of basic concepts such as those of quantity, time, and space. Again, the effects of hearing loss are quickly seen in

Table I

| | Performance on Receptive Language Tests | | | |
|---|---|---|---|---|
| | Receptive Vocabulary Quotient | Reading Grade Equivalent | | |
| Subjects | | (Word) | (Paragraph) | (Total) |
| Normal | 118 | 6.7 | 6.9 | 6.9 |
| HH-HF | 91 | 4.1 | 4.5 | 4.3 |
| HH-F | 77 | 3.7 | 4.1 | 3.8 |
| Deaf | 62 | 3.2 | 2.9 | 3.0 |

7

these data. It was found that 58 percent of those youngsters with mild hearing impairments scored below the 10th percentile. In the moderate hearing loss category, 91 percent of the youngsters scored below the 10th percentile.

In short, a cursory review of selected language and learning studies reveals that even mild sensorineural hearing losses create significant deficits, not only in oral language competence, but in auditory memory, concept development, reading, and writing skills. In view of the fact that the language studies by Watson and by Wohlner were completed with carefully chosen samples of hearing-impaired children from middle-income families who were free of additional handicapping conditions and environmental deprivation, the data reviewed here may underestimate the difficulties encountered by many children with similar hearing losses.

Numerous studies, including a recent longitudinal investigation of 718 children by Schery (1985), have highlighted the relationship between a child's hearing status and both receptive and expressive language development. However, as mentioned earlier, numerous additional factors are believed to affect language acquisition during early childhood. Unfortunately, much of the child language literature is flawed by the failure of researchers to adequately describe and control these additional variables. Without adequate subject descriptions, the ability to replicate existing studies as a means of determining the generality of findings is not possible. Wickstrom, Goldstein, and Johnson (1985) reviewed 40 articles concerned with child language that were published in seven journals between 1978 and 1980. Inconsistent subject descriptions in child language intervention studies were more the rule than the exception. Beyond a notation of age, sex, and initial diagnosis, the control of additional variables during subject selection appeared haphazard at best. Thus, the validity of the conclusions reached in many recent child language studies must be questioned. In 1980, Ventry raised the same concern relative to the studies of language delay and recurrent otitis media in childhood. Despite the importance of a comprehensive description of research subjects, there apparently is no accepted standard for describing children included in language studies.

One of the major problems faced by current investigators is lack of agreement as to the primary variables that should be controlled during subject selection. In other words, there is a pressing need for a working model when describing children included in studies of language development. As noted by Dale, normal children vary a great deal in their rate of language development (1976). Which variables correlate with rate are not well understood. Yet, the average performance of hearing-impaired children on language and learning measures frequently is cited without consideration of the variability seen among children having similar degrees of hearing loss (Matkin 1979). Hubatch et al., in a recent article on early language development of high-risk infants suggest that seven factors have potential effects on language development (1985). In contrast, Wickstrom et al. (1985), propose a set of guidelines for describing children in language studies that includes 20 different factors. In my judgment, the importance of some variables is well documented, while others are cited on a theoretical basis.

It is not feasible in this short article to describe and document the research relative to each of these potentially contaminating variables. Table II has been included to facilitate discussion, but is viewed only as an outline. Certainly additions and deletions may be in order. My goal, however, is to highlight the number of factors *in addition to hearing loss* that if not controlled, may influence early childhood language development and that may contaminate childhood language studies.

Using a model proposed by Kirk and Chalfant (1984), the various factors in Table II have been grouped under two major areas: intrinsic and extrinsic variables. In this context, intrinsic refers to conditions within the child, while extrinsic conditions refer to contributing factors in the environment. Included in the latter category are socio-economic conditions, cultural factors, and lack of opportunity. Many of these primary variables are broad in scope and various characteristics must be considered for each. For example, a host of characteristics including age of onset, etiology, degree, symmetry and configuration of the hearing impairment, as well as the history of hearing aid use and educational intervention, can affect language development in the presence of a hearing loss.

Table II

Primary Variables Which May Relate to Early Childhood Language Development

| Intrinsic Factors: | Extrinsic Factors: |
| --- | --- |
| Age | Social/Economic Status |
| Sex | Dialect/Language Exposure |
| Hearing Status | Parent/Child Interaction |
| Visual Status | Birth Order/Number of Siblings |
| IQ | Speech-Language Assessment Measures |
| Language Dimensions | Receptive: Form, Content, Use |
| cognitive capacity | Expressive: Form, Content, Use |
| linguistic capacity | |
| communicative capacity | |
| Physical/Motor Development | |
| Social/Emotional Development | |
| Nutritional Status | |
| History of Illnesses and Medications | |

9

## Summary:

The pervasive effects of severe and profound bilateral hearing impairments upon language development have been well documented since the early 1900's. In contrast, investigations of the impact of mild and moderate hearing losses in early childhood are limited. Nevertheless, there is growing evidence that such bilateral impairments, when permanent, do result in significant language delays. Currently, there are contradictory findings relative to the influence of unilateral hearing loss.

While normal hearing and consistent exposure to speech are prerequisites to optimal language comprehension and use, a number of additional factors also may influence the development of this most human and complex behavior. It is recognized that the preceding comments reflect only a few salient points relative to the complexity of the topic, as well as my bias as a pediatric audiologist. As noted by Rees (1980), the study of language development in children is an area where a number of disciplines overlap. Members of each discipline bring different perspectives, techniques for investigation, and knowledge of the extensive literature to bear upon this topic. It is encouraging to note the number of disciplines represented in this publication as the influence of recurrent otitis media, associated hearing loss, and the speech-language development of young children are considered.

## References

Bloom, L. and Lahey, M. 1978. *Language Development and Language Disorders*. New York: John Wiley & Sons, Inc.
Dale, P. S. 1976. *Language Development: Structure and Function*. New York: Holt, Rinehart and Winston, Inc.
Davis, J. 1974. Performance of young hearing-impaired children on a test of basic concepts. *Journal of Speech and Hearing Research* 17:342–351.
Hubatch, L. M., Johnson, C. J., Kistler, D. J., Burns, W. J. and Moneka, W. 1985. Early language abilities of high-risk infants. *Journal of Speech and Hearing Disorders* 50: 195–206.
Kirk, S. A. and Chalfant, J. S. 1984. *Academic and Developmental Learning Disabilities*. Denver-Foudours: Love Publishing Company.
Lenneberg, E. H. 1967. *Biological Foundations of Language*. New York: John Wiley & Sons, Inc.
Matkin, N. D. 1979. Language delay in chronic otitis media. *In* R. J. Wiet and S. W. Coulthard (eds.). *Proceedings of the Second National Conference on Otitis Media*. Columbus, Ohio: Ross Laboratories.
Myklebust, H. R. 1960. *The Psychology of Deafness*. New York: Grune and Stratton.
Olsen, W. O. 1984. Speech spectrum, audiograms and functional gain. *The Hearing Journal* 37:24–26.
Pascoe, D. P. 1980. Clinical implications of non-verbal methods of hearing aid selection and fitting. *Seminars in Speech, Language and Hearing* 1:217–229.
Ramsdell, D. A. 1960. The psychology of the hard-of-hearing and the deafened adult, *In*

H. Davis and S. R. Silverman (eds.). *Hearing and Deafness* (2nd Ed.). New York: Holt, Rinehart and Winston, Inc.

Rees, N. S. 1980. Learning to talk and understand. *In* T. J. Hixson, L. D. Shriberg, and J. H. Saxman (eds.). *Introduction to Communication Disorders.* Englewood Cliffs, N. J.: Prentice-Hall, Inc.

Schery, T. K. 1985. Correlates of language development in language-disordered children. *Journal of Speech and Hearing Disorders* 50:73–83.

Skinner, M. W. 1978. The hearing of speech during language acquisition. *Otolaryngologic Clinics of North America* 11:631–650.

Ventry, I. M. 1980. Effects on conductive hearing loss: Fact or fiction. *Journal of Speech and Hearing Disorders* 45:143–156.

Watson, C. G. 1975. A Study of Short Term Visual Memory Skills and Relationship to Certain Aspects of Language in Selected Groups of Hearing Impaired Children. Dissertation, Northwestern University, Evanston, Illinois.

Wellen, C. J. 1985. Effects of older siblings on the language young children hear and produce. *Journal of Speech and Hearing Disorders* 50:84–99.

Webster, D. B. and Webster, M. 1977. Neonatal sound deprivation affects brain stem auditory nuclei. *Archives of Otolaryngology* 103:392–396.

Wickstrom, S., Goldstein, H., and Johnson, L. 1985. On the subject of subjects: Suggestions for describing subjects in language intervention studies. *Journal of Speech and Hearing Disorders* 50:282–286.

Wohlner, L. R. 1975. An Investigation of Certain Verbal and Gestural Communication Abilities in Hard of Hearing and Normal Hearing Children. Dissertation, Northwestern University, Evanston, IL.

# 2

# Speech Input and the Development of Speech Perception

*Winifred Strange*

This chapter provides an overview of the normal development of speech perception from birth through the preschool years. A considerable body of research exists on the perception of speech and speech-like sounds by "prelinguistic" infants in the first year of life. From these studies we can conclude that infants as young as one to two months old possess rather remarkable capabilities for discriminating many of the acoustic parameters that specify the consonants and vowels of languages of the world. This research has been reviewed extensively elsewhere (Eimas 1975, 1978; Kuhl 1978, 1980; Jusczyk 1981; Aslin, Pisoni, and Jusczyk 1983) so I will only briefly summarize the data here, and take this as a starting point for a discussion of receptive phonological development. Specifically, I want to focus on the role of linguistic input in the development and modification of these inborn perceptual capabilities.

In contrast to the infant research, much less is known about how speech perception develops during the crucial years of language acquisition. In part, this dearth of experimental evidence is due to the considerable methodological difficulties encountered when testing the receptive abilities of very young children. However, there is a growing number of well-controlled studies from which we can start to piece together the course of change over the first six years of life. During this time, speech perceptual skills are molded and modified as children are exposed to a particular language environment and master the sound system of their native language. The end result of this development is an adult language user whose perception, as well as production, of speech is very much determined by the specific phonological structure of that native language. It is now well established that adults perceive speech in terms of the functional speech-sound categories (the phonemes) of their language and according to the rules under which those categories combine and contrast to form the words of that language. In order to understand the relevance of the developmental research to the issues addressed in this volume, it will be helpful to describe briefly the psychological processes involved in speech perception, and to set forth a theoretical framework within which the developmental research may be interpreted.

## THEORETICAL OVERVIEW

The sound systems of all human languages can be described in terms of a universal phonetic inventory, a relatively small set of speech sounds (called *phones*) that can be produced by the human articulatory system and perceptually differentiated by the human auditory system. Phones are further characterized as consisting of a set of *phonetic features* which describe variations in the way they are produced. So, for instance, consonants are described in terms of voicing (the timing of the action of the vocal cords), place-of-articulation (where in the vocal tract a constriction occurs) and manner-of-articulation (what kind of constriction occurs in the vocal tract). Phones can thus differ by one or more of these phonetic features, and contrasts between phones can be described in terms of which features differ.

The phonological system of a particular language defines the subset of the universal phonetic inventory which is used in that language and the rules by which these segments are combined and sequenced to form larger units, such as syllables and words. The set of phones that are functional in a particular language are referred to as the *phonemes* of the language; the features which contrast those phonemes are called *distinctive features*. Other contrasts either do not occur at all in the language or occur as optional ways of articulating words. In addition, each language has a set of rules that determine how phonemes are produced in different syllabic contexts (e.g., at the beginning or end of a syllable) and in different phonetic contexts (preceding or following certain other phonemes).

As an auditory stimulus, speech is a very complex, rapidly-changing pattern of acoustic energy. Any particular phonetic contrast is signaled acoustically by differences in many aspects of the physical signal. That is, a difference in articulation that can be described in terms of a single phonetic feature results in multiple variations in the frequency, intensity, and duration of components of the acoustic pattern. These multiple variations are integrated by the perceiver in rather complex ways that are just beginning to be understood.

To take an example, consider the phonetic contrast of voicing in stop consonants (e.g., the difference between /b/ and /p/ or /d/ and /t/). This phonetic feature refers to the temporal relation between laryngeal gestures (closing the vocal cords) and the oral gesture (the release of the total constriction of the vocal tract). For voiced stops in English (/b/ or /d/), the vocal cords close before or at the time of the release, while for voiceless stops (/p/ or /t/), the vocal cords close sometime after the release. Acoustically, this contrast is distinguished in word-initial position by the relative onset time of low frequency periodic energy and the burst of high frequency noise associated with the release. However, accompanying this temporal parameter are several other acoustic variables: frequency at onset of the first oral formant[1], amount of change over time in the frequency of the first formant, duration of periodic energy preceding the burst, and duration of aspiration noise after the burst. When this contrast occurs in syllable-final position, the acoustic parameters which signal the contrast include the duration of silence preceding the burst, the duration and intensity of periodic energy during the time the vocal tract is constricted, and even the duration of the vowel preceding the stop consonant. Furthermore, although many languages make phonemic use of the voicing contrast, the particular acoustic variations used to distinguish the phonemes vary across languages and the relative importance of the particular variations differs from language to language.

Phonetic contrasts in place-of-articulation of consonants (e.g., between /b/ and /d/, or between /r/ and /l/ in English) are signalled acoustically by differences in the frequency pattern of very brief segments (from 30 to 100 ms) of the speech signal. These segments are quite low in intensity, relative to the vowel portion of a syllable, and often differ from each other only in the high frequency portion of the signal. Differences in manner-of-articulation of consonants (e.g., /d/ versus /z/ in English) are signaled by the duration and frequency characteristics of both periodic and noisy portions of the speech pattern. Again, these segments of the speech signal are quite low in intensity relative to the vowel portion of the signal.

Thus, the perception of speech involves the detection of

---

[1]Formants are bands of relative intense energy at particular frequencies in the speech spectrum (i.e., spectral peaks). These peaks are numbered consecutively from lowest to highest frequency; speech contains approximately five such peaks within the range of 100 Hz to 8000 Hz. The frequencies of the formants are determined by the resonance characteristics of the vocal tract, acting like an acoustic filter, and change as the articulators move. The first three formants are the most important in specifying the phonetic structure of speech.

subtle differences in a complex acoustic signal and the integration and "interpretation" of this information by the perceptual system in order that the listener can identify and categorize the phonetic sequences uttered by the speaker. The processes by which this takes place are not yet fully understood, but clearly involve attentional and memorial factors, in addition to basic auditory sensory processes. The role of linguistic experience (exposure to speech input and active interaction with speakers of a particular language) in shaping these perceptual processes during first language acquisition and subsequent language learning is a topic of continuing research interest.

Current theories of speech perception differ somewhat with respect to their characterization of the processes by which the listener recovers the linguistic message from the speech signal. Specifically, there is continuing debate about the extent to which the phenomena of speech perception require the postulation of specialized processes unique to the human species. Typically, theorists have distinguished between "general" auditory perceptual processes, thought not to involve any species-specific specialization of function, and a phonetic level of processing, wherein the auditory representation of the acoustic signal is "interpreted" in terms of linguistically defined categories. (cf., Cutting and Pisoni 1978.) More recently, Janet Werker and her colleagues (Werker and Tees 1984; Werker and Logan 1985) have postulated three processing modes, two of which involve linguistic capabilities. In addition to a nonlinguistic auditory level of analysis, these researchers distinguish between *phonetic* and *phonemic* modes of perception of speech and speech-like stimuli. This distinction will be utilized here in characterizing the perceptual abilities of infants and children, and in discussing the role of linguistic experience in receptive phonological development.

Perception in the phonetic mode refers to the ability to discriminate acoustic differences in speech sounds that vary as a function of articulatory feature distinctions. Phonetic perception thus involves processes that may be specialized for interpreting complex acoustic patterns produced by the human vocal system. However, perception in this mode does not reflect, and is not constrained by, the functional categories of any particular language. Rather, perception in this mode reflects language-universal dimensions of contrast, or "natural phonetic boundaries."

In contrast, phonemic perception refers to the identification and categorization of speech in terms of language-specific (learned) categories. In this mode, acoustic parameters that are not used to distinguish phonemes in the perceiver's native language are not differentiated perceptually, while acoustic parameters that are phonemic are differentiated effortlessly and automatically. This refers to the familiar *categorical perception* phenomenon demonstrated by adult language users. (See Strange and Jenkins 1978; Repp 1983 for detailed reviews of this phenomenon.)

From this theoretical viewpoint, the development of speech perception can be characterized as the development of phonemic perception as the primary mode used in processing speech under ordinary circumstances. This is conceived of as the "education of selective perceptual processes," (cf. Gibson 1969; Strange and Broen 1980). According to this conception, the underlying auditory sensory processes do not change with linguistic experience. However, the child does learn to pay attention to the patterns in the acoustic signal that specify native-language phonemic categories, while filtering out or ignoring irrelevant phonetic variation. With development, these selective processing strategies become automatic and highly efficient (cf. Walley, Pisoni, and Aslin 1981; Soli 1983).

Thus, in acquiring phonemic perception, a child must develop the ability to identify and categorize complexes of acoustic parameters in language-appropriate ways. This process is conceived of as the attunement of biologically endowed phonetic perceptual capabilities.

## EXPERIMENTAL EVIDENCE

In this section, a brief review of the data on the development of speech perception is presented within the framework outlined above. The first question addressed is, how do "prelinquistic" infants, one to ten months old, perceive speech and speech-like signals?

Paradigms for testing these very young infants are varied, but have in common the fact that the subjects reveal, by some physiological or behavioral response (heart rate deceleration, auditory evoked potential, sucking rate, head turn), that they detect a change in a repeating acoustic stimulus. (See Eilers 1980, for a good review of methods used to test infants.) Both recorded natural speech stimuli and synthetic stimuli, generated by computer to simulate speech sounds, have been employed. In studies with natural speech, the repeating stimulus changes from instances of one phonetic category (e.g., the syllable, "ba") to repeated instances of another category (e.g., "pa") which differ from the first in one or more phonetic features (in this example, by the feature of voicing). Control conditions are those in which the category does not change. In studies using synthetic speech, the change to be detected can be either from one phonetic category to another, simulating the natural speech condition, or it can constitute an *intra*category acoustic change. Paradigms which employ synthetic speech allow the experimenter to vary a single acoustic parameter along a continuum from values appropriate to one pho- neme, through acoustically intermediate values, to values appropriate for the contrasting phoneme. Other acoustic differences, which occur redundantly in natural speech, can be held constant.

The ability of infants (and adults) to discriminate acoustic parameters which signal phonetic feature contrasts of voicing, place- of-articulation, and manner-of-articulation has been studied quite extensively, using both natural speech and synthetic speech continua in the change-detection paradigm. (See Jusczyk 1981; Aslin, Pisoni, and Jusczyk 1983 for recent reviews.) In general, results have shown that infants as young as one to two months of age can discriminate many phonetic contrasts on the basis of multiple acoustic parameters and also on the basis of individual acoustic parameters known to be sufficient "cues" to the contrasts for adults. Furthermore, studies with synthetic speech indicate discontinuities in discriminability along sev- eral acoustic dimensions. That is, acoustic differences that distinguish phonemes in at least one language are discriminated, while intracat- egory differences of the same physical magnitude, but which do not correspond to a phonemic contrast in any language, are not discrim- inated. It thus appears that infants respond to acoustic variations in speech or speech-like stimuli according to the natural phonetic bound- aries used by languages of the world to distinguish functional categories.[2]

But do infants perceive in a phonetic mode or a phonemic mode? To answer this question, one must look to cross-language studies in which infants from different language environments are tested. In one language, the phonetic contrast under study is pho- nemic and is perceptually and productively differentiated by adult speakers of that language. In the other language, the contrast is not functional; the two categories either are not produced and thus are not present in the child's linguistic environment, or they are produced but as variations of a single phoneme category.

Studies of this kind are relatively few in number, but the existing data suggest that infants from two to about ten months of age respond according to language-universal phonetic boundaries. That is, infants from both linguistic environments discriminate the phonetic contrast, regardless of the functional status or presence or absence of phonetic contrast in the infant's language environment. This has been shown in studies of voicing contrasts with infants from English (Eimas 1975; Aslin et al. 1981), Spanish (Lasky, Syrdal-Lasky, and Klein 1975)

---

[2]In addition to their ability to discriminate speech sounds on the basis of multiple acoustic cues, prelinguistic infants also demonstrate the ability to recognize different instances of a phoneme category as "the same phoneme." That is, they show *perceptual constancy* over variations in pitch and intonation, and in the identity of the speaker producing the phonemes (see Kuhl 1980).

and Kikuyu (Streeter 1976) language environments (but see Eilers, Gavin, and Wilson 1979). In all of these studies, synthetic speech stimuli were utilized. In an early study using natural speech, Trehub (1976) demonstrated that one- to four-month-old infants from an English-speaking environment could discriminate a (non-English) contrast between oral and nasal vowels in French and a (non-English) Czech place-of-articulation contrast between fricatives. Eilers, Gavin, and Oller (1982) replicated Trehub's results on the Czech contrast with six- to eight-month-old infants from both Spanish- and English-speaking homes. In addition, they demonstrated discrimination by infants from Spanish-speaking homes of the English voicing contrast between the fricatives /s/-/z/, a contrast that is not phonemic in Spanish.

More recently, Werker and her colleagues (Werker et al. 1981; Werker and Tees 1984) examined the perception of two place-of-articulation contrasts, one from Salish (a North American Indian language) and one from Hindi. Neither contrast is phonemic in English, nor are the phones produced as variants in English. However, six- to eight-month-old infants from English-speaking environments discriminated both contrasts as well as infants from Salish- and Hindi-speaking homes. Tests of English-speaking adults showed the typical language-specific results; these non-native contrasts were not differentiated perceptually under identical stimulus conditions as used with the infants!

Thus, we can conclude, at least tentatively, that "prelinguistic" infants, up to the age of about eight months, perceive in a phonetic mode. They discriminate phonetically relevant acoustic parameters independent of their linguistic function in the language to which they have been exposed; indeed, they discriminate these parameters even if they have not been exposed to them at all. These perceptual processes thus appear to reflect universal phonetic categories.

But when does this begin to change? When does speech perception become specific to the native language phonology? Again, the research of Werker and her colleagues is exceedingly interesting with respect to this question. She extended her study of the Salish and Hindi contrasts to infants between eight and ten months old and between ten and twelve months old, in both cross-sectional and longitudinal designs (Werker and Tees 1984). She reported that the eight- to ten-month-old infants from English-speaking environments yielded inconsistent performance; some children showed good discrimination of both contrasts, while others failed to discriminate one or both contrasts. By the time they were ten to twelve months old, the English group was *no longer* able to discriminate the Hindi and Salish contrasts, while infants from Hindi- and Salish-speaking environments maintained good discrimination of their respective contrasts!

English infants of all ages performed well on a native English place-of-articulation control contrast (/b/ vs /d/).

In the study previously cited, Eilers, Gavin, and Oller (1982) reported that six- to eight-month-old infants from English-speaking homes as a group showed only marginal discrimination of the Spanish flapped vs. trilled /r/ contrast whereas a group of infants the same age coming from Spanish-speaking homes produced significantly better discrimination of this contrast. However, the infants from Spanish-speaking homes also performed better than the infants from English-speaking homes on the Czech contrast, which is not phonemic in either language. Thus, we cannot attribute their superior performance on the Spanish contrast directly to linguistic experience.

These initial bits of evidence suggest that language-specific perceptual patterns emerge right around the first birthday—just about the time the child is beginning to produce first words. Discrimination of native language contrasts continues to be highly sensitive. However, phonetic contrasts that are not functional in the native language are no longer discriminated under identical stimulus conditions.

It would appear then, that phonemic perception begins to develop during the second year, in tandem with expressive phonological development. Unfortunately, studies of speech perception are sadly lacking in this age group, due to the extreme difficulty of designing experimental paradigms for testing these children. The experimental evidence resumes with studies of children in the third year—from about 24–30 months of age.

Early studies by Shvachkin (1973), Garnica (1973) and Edwards (1974) were well-motivated efforts to assess speech perceptual skills in two- to three-year olds. However, because of the use of rather informal methodology and "live voice" presentation of stimulus materials, their results are somewhat less interpretable than studies with controlled materials and procedures. Studies by Menyuk and Anderson (1969); Locke (1971); Barton (1978); Strange and Broen (1980, 1981); Zlatin and Koenigsknecht (1975) and others have employed forced-choice identification tasks in which the child must choose between two or three alternatives (either pictures or real objects) upon presentation of recorded stimuli. This requires that the child identify each stimulus by comparing the input pattern to "stored" representations of the phonetic categories. These studies almost exclusively have investigated children's perception of phonemic contrasts, i.e., contrasts that are functional in the child's native language.

In general, results suggest that children as young as two can perceptually differentiate many native-language phonemic contrasts, including contrasts of voicing, place-of-articulation and manner-of-articulation (cf. Barton 1978). However, children at this age may not differentiate all phonemic contrasts with the same ease. A study that

Patricia Broen and I performed can serve as an illustration (Broen et al. 1981).

Children from 24 to 30 months old were tested on a /w/-/r/ place-of-articulation contrast (*wing-ring*), as well as on two control pairs, /w/-/k/ and /r/-/k/, which differed in both place and manner of articulation. Upon presentation of the recorded stimulus, the child had to choose between two objects depicting the response alternatives. A token reinforcer was placed under the correct object. (Children who could not learn the task using a *wing* or *ring* vs. *cup* pairing were excluded from the study.) Of the 12 children who completed the experiment, all but one differentiated the /w/-/k/ and /r/-/k/ contrasts above chance levels, demonstrating that they knew the stimulus alternatives and could do the task. However, only 7 of the 12 subjects performed above chance on the /w/-/r/ contrast, even though it is phonemic in English.

It is well known that the phonemes /w/ and /r/ are confused in production; /w/ is produced for both /r/ and /w/ by many normally developing children and remains the most frequent substitution in children with /r/ articulation problems. These findings thus suggest that children's perception of phonetic contrasts, as tested in this kind of identification paradigm, may sometimes reflect the (temporary) collapsing of a contrast that is used in the adult native language, but which is not yet distinguished in the child's own expressive phonology.

A very promising study by Oller and Eilers (1983) investigated the perceptual differentiation by two-year-olds of native and non-native phonetic contrasts. English-learning and Spanish-learning children were tested on the English /w/-/r/ contrast and the Spanish flapped vs. trilled /r/ contrast, using an identification paradigm in which a real word and a minimally-contrasting nonsense word were the alternatives (e.g., *rabbit* vs. *wabbit* in English). The /w/ occurs in both languages. However, the English liquid [ ɹ ] does not occur in Spanish and the trilled [r] does not occur in American English. The flapped [ ɾ ] occurs in American English as a phonetic variant of /d/ between vowels, as in "ladder." Unfortunately, the stimuli were presented "live voice" (albeit by a bilingual phonetician) so control of stimulus variables was less than optimal.

The results suggest a clear language-specific advantage in perception. Five of the seven English-speaking children differentiated the English /w/-/r/ contrast above chance levels, while none of the seven Spanish-learning children did. Likewise, four of the seven Spanish children differentiated the Spanish flap-trill contrast, while only one of the seven English-learning children did. These results again show that even native contrasts may present perceptual difficulties for some two-year-olds when the task involves identification of stimuli presented one at a time rather than discrimination of a phonetic change in a repeating sequence of stimuli. (As noted above, the Spanish flap-trill distinction was discriminated well by six- to eight-month-old infants from Spanish-speaking environments.) However, perceptual differentiation of native contrasts was consistently better than non-native contrasts, again showing the influence of the particular language being heard and learned by the children.

Perceptual studies with synthetic speech have been performed with children from three through six years old and provide a more analytical look at how specific acoustic parameters and combinations of parameters are processed (Wolf 1973; Zlatin and Koenigsknecht 1975; Strange and Broen 1981; Krause 1982). Again, these studies examine the perception of native phoneme contrasts. As an illustration, my colleagues and I have done a number of experiments on the perception of contrasts among /w/, /r/, and /l/, using synthetic speech series in which multiple acoustic parameters vary concurrently in small steps from one phoneme to another. Results with 36- to 42-month-olds suggest that there may be minor differences in the location of phonetic boundaries along the acoustic dimensions and less consistency in identifying acoustically intermediate variants than for older children and adults. In general though, we can say that by the age of four years, normally developing children produce nearly adult-like identification functions of synthetic speech series that contrast these phonemes. Furthermore, this was, in general, true even for those children who did not yet produce all the phonemes correctly. That is, for these contrasts, perceptual differentiation generally preceded articulatory differentiation.

Studies of voicing contrasts have reported developmental trends from three to six years old in location of phonetic boundaries and in the abruptness of the shift in identification from one phoneme to another along the acoustic dimensions underlying the phonetic contrasts (Zlatin and Koenigsknecht 1975; Krause 1982). These systematic shifts with age may reflect continuing fine tuning of phonemic perception through the preschool years.

Recently, a new experimental technique, called the "trading relations" paradigm, has been developed to examine how multiple acoustic parameters underlying phonetic contrasts interact in perception (Fitch et al. 1980; see also Repp 1982). This paradigm has been extended to developmental studies with infants and preschool children (Morrongiello et al. 1984; Eimas 1985; see also Eimas and Clarkson this volume). For example, a study just completed in our laboratory with five-year-olds investigated the integration of temporal and spectral parameters differentiating /r/ and /l/ (Manji et al. 1985). Synthetic stimuli were generated in which the two acoustic parameters were varied independently. Results indicated that the children produced the same pattern of integration of the acoustic parameters as did adults. This study and others like it (see also, Mann, Sharlin, and Dorman 1985) suggest that phonemic perception is adult-like in normal five- to six-year-old children, despite the fact that expressive phonology may still be characterized by non-adult patterns.

There have been only a few cross-language studies with preschool children in which phonetic versus phonemic perceptual modes might be distinguished. Shimizu and Dantsuji (1983) recently studied perception of the English /r/-/l/ contrast by five-year-old monolingual Japanese speakers. It is well established that Japanese adults learning English have a great deal of difficulty differentiating these phonemes perceptually, neither of which occur in Japanese (Miyawaki et al. 1975; MacKain, Best, and Strange 1981; Strange and Dittmann 1984). Shimizu and Dantsuji replicated this result with adults using a synthetic speech continuum and the traditional identification and discrimination tests of the categorical perception paradigm. (See Strange and Jenkins 1978, for a detailed description of these procedures.) They reported, however, that discrimination performance by four five-year-olds showed a pattern of relative discrimination similar to American adults. That is, discrimination of stimuli drawn from different phonetic categories was better than for stimuli drawn from within a single category. While the results are inconclusive at this point due to the very small number of subjects tested, they do suggest that preschool children may (still) be able to perceive non-native speech sounds in a phonetic mode while adults' performance reflects only language-specific phonemic perception.

Werker and Tees (1983), on the other hand, reported that English-speaking children as young as four years old did not differentiate Hindi place-of-articulation or voicing contrasts that are not phonemic in English. Interestingly, they reported that eight-year-olds and twelve-year-olds actually did somewhat *better* on the voicing contrast than did the four-year-olds, although still not as well as infants under ten months of age. Much more work of this kind is needed before we will be able to make any definitive statements about the maleability of phonemic perception in childhood and later.

One final intriguing result reported by Tees and Werker (1984) speaks to the issue of the long-range effects of speech input in shaping phonemic perception. In examining native English-speaking adults' ability to learn the Hindi place-of-articulation contrast, they compared three groups of college students: students who had taken five years of Hindi, and two groups of beginning Hindi students. The latter groups differed in that one set had been exposed to Hindi in the first one or two years of life, while the other group had not. The group with five years of formal training did show good perceptual differentiation of the contrast, while the beginning students without early exposure had very poor perception, even after one year of instruction.

However, the students with early experience could perceive the contrast after only two weeks of instruction as well as the five-year students! Furthermore, they continued to be able to do it at the end of the first year of instruction. Thus, it would seem that early exposure to particular language environments may have lasting effects on phonemic perception.

## Conclusions and Implications

Let me summarize the facts as we know them about the development of phonemic perception in normal children. Prelinguistic infants appear to have the capacity to discriminate all or most of the acoustic parameters of speech that differentiate the phonemes of the languages of the world. They perceive speech in terms of language-universal phonetic categories. By the end of the first year of life, as the child begins to use speech productively to convey meaning, speech perceptual patterns have already been constrained to some extent by the specific phonological structure of the native language. Native language contrasts continue to be perceptually differentiated (although there may be some collapsing of adult phonemic categories), while non-native contrasts are no longer discriminated easily.

Phonological processes in normal children continue to be refined throughout the early preschool years with perceptual differentiation of native contrasts usually preceding articulatory differentiation. By the time the child is four to five years old, adult-like language-specific perceptual patterns appear to be well learned and perhaps automatic, although there are questions remaining about the maleability of such processes in the preadolescent years and beyond.

Consider now, the child with a fluctuating hearing loss which begins in the first year of life and continues throughout the first several years (See Klein this volume). For this child, the pattern of speech input is distorted; subtle acoustic differences that provide information for phonetic contrasts may not be audible during periods of effusion. However, since there is considerable redundancy in the acoustic signal and since speech is normally used within a situational context that often disambiguates phonemic confusions, the child may show no obvious deficit in speech comprehension. However, we can speculate that there may indeed be subtle differences in the selective perceptual processes of these children (see Feldman and Gelman and Menyuk this volume). The formation of phonemic categories may progress more slowly, and "intepretation" of multiple acoustic parameters may show patterns of integration that are different from those seen in children without such fluctuating hearing losses. Tests of speech discrimination that employ redundantly specified natural speech materials in optimal listening conditions may not be sensitive enough to detect these subtle differences in processing. More analytical tests employing procedures that have been developed in the laboratory may be needed to assess these differences (see Eimas and Clarkson this volume).

The conception of the development of speech perception as the education of selective perception or attention leads to other hypotheses about the possible effects of fluctuating hearing loss on this development. If (auditory) speech input is an unreliable source of information about the phonetic message, as it might be with a fluctuating hearing loss, the child may adopt attentional strategies that are different from those of children with consistently good hearing (see Feagans this volume). When the speech signal is low in intensity or when the environment is noisy, they may learn to depend more on visually-conveyed information or on contextual cues that disambiquate the message. These are strategies adopted by all listeners under degraded acoustic conditions. However, visual information is relatively impoverished with respect to many phonetic contrasts. Furthermore, unlike the sophisticated language user, very young children do not yet have the knowledge of semantic and grammatical structures of their language by which the phonetic message might be disambiguated. Thus, they are left with an unreliable signal and an effortful and error-prone task which must often prove too difficult for them. Such strategies of nonattention to auditory inputs may be generalized even to good listening conditions, leading to a pattern of auditory inattention that characterizes some learning disabled children (see Zinkus this volume).

In concluding this review of the role of speech input in the normal development of speech perception, it is important to re-emphasize a final point. Experimental results suggest strongly that infants' phonetic perceptual processes begin to undergo significant modification in the latter half of the first year of life. The phonological structure of the particular language to which the child is exposed shapes the processes by which the child identifies and classifies speech sequences into meaningful categories, i.e., perceives in the phonemic mode. It is an ominous coincidence that this period is also marked by the greatest incidence of otitis media with effusion (see Klein this volume). When we ask whether this disease, and the fluctuating hearing loss that often accompanies it, affects speech and language development, we must not ignore this important "prelinguistic" period.

## REFERENCES

Aslin, R. N., Pisoni, D. B., and Jusczyk, P. W. 1983. Auditory development and speech perception in infancy. *In* M. M. Haith and J. J. Campos (eds.). *Carmichael's Manual of*

*Child Psychology, 4th edition: Vol. II, Infancy and the Biology of Development.* New York: Wiley and Sons.

Aslin, R. N., Pisoni, D. B., Hennessy, B. L., and Perey, A. J. 1981. Discrimination of voice onset time by human infants: New findings and implications for the effects of experience. *Child Development* 52:1135–1145.

Barton, D. P. 1978. *The Role of Perception in the Acquisition of Phonology.* Bloomington, IN: Indiana University Linguistics Club.

Broen, P. A., Strange, W., Metz, S. V., and Weber, S. 1981. Perception of the w-r contrast by 2-year-old children. Paper presented at the American Speech-Language-Hearing Association, Los Angeles.

Cutting, J. E., and Pisoni, D. B. 1978. An information-processing approach to speech perception. *In* J. F. Kavanagh and W. Strange (eds.). *Speech and Language in the Laboratory, School and Clinic.* Cambridge, MA: The MIT press.

Edwards, M. L. 1974. Perception and production in child phonology: The testing of four hypotheses. *Journal of Child Language* 1:205–220.

Eilers, R. E. 1980. Infant speech perception: History and mystery. *In* G. H. Yeni-Komshian, J. F. Kavanagh and C. A. Ferguson (eds.). *Child Phonology: Vol. 2. Perception.* New York: Academic Press.

Eilers, R. E., Gavin, W. J., and Oller, D. K. 1982. Cross-linguistic perception in infancy: Early effects of linguistic experience. *Journal of Child Language* 9:289–302.

Eilers, R. E., Gavin, W. J., and Wilson, W. R. 1979. Linguistic experience and phonemic perception in infancy: A cross-linguistic study. *Child Development* 50:14–18.

Eimas, P. D. 1975. Speech perception in early infancy. *In* L. B. Cohen and P. Salapatek (eds.). *Infant Perception: Vol. 2. From Sensation to Cognition.* New York: Academic Press.

Eimas, P. D. 1978. Developmental aspects of speech perception. *In* R. Held, H. Leibowitz and H. L. Teuber (eds.). *Handbook of Sensory Physiology: Perception* (Vol. 8). Berlin: Springer-Verlag.

Eimas, P. D. 1985. The equivalence of cues in the perception of speech by infants. *Infant Behavior and Development* 8:125–138.

Fitch, H. L., Halwes, T., Erickson, D. M., and Liberman, A. M. 1980. Perceptual equivalence of two acoustic cues for stop-consonant manner. *Perception & Psychophysics* 27:343–350.

Garnica, O. K. 1973. The development of phonemic speech perception. *In* T. E. Moore (ed.). *Cognitive Development and the Acquisition of Language.* New York: Academic Press.

Gibson, E. J. 1969. *Principles of Perceptual Development.* New York: Appleton-Century-Crofts.

Jusczyk, P. W. 1981. Infant speech perception: A critical appraisal. *In* P. D. Eimas and J. L. Miller (eds.). *Perspectives on the Study of Speech.* Hillsdale, N. J.: Lawrence Erlbaum Associates.

Krause, S. E. 1982. Vowel duration as a perceptual cue to postvocalic consonant voicing in young children and adults. *Journal of the Acoustical Society of America* 71:990–995.

Kuhl, P. K. 1978. Predispositions for the perception of speech-sound categories: A species-specific phenomenon? *In* F. D. Minifie and L. L. Lloyd (eds.). *Communicative and Cognitive Abilities: Early Behavioral Assessment.* Baltimore: University Park Press.

Kuhl, P. K. 1980. Perceptual constancy for speech-sound categories in early infancy. *In* G. H. Yeni-Komshian, J. F. Kavanagh and C. A. Ferguson (eds.). *Child Phonology: Vol. 2. Perception.* New York: Academic Press.

Lasky, R. E., Syrdal-Lasky, A., and Klein, R. E. 1975. VOT discrimination by four and six and a half month old infants from Spanish environments. *Journal of Experimental Child Psychology* 20:215–225.

Locke, J. R. 1971. Phoneme perception in two- and three-year-old children. *Perceptual and Motor Skills* 32:215–217.

MacKain, K. S., Best, C. T., and Strange, W. 1981. Categorical perception of English /r/ and /l/ by Japanese bilinguals. *Applied Psycholinguistics* 2:369–390.

Manji, S., Strange, W., Polka, L., and Steffens, M. L. 1985. Trading relations in the perception of /r/-/l/ by articulation-delayed children. *Journal of the Acoustical Society of America* 78: Suppl. 1, S68 (abstract).

Mann, V. A., Sharlin, H. M., and Dorman, M. F. 1985. Children's perception of sibilants: The relation between articulatory and perceptual development. *Journal of Experimental Child Psychology* 39:252–264.

Menyuk, P., and Anderson, S. 1969. Children's identification and reproduction of /w/, /r/, and /l/. *Journal of Speech and Hearing Research* 12:39–52.

Miyawaki, K., Strange, W., Verbrugge, R. R., Liberman, A. M., Jenkins, J. J., and Fujimure, O. 1975. An effect of linguistic experience: The discrimination of [r] and [l] by native speakers and Japanese and English. *Perception & Psychophysics* 18:331–340.

Morrongiello, B. A., Robson, R. C., Best, C., and Clifton, R. R. 1984. Trading relations in the perception of speech by 5-year-old children. *Journal of Experimental Child Psychology* 37:231–250.

Oller, D. K., and Eilers, R. E. 1983. Speech identification in Spanish- and English-learning 2-year-olds. *Journal of Speech and Hearing Research* 26:50–53.

Repp, B. H. 1982. Phonetic trading relations and context effects: New experimental evidence for a speech mode of perception. *Psychological Bulletin* 92(1):81–110.

Repp, B. H. 1983. Categorical perception: Issues, methods, findings. *In* N. J. Lass (ed.). *Speech and Language: Advances in Basic Research and Practice.* Vol. 10. New York: Academic Press.

Shimizu, K., and Dantsuji, M. 1983. A study on the perception of /r/ and /l/ in natural and synthetic speech sounds. *Studia Phonologica* XVII: 1–14.

Shvachkin, N. Kh. 1973. The development of phonemic perception in early childhood. *In* C. A. Ferguson and D. I. Slobin (eds.). *Studies of Child Language Development.* New York: Holt, Rinehart, and Winston.

Soli, S. D. 1983. The role of spectral cues in discrimination of voice onset time differences. *Journal of the Acoustical Society of America* 73:2150–2165.

Strange, W., and Broen, P. A. 1980. Perception and production of approximant consonants by 3-year-olds: A first study. *In* G. H. Yeni-Komshian, J. F. Kavanagh and C. A. Ferguson (eds.). *Child Phonology: Vol. 2. Perception.* New York: Academic Press.

Strange, W., and Broen, P. A. 1981. The relationship between perception and production of /w/, /r/, and /l/ by three-year-old children. *Journal of Experimental Child Psychology* 31:81–102.

Strange, W., and Dittmann, S. 1984. Effects of discrimination training of the perception of /r-l/ by Japanese adults learning English. *Perception & Psychophysics* 36:131–145.

Strange, W., and Jenkins, J. J. 1978. Role of linguistic experience in the perception of speech. *In* R. D. Walk and H. J. Pick, Jr. (eds.). *Perception and Experience.* New York: Plenum.

Streeter, L. A. 1976. Language perception of two-month old infants shows effects of both innate mechanisms and experience. *Nature* 259:39–41.

Tees, R. C., and Werker, J. F. 1984. Perceptual flexibility: Maintenance or recovery of the ability to discriminate non-native speech sounds. *Canadian Journal of Psychology* 38:579–590.

Trehub, S. E. 1976. The discrimination of foreign speech contrasts by infants and adults. *Child Development* 47:466–472.

Walley, A. C., Pisoni, D. B., and Aslin, R. N. 1981. The role of early experience in the development of speech perception. *In* R. N. Aslin, J. R. Alberts and M. F. Peterson (eds.). *Development of Perception:* (Vol. 1). New York: Academic Press.

Werker, J. F., Gilbert, J. H. V., Humphrey, K., and Tees, R. C. 1981. Developmental aspects of cross-language speech perception. *Child Development* 52:349–355.

Werker, J. F., and Tees, R. C. 1983. Developmental changes across childhood in the perception of nonnative speech sounds. *Canadian Journal of Psychology* 37:278–286.

Werker, J. F., and Tees, R. C. 1984. Phonemic and phonetic factors in adult cross-language speech perception. *Journal of the Acoustical Society of America* 75:1866–1878.

Werker, J. F., and Logan, J. S. 1985. Cross-language evidence for three factors in speech perception. *Perception & Psychophysics* 37:35–44.

Wolf, C. G. 1973. The perception of stop consonants by children. *Journal of Experimental Child Psychology* 16:318–331.

Zlatin, M. A., and Koenigsknecht, R. A. 1975. Development of the voicing contrast: Perception of stop consonants. *Journal of Speech and Hearing Research* 18:541–553.

# 3

# Otitis Media and Cognitive Development: Theoretical Perspectives

*Heidi Feldman* and *Rochel Gelman*

This paper explores the theoretical positions underlying predictions that the hearing loss associated with otitis media affects cognitive and language development. The relationship between sensory input and higher mental processes has been the topic of a long-standing theoretical debate in the fields of psychology and philosophy. Our current interest in theory is more than academic; researchers or clinicians make predictions about the effects of otitis media as a function of the theory of development they hold, implicitly or explicitly.

In this paper we will discuss three current classes of theories of cognitive development. All assume that cognitive development is a function of experience and all assume that the absence of experience has deleterious effects.[1] Yet, they differ in their assumptions about the nature and role of experience, the effects of disruptions of sensory input, and the mechanisms mediating those effects. There is a growing sense in the field of developmental psychology that the most satisfying overriding theory is one in which the infant is born with a biological endowment that organizes sensory experience and that shapes learning about language and certain kinds of concepts. In this view, the

Partial support for preparation of this manuscript came from Grant NSF-BNS-80-04881 to Rochel Gelman. We thank Dena Hofkosh, Richard Michaels, and Jack Paradise for their helpful criticisms of an earlier version of the paper and Carol Hallberg for her careful preparation of the manuscript.

[1]An excellent discussion of the role of experience in different developmental theories can be found in Gottlieb (1983). This would be a valuable reference for researchers or clinicians who desire a more general review of the issues.

infant actively searches the environment for experiences that will support this learning. Since this position is less familiar in otitis media research, we will review it in more detail than the other two positions and will discuss research designs suggested by it.

## DEFINITIONS AND ASSUMPTIONS

Cognitive development involves the acquisition of knowledge about the world and the development of devices for processing that knowledge. The field includes the development of concepts such as number and causality and the development of processes such as memory and language. The task of the developmental psychologist is to discover the principles of acquisition: the sequence of changes, mechanisms of acquisition, and functions of new knowledge and new reasoning devices. In studying the effects of otitis media on cognitive development, we are interested in more than describing outcomes. We are also interested in how otitis media might influence the developmental sequence, whether similar outcomes might be preceded by different developmental sequences, whether different outcomes can follow the same illness, and which factors might influence development favorably or unfavorably during periods of illness and good health.

In reviewing studies on developmental effects of otitis media we make several basic assumptions. The first is that although we may call the condition simply "otitis media," we are referring to a history of chronic or recurrent bouts of symptomatic or asymptomatic effusion with resulting intermittent, variable, mild to moderate hearing loss (Bluestone et al. 1983). We assume that, unless otherwise stated, studies are restricted to the pure cases, where the only thing wrong with the subjects is a history of otitis media. Chronic otitis media is associated with Down syndrome, cleft palate, and possibly with subtle unrecognized CNS disorders (Paradise 1981), conditions which themselves are associated with poor developmental outcome. It is important to rule out the possibility that other factors, such as these medical conditions, mediate reported consequences of otitis media. We acknowledge that there are many possible explanations for an association of otitis media and developmental sequelae (Leviton 1980 and this volume; Paradise 1981). We will concentrate only on the hypothesis that otitis media compromises hearing acuity which in turn compromises cognitive and language development.

## DEVELOPMENTAL THEORIES
THE EMPIRICIST THEORY.

The Empiricist position, simply stated, is that all knowledge comes in through the senses and is built up by our capacity to form associations. The infant's mind is characterized as a blank slate, upon which will be written the record of her sensory and association history. It is a mind that has no initial capacity to interpret, select, or organize incoming data. The infant's world is a set of fragmentary sensory data.

There are several corollaries to the basic position. First, the greater the degree of sensory input, the greater the opportunity to build associations and thus, the greater the degree of knowledge about objects of the world. Second, the greater the diversity of sensory data, the greater the opportunity to build associations representing objects and the greater the understanding of objects in the world. Objects have sounds as well as sights and smells, and our understanding of these objects must integrate all of the sensory modalities.

The predicted consequences of an Empiricist theory for the effects of low level hearing loss are straightforward. Even limited hearing loss should have a definite negative impact on the course of cognitive development. The decrement in auditory information decreases the amount and the diversity of sensory experience and thus the amount of knowledge about objects in the world. Sensory deprivation may influence any and all types of cognition. If the infant's mind is a *tabula rasa*, without structures to determine differential developmental patterns in different domains, then the effects of a specific deprivation such as hearing loss may be nonspecific, apparent in multiple areas.

THE CRITICAL PERIOD THEORY.

Critical Period theory differs from the Empiricist view in that the infant's mind is not a blank slate. The child is created with a biological endowment, albeit an immature one, which allows for the selection of complex, organized sensory data for input to specific processing mechanisms. It is assumed that the child is maximally sensitive to this stimulation at a particular point in the life cycle, and that exposure to the requisite sensory data must occur if normal development of the underlying processing mechanisms is to occur. In its strongest interpretation, specific experiences must occur during a critical time; otherwise, there will be irreversible damage to physiological mechanisms and the behaviors of interest. In a weaker interpretation of the theory, there are Optimum or Sensitive rather than Critical Periods; full expression of an ability is facilitated by specific exposures at the proper times, but some potential for development continues for considerably longer time spans (Gottlieb 1983).

Critical Period theory is derived from animal studies of sensory development, especially the development of vision. These studies provide evidence that a critical period, in the strongest interpretation, governs the anatomical and physiological development of the feline visual system. In the case of human cognitive development, the only example of a potential critical period is in language development. Here the weaker interpretation is more appropriate. Language is learned with greater ease by the young, that is, by toddlers and preschoolers. Acquisition in later life is possible (as some of us learned in high school French), but the process may be more difficult (Lenneberg 1967), and the product a less well developed formal system, even for the acquisition of sign language (Newport 1984).

As applied to the case of otitis media, the Critical Period theory states that specific auditory experiences are necessary early in life for the full development of the higher mental processes. Since the hearing loss associated with otitis media is variable and almost always mild (Bluestone et al. 1983), the underlying theory would have to be that auditory input must develop. In this view, bouts of hearing loss early in life deprive the child of the required inputs to other functions during the presumed sensitive period in their development.

THE RATIONAL-CONSTRUCTIONIST THEORY.

We coin the phrase Rational-Constructionist theory to capture the fact that this theory differs from the Empiricist theory in two fundamental ways. The first way is that infants' minds are not seen as blank slates on which sensory experiences are passively imprinted. This position, like the Critical Period theory, grants the child an initial biological endowment to select organized aspects from the diversity of sensory experience. Selection is guided by mental structures that interpret the environment such that the sensory data are classified, transformed, even altered as they are processed by the child. Unique to this Rational-Constructionist theory is the second fundamental principle that infants and young children have an active role in their own cognitive development, one that involves their seeking out experience to nourish nascent capacities. The child is not given preformed, full-blown knowledge, triggered as soon as a particular stimulus is encountered. The child has available only initial structures that begin the process of assimilating the environment and that determine the kind of experience that must be assimilated to construct concepts of the world.

Moreover, in this theory, infants are motivated to seek out relevant inputs that will feed developing structures. This Constructionist assumption contrasts with the Empiricist and Critical Period theories that have the infant taking in only that which is presented but doing nothing to search for, alter, or even reject inputs. This formulation follows Piaget (1975); the infant works hard to get an environment that supports cognitive development in domains in which nature has provided some initial preparation. Infants and young children may even create their own environments for cognitive development.

There is a growing body of evidence in developmental psychology to support the Rational-Constructionist position in cognitive and language development.[2] Experiments with infants of very young ages demonstrate that they select sensory input for particular processing and handle the data in an organized fashion. For example, as discussed elsewhere in this volume (see chapters by Strange and Eimas and Clarkson) one-month-old infants do not handle speech sounds as mere auditory signals but as phonemes, units of language which alter the meaning of words. Their performance is akin to adult performance in similar paradigms. Similarly, young infants demonstrate that they understand the coordination of cross-modal sensory data from the eyes, hands, and mouth that indicate properties of real objects such as rigidity or malleability (Gibson and Walker 1984). Finally, young children are motivated, even after succeeding on tasks with trial and error solutions, to generate systematic approaches to problems and to improve their performance (Karmiloff-Smith and Inhelder 1974/5; DeLoache, Sugarman, and Brown 1985). They continue to search for new solutions without rewards, or modelling, or even prompting.

More support for this theoretical position comes from empirical data that demonstrate that a given set of sensory experiences is not absolutely necessary for aspects of cognitive development. One such demonstration comes from the study of deaf children of hearing parents (Feldman, Goldin-Meadow, and Gleitman 1977). These children were deprived of verbal language experience by their biological condition and sign language experience by their parents' commitment to an oral education. In these families, the children lacked sensory experience associated with learning a formal language system. Nonetheless, the children invented their own system of manual communication. Their system was based on elements available to them, movements of hands, body, and face, but used in a novel symbolic fashion. The system was functional; it was possible for their families to respond to the gestures appropriately (Goldin-Meadow and Mylander 1984),

[2]An extensive review of the empirical support for this position can be found in Gelman and Brown (1986).

and for the researchers to translate them into an understandable form. Furthermore, in both structure and content, the early gestural system was reminiscent of the earliest stages of verbal language learning in young hearing children. They talked, or rather gestured, about small objects before large objects and actions before attributes.

Another illustration comes from the study of blind children. It has often been assumed that concepts of the visual world derive from the visual inputs and that the child learns the meaning of words in particular, and language in general, by having someone point to objects or actions and label them. It follows that a blind child should not only have trouble learning language, she should be especially at risk when it comes to learning vocabulary terms related to vision, e.g., *look* and *see*. Her knowledge of objects should be limited to those features that are defined by touch or by sound. A dramatic set of demonstrations to the contrary are present in Landau and Gleitman (1985) who found that acquisition of syntax, early vocabulary, and functional uses of language in congenitally blind children is remarkably like the acquisition of the same abilities in normal, sighted children. These authors provide compelling demonstrations that Kelli, one of their congenitally blind subjects, came to understand the words *look* and *see* in a fashion similar to sighted children. To explain the preserved abilities, the authors suggest that Kelli substituted the verbal environment for the visual environment, that she used linguistic context to acquire these words. The absence of the presumed sensory requisites did not block development.

This position leads to a very different notion of what constitutes a supporting environment. A supporting environment is not simply that environment with the greatest amount of sensory input of the kind that bears a surface resemblance to the concept. Presumably a supporting environment is one with a diversity of sensory experience. But ultimately, the child must define for us the environment that she needs for optimal development. Our adult preconceptions that vision is necessary to learn about objects beyond the size of our hands or that hearing is necessary to begin a symbolic language system have been severely challenged by the very children whose receptors cannot process such sensory information, but who nevertheless learn.

The Rational-Constructionist position thus makes very different predictions about the effects of otitis media on cognitive and language development. A decrement in the amplitude of auditory stimulation or some inconsistencies in the nature of the input need not interrupt the acquisition of knowledge since the infant can actively search out alternative sources of information or alternative approaches to management of that sensory system. This position does not take the stand that the environment is irrelevant for cognitive development. On the contrary, the environment is fundamental for adequate cognitive growth. However, the features of the environment which are critical for cognitive development are not obvious. Input need not be specific to a single sensory domain. Children may be able to substitute alternative environmental stimulation if the usual input is degraded or unavailable and may be motivated to overcome or to compensate for the special environmental circumstances with which they live. In the research on effects of otitis media, there is no clearly articulated theory of the role of environment. Theorists and researchers must develop such a theory if they are to understand environmental effects. Watching how impaired children cope is one way to start developing such a theory.

## STUDIES OF EFFECTS OF OTITIS MEDIA ON COGNITIVE DEVELOPMENT

*The Empiricist position* leads to hypotheses that the child is vulnerable to even minor disruptions of sensory input. Thus, the studies following this theoretical position would predict a correlation between the severity of otitis, presumably a function of frequency and duration, and developmental outcome. Disruptions wherever they occur during acquisition limit the auditory input and hence the opportunity to learn in multiple domains (Howie 1980).

One study based in part on an Empiricist theory is that of Teele, Klein, and Rosner (1984). Children were selected for study based on an estimate of the severity of their otitis media with effusion. The prediction was that the longer the time with effusion the greater the negative developmental consequences. The theory seemed to determine the interpretation of results. Statistically significant effects of otitis media were found in the high socioeconomic status (SES) group only on three formal test measures. There were no significant effects in the low SES group on these measures. There were also no effects in either SES group on any of the measures apparently derived from a language sample, including intelligibility, the number of grammatical transformations, the mean length of the utterances, or articulation. Yet, the authors did not discuss the complicated patterns of results. The discussion revolved around the positive findings, differences which supported the implicit developmental theory. The lack of any differences in the low SES group and in measures from language samples in both SES groups were dismissed without serious discussion. There was no consideration of the educational or functional significance of these findings. The demonstration of any differences seemed to herald such profound and pervasive effects that the authors alerted pediatricians to the possible need to reconsider medical practice on the basis of these data.

*The Critical Period theory* also predicts that children will be vulnerable to the effects of early otitis media. However, the timing and degree of sensory disturbance is deemed crucial to the developmental outcome. Episodes of otitis media outside the critical period should have less impact on the developmental course than episodes within the critical period. If the critical period is between two and four years, the bouts which are restricted to infancy or middle childhood (and leave no physiological damage) should have no lasting effects on language and cognitive skills. Of course, for cognitive and language development it is difficult to guess the length of any critical period. The critical period for language development has been posited to last at least several years, possibly into adolescence (Lenneberg 1967).

There is some evidence to support a Critical Period theory for the development of auditory processing and speech perception mechanisms in humans. Work by Eimas on speech perception (reported in this volume), suggests that early auditory experience may affect the way that speech signals are processed.

However, the evidence for a critical period for higher level cognitive development is less convincing. The otitis media literature frequently assumes that the critical periods for sensory processing are critical periods for cognitive processes as well. The implicit theoretical position is that early sensory experience affects processing mechanisms that in turn impair cognitive processes. The Critical Period hypothesis thus merges with the Empirical position, despite the former's commitment to an innate endowment for a particular behavior. Optimal sensory data is necessary in both theories for optimal cognitive development.

One representative study based on a Critical Period theory is that of Zinkus, Gottlieb, and Schapiro (1978) who wrote that chronic middle ear disease may have particular significance before four years of age, which they posited as critical periods for speech and language development. They hypothesized that developmental, psychological, and educational delays in school age children may represent the residual complications of otitis media in early childhood, due to irreversible changes in a central auditory processing mechanism. Their subjects came from the population of patients attending a multidisciplinary clinic for learning disabilities. They compared children with histories of severe otitis media and matched subjects with histories of mild otitis media on several measures: the history of language milestones, IQ testing, and reading, mathematics and spelling achievement. Children with severe otitis media were reported to have very substantial delays in the acquisition of single words and sentences. These same children did worse than those with histories of mild otitis on many of the subtests of the IQ examination and on reading and spelling achievement tests.

The theoretical perspective again affected the interpretation of results. Children with histories of severe otitis scored at the population mean for full scale, verbal, and performance IQ. Thus, despite serious language delays, their eventual intellectual performance was solidly average. The group with mild otitis performed slightly above the population mean accounting for the group differences. The authors did not discuss this impressive ability of children with severe language delays to achieve normal intelligence. Furthermore, there were significant differences on only some of the subtests of the WISC-R which the authors attributed to disturbances of auditory processing. However, they explain in a rather *post hoc* fashion why some of the subtests on the performance section of the WISC-R such as visual-motor coordination showed group differences whereas vocabulary on the verbal subsection did not. Later work by this group (Zinkus and Gottlieb 1980), aimed at describing the nature of the presumed auditory processing deficit in the group with a history of early and severe otitis media, seems to suffer from a logical circularity; the diagnostic criteria for auditory processing deficit were never described and it is not clear what were the independent variables for subject selection and how they differed from dependent variables used to describe the nature of the processing difficulties.

The test of the Critical Period theory requires that differential processing resulting from the non-optimal early sensory exposure have life-long consequences. Zinkus, et al. (1978), though open to alternative interpretation, did attempt to relate the early history of language milestones and the later evidence of auditory processing problems as evidence of irreversible effects. The mere demonstration of early differences between groups cannot speak to the issue of irreversibility. In general, a longitudinal design or age dependent cross sectional design allows for the analysis of reversibility or irreversibility. Needleman and Menyuk (1979) tested aspects of phonological development, skills related to the production and comprehension of the sounds in the language, in children aged three to eight years of age. Although there were some differences at all ages, the magnitude of the differences decreased with age. This study suggested that early differences between the otitis media group and controls might not persist after a period of improved health and hearing. Some studies that include a longitudinal data collection analyze each point in time separately and do not test for interactions over time (Schlieper et al. 1985); the additional statistical measures about interactions over time would provide more evidence about changing trends and more evidence about reversibility or irreversibility of effects.

*The Rational-Constructionist position* predicts that some high level abilities will develop in a rather normal fashion even if auditory input is limited. How resilient a particular cognitive or language function will be, given repeated bouts of hearing loss, depends, in part, on whether the function in question depends on auditory input alone for its development. We have already seen that the assumption that blind children need to see to develop concepts about the visual world turns out to be in error because the children use their linguistic environment to solve the problem of induction. Similarly, children who are hard of hearing might make use of inputs we have yet to consider. In order to predict how resilient a particular skill will be, we need to know more about the kinds of environments children can use, their proclivities to seek out or create inputs they need to develop specific domains of abilities, and their abilities to compensate in other ways to a less than ideal condition.

There is some evidence of developmental resiliency of high level functions. Hubbard et al. (1985) studied two groups of children with cleft palates, one of whom underwent myringotomy early in infancy and presumably enjoyed improved hearing, and one of whom underwent myringotomy late in infancy or later during the toddler years and presumably suffered from chronic otitis media and conductive hearing loss. They found differences between the groups in articulation but no differences in IQ scores. These data suggest that early sensory experience may be important to some aspects of language function but not necessarily to measured intelligence.

When cognitive development is viewed from a Constructionist perspective, it is necessary to grant the child an active role in the creation of her own environments. On the assumption that she will do this work, we must be prepared in turn to follow her inclinations. Children who suffer from otitis media may gravitate to less noisy environments so as to maximize the ratio of signal over noise (see Davis this volume); similarly, they may prefer one style of conversation over another, such as face-to-face interaction, frequent repetitions, and simplified linguistic style (Menyuk 1980; Horowitz and Leake 1980). Careful attention to what kinds of environments make them comfortable and maximize their performance could provide clues for nonintrusive interventions.

Another valuable research strategy is to study the children with otitis media who develop completely normal cognitive function. Just as the deaf and blind children provided major clues regarding the nature of a development and the kinds of environments which nurture specific skills, similar studies of children with otitis media who succeed at performing well on the skills in question might provide both theoretical and clinical insights into the factors that protect the child from serious consequences of otitis media.

The Rational-Constructionist hypothesis does not predict that all abilities will necessarily develop normally even if the environment is rendered optimal. Severe and protracted cases of otitis media may take their developmental toll. However, the theoretical position focuses attention on the need to know much more about the kinds of experiences that could encourage the child's active participation in her own cognitive development. Further, it focuses attention on the need to consider in detail how different aspects of cognition may be at risk. On the assumption that what counts as input for one capacity need not count as input for another, it is crucial that we analyze the nature of skills that may be influenced by limits in auditory function (Menyuk 1980). Menyuk (this volume) concludes that all aspects of language acquisition are not affected equally by otitis media and, therefore, presumably are not controlled by a single mechanism. Hearing loss might influence the ability to discriminate beginning sounds of words and unstressed functors of sentences such as prepositions and articles, but it need not stop the child from developing the ability to use the rules of the language called syntax (Gleitman and Wanner 1982). Similarly, hearing loss may limit the number of different novel words children can hear and learn but it need not stand in their way of forming concepts. Research designs should include a comparison of abilities, some that we suspect will be spared and some that we suspect will be at risk.

The research strategy just outlined is seldom used in the literature on the effects of otitis media on cognitive development. Instead, much of the research to date has considered intelligence testing or academic achievement. These are useful measures for some purposes, since they offer a quantitative prediction of school performance. However, they are empirically derived measures that were not designed to understand underlying mechanisms or structures of thought. They are particularly problematic in the preschool population where even predictive validity is limited. Thus, the results on IQ or achievement tests do not indicate the locus of any cognitive lesion.

The alternative we propose would be to demonstrate that the variable hearing loss associated with otitis media interacts with the acquisition of key concepts or basic cognitive processes. (See Kagan this volume, for some discussion of this point and the need for new assessments of this type). A direct prediction from the above discussion would be that language-dependent cognitive structures would show an effect of hearing loss whereas language-independent tasks would not. The logic of this research design is to find statistical interactions between groups and tasks. If a history of hearing loss had only general effects such as motivation, then the performance of an otitis media group would be shifted downward compared to controls, regardless of task. If hearing loss had specific effects in specific domains, then performance of an otitis media group would be normal in some tasks and below normal in others. It would be important to predict, before testing, the pattern of results to avoid *post hoc* explanations.

A concrete example of this research design would be the comparison of an otitis media group and a control group on tasks of classification versus causal reasoning. Classification appears to be a cognitive skill with dependence on language whereas causal reasoning is a cognitive skill with little relation to language. Let us explain in detail.

In classification tasks, verbal labels seem to serve as a constraint that tells children that the object should be thought of in terms of its categorical membership rather than functions or story themes. If you show a two year old a cup, and label it as such, then when asked to "show me another" the child is likely to choose on the basis of category, another cup. If no such label is used, then the child is more likely to choose on the basis of a thematic relationship, for example, a pitcher or plate or person who can drink, rather than another cup. Waxman and Gelman (in press) showed that normal three-year-old English speaking children used this classification strategy even when the labels were in Japanese, a language they did not know. There were two conditions in their experiment. In one condition, called the "label" condition, children were told that a puppet liked a specific picture object called a "dabootsu," but the term was not defined for them. In the other condition, known as the "instance" condition, it was the puppet who was given the Japanese name (to control for the effects of using a strange word with the children), but the object that the puppet liked was unnamed. The task for the children was to find additional objects that the puppet would like. The children did much better in the label condition than in the instance condition at classifying new exemplars according to class membership.

On the other hand there are many cognitive tasks performed by young children where language seems to play no major role. One is in the development of causal reasoning, one aspect of which is the ability to understand how objects undergo transformations of state via specific instruments. Premack (1976) has developed a non-verbal technique to study what children and non-verbal primates understand about the state-state transformation relationship. The method involves the use of unfamiliar picture sequences. Two of three pictures of this causality sequence are presented and the child's task is to choose, from three candidates, the one that best completes the sequence. For example, the child is shown a picture of a pair of glasses followed by a hammer and asked to choose which picture completes the sequence. The correct answer is obviously a pair of shattered lenses. Since both the reasoning process and the method for assessing it are not language dependent, we would expect otitis patients to be indistinguishable from controls on this task.

## CONCLUSIONS

Our suggestion to the research community is to generate specific hypotheses about possible effects and non-effects of otitis media on cognitive development. Much of the research to date seems predicated on an implicit Empiricist position or Critical Period theory that predicts deleterious effects of otitis media and resultant sensory impairment on cognitive development. In its strongest form the Empirical theory predicts the analogue to the dose response curve; the worse the otitis the more serious the effects. The Critical Period theory predicts life-long irreversible changes in auditory processing mechanisms which are often predicted to disrupt higher level functioning in much the same way as the Empirical theory predicts. Studies based on these theoretical positions often minimize complexity of their own results and ignore alternative interpretations of their data. The authors rush to suggest radical interventions such as surgery in order to prevent these sequelae.

We feel that the goal of research on otitis media and cognitive development should be more than just the demonstration of slight group differences on global measures of auditory processing or intelligence quotients. We have offered support for a Rational-Constructionist theory of cognitive development. We feel that this position predicts developmental resiliency under many untoward conditions including some cases of otitis media. The position suggests that a few bouts of ear infection might not suffice to interfere with developmental progress in a biologically prepared and active organism. Of course, there may be deleterious developmental effects under some conditions, presumably protracted or very frequent infections. But the research emphasis under a Rational-Constructionist position would focus on factors that offer protection as well as factors that increase risk and on functions that develop normally as well as those that develop abnormally. The position supports the notion that there is as much to learn from children with otitis who develop normally as from those who develop abnormally.

We strongly support a research enterprise that carefully defines the patient population and documents the severity of illness not only in otologic but in audiometric terms. We also feel that other host and environmental factors should be considered carefully as they interact with the illness and subsequent development. We favor a longitudinal design to determine if short term consequences become permanent. Finally, we recommend the use of hypothesis-driven measures of cognitive development that assess basic concepts and cognitive process in addition to traditional assessments of intelligence quotient and academic achievement.

## REFERENCES

Bluestone, C. K., Klein, J. O., Paradise, J. L., Eichenwald, H., Bess, F. H., Downs, M. P., Green, M., Berko-Gleason, J., Ventry, I. M., Gray, S. W., McWilliams, B. J., and Gates, G. A. 1983. Workshop on effects of otitis media on the child. *Pediatrics* 71:639–652.

DeLoache, J. S., Sugarman, S., and Brown, A. L. 1985. The development of error correction strategies in young children's manipulative play. *Child Development* 56: 928–939.

Feldman, H. M., Goldin-Meadow, S., Gleitman, L. R. 1977. Beyond Herodotus: The creation of language by linguistically deprived deaf children. *In* A. Lock (ed). *Action, Symbol, and Gesture: The Emergence of Language.* London: Academic Press.

Gelman, R., and Brown, A. 1986. Changing view of cognitive competence in the young. *In* N. J. Smelser and D. R. Gerstein (eds). *Behavioral and Social Science: Fifty Years of Discovery.* Washington, DC: National Academy Press.

Gibson, E. J., and Walker, A. S. 1984. Intermodal perception of substance. *Child Development* 55:453–460.

Gleitman, L. R., and Wanner, E. 1982. *Language Acquisition: The State of the Art.* Cambridge, England: Cambridge University Press.

Goldin-Meadow, S., and Mylander, C. 1984. Gestural communication in deaf children: The effects and noneffects of parental input on early language development. *Monograph of the Society for Research in Child Development*, Serial No. 206. Chicago: University of Chicago Press.

Gottlieb, G. 1983. The psychobiological approach to developmental issues. *In* M. M. Haith and J. J. Campos *Handbook of Child Psychology Volume II: Infancy and Developmental Psychobiology.* New York: John Wiley and Sons.

Horowitz, E. D., and Leake, H. 1980. Effects of otitis media on cognitive development. *The Annals of Otology, Rhinology & Laryngology,* Supp. 68. 89:264–268.

Howie, M. D. 1980. Developmental sequelae of chronic otitis media: A review. *Developmental and Behavioral Pediatrics* 1:34–38.

Hubbard, T. W., Paradise, J. L., McWilliams, B. J., Elster, B. A., and Taylor, F. H. 1985. Consequences of unremitting middle-ear disease in early life. *New England Journal of Medicine* 312:1529–1534.

Karmiloff-Smith, A., and Inhelder, B. 1974/75. 'If you want to get ahead, get a theory.' *Cognition* 3:95–212.

Landau, B., and Gleitman, L. R. 1985. *Language and Experience: Evidence from the Blind Child.* Cambridge, MA: Harvard University Press.

Lenneberg, E. H. 1967. *Biological Foundations of Language.* New York: John Wiley and Sons.

Leviton, A. 1980. Otitis media and learning disorders. *Developmental and Behavioral Pediatrics* 1:58–63.

Menyuk, P. 1980. Effect of persisitent otitis media on language development. *In* B. H. Senturia, C. D. Bluestone, D. J. Lim, and W. H. Saunders. *Recent Advances in Otitis Media with Effusion.* Proceedings of the Second International Symposium. St. Louis, Missouri: The Annals Publishing Company.

Needleman, H., and Menyuk, P. 1977. Effects of hearing loss from early recurrent otitis media on speech and language development. *In* B. F. Jaffe (ed). *Hearing Loss in Children.* Baltimore: University Park Press.

Newport, E. 1984. Constraints on learning: Studies on the acquisition of American sign language. *Papers and Reports on Child Language Development* Vol 23:1–22.

Paradise, J. L. 1981. Otitis media during early life: How hazardous to development? A critical review of the evidence. *Pediatrics* 68:869–873.

Piaget, J. P. 1975. *L'equilibration des Structures Cognitives,* Etudes d'epistemolgie genetique, Vol. 33. Paris: Presses Universitaires de France.

Premack, D. 1976. *Intelligence in Ape and Man.* New York: Halstead Press.

Schlieper, A., Kisilevsky, H., Mattingly, S., and Yorke, L. 1985. Mild conductive hearing loss and language development: A one year follow-up study. *Developmental and Behavioral Pediatrics* 6:65–68.

Teele, D. W., Klein, J. O., Rosner, B. A., 1984. Otitis media with effusion during the first three years of life and development of speech and language. *Pediatrics* 74:282–287.

Waxman, R., and Gelman, R. In press. Preschooler's use of superordinate relations in classification and language. *Cognitive Development.*

Zinkus, P. W., and Gottlieb, M. I. 1980. Patterns of perceptual and academic deficits related to early chronic otitis media. *Pediatrics* 66:246–253.

Zinkus, P. W., Gottlieb, M. I., and Schapiro, M. 1978. Developmental and psychoeducational sequelae of chronic otitis media. *American Journal of the Disabled Child* 132:1100–1104.

# Otitis Media: Identification and Diagnosis

# 4

# Risk Factors for Otitis Media in Children

*Jerome O. Klein*

Acute otitis media is defined by the presence of fluid in the middle ear accompanied by a recent sign of illness. The sign may be specific for ear disease such as otalgia, otorrhea, or hearing loss or it may be non-specific including fever, irritability, anorexia, vomiting, or diarrhea. Most children have at least one episode of acute otitis media and many have severe and recurrent disease. In addition to the morbidity of the acute infection, fluid persists in the middle ear for weeks to months after each episode of otitis media. The persistent middle ear effusion may be unrecognized by parents and physicians because the acute signs of disease resolve within a few days after the child receives appropriate antimicrobial therapy. The frequency of middle ear infections and prolonged time spent with middle ear effusion is of concern because most children have impaired hearing when fluid is present.

Certain host factors are associated with risk for acute and recurrent otitis media including young age, male sex, having a sibling with chronic ear disease, being bottle-fed in infancy, and having the onset of disease during the first year of life. Environmental factors such as those associated with season, crowding, poor hygiene, and day care play a role in increased incidence of respiratory infections including otitis media. The purpose of this paper is to review the factors that place children at risk for severe and recurrent infections of the middle ear.

## AGE

Otitis media is most frequent during the first three years of life. The peak incidence occurs between 6 and 18 months. A prospective study of 2500 Boston children revealed that by three years of age more than two thirds had at least one episode of otitis media and one third of children had three or more episodes of otitis media (Teele et al. 1980). By three years of age, children could be subdivided into three categories relative to ear infections: one-third had no problems, one third had occasional episodes associated with upper respiratory infections, but one-third had significant experience with severe and recurrent disease (Table 1). After age three the incidence of otitis media declines with age except for a limited reversal of the downward trend between five and six years of age, the time of entrance into school. Otitis media is relatively uncommon in children seven years of age and older.

Otitis media during the first year of life is of particular concern. In the Boston study, 9 percent of children had otitis media by three months of age and 25 percent by six months of age. Children who have infection early in life are most likely to have severe and recurrent disease. Infection of the middle ear in infancy is probably similar to infection of the urinary tract; early onset of infection identifies those children with an underlying anatomic or physiologic disability which is often first recognized by signs of infection. An alternative hypothesis is that otitis media in infancy damages the mucosa of the middle ear or eustachian tube leading to recurrent infections.

Age did not appear to be a significant factor in the duration of effusion after acute infections in Boston children. Fluid persisted for weeks to months in each of the first three years of life. The mean period of time spent with middle ear effusion after first, second, and third episodes of acute otitis media was similar—approximately 40 days.

## SEX

In most studies the incidence of acute episodes of otitis media was not significantly different in boys from that in girls. However, recent studies in Boston (Teele et al. 1980) and Finland (Pukander et al. 1982) identified significantly more episodes in males than in females. Males also have more myringotomies and tympanoplasties than do females, a fact suggesting that chronic or severe infections of the middle ear may be more common among males (Solomon and Harris 1976).

Table 1

Cumulative Incidence of Acute Otitis Media In Boston Children

| Age (Months) | Number of Episodes ≥ 1 | ≥3 |
|---|---|---|
| 3 | 9% | 0 |
| 6 | 25% | 0 |
| 12 | 47% | 9% |
| 24 | 65% | 24% |
| 36 | 71% | 33% |

## RACE

Studies of American Indians and Alaskan and Canadian Eskimos indicate an extraordinary incidence and severity of otitis media. Otorrhea is frequent although persistent effusion is uncommon. Some of these data are described by Todd elsewhere in this volume.

American Black children appear to have less disease due to middle ear infection than do White American children (Kessner, Snow, and Singer 1974; Bush and Rabin 1980). The higher incidence of ear disease may be associated with differences in anatomy of the bony eustachian tube. Significant differences in the length, width and angle of the tube was identified by Doyle (1977) in skulls of American Blacks, Americans of Caucasian ancestry, and American Indians. Beery and colleagues (1980) noted altered function of the eustachian tube in Apache Indians living in Arizona. Indians had lower forced opening pressures during inflation-deflation tests than had been measured previously in a group of Caucasians. The test results in the Apache group were interpreted as impairment of the protective function of the tube.

Few inter-racial studies have been done. Poverty is a common factor among many of the nonwhite populations that have been studied. Other variables, including extremes of climate, crowding, inadequate hygiene, poor sanitation, and lack of medical care need to be considered in evaluating the data about race as a risk factor for otitis media.

## SEASON

The seasonal incidence of infections in the middle ear parallels the seasonal variations of upper respiratory tract infections. Acute episodes peak during the winter and are least frequent in the summer. The incidence of episodes of otitis media also increases during outbreaks of viral infections of the respiratory tract; these are most likely to occur in the winter and spring (Henderson et al. 1982). Surveys of middle ear effusions in asymptomatic children indicate a greater prevalance in winter and fall than in summer (Shy et al. 1980) and effusions occurring in the winter persist longer than effusions occurring in summer (Lous and Fiellau-Nikolajsen 1981).

## GENETIC AND FAMILIAL FACTORS

A genetic predisposition to frequent and severe otitis media has been suggested. Children enrolled in the Boston study who had single or recurrent episodes of otitis media were more likely to have siblings with histories of significant middle ear infections than were children who had had no episodes of otitis media (Teele et al. 1980). Adopted Apache children had more episodes of acute otitis media than their non-Apache siblings and had an illness rate similar to that of Apache children who remained on the reservation (Spivey and Hirschorn 1977). The data of Prellner and colleagues (1985) suggest that genetic immunoglobulin markers may be present in some children with recurrent otitis media and in their parents.

## FEEDING TECHNIQUES

Breastfeeding has been suggested as an important factor in prevention of respiratory and gastrointestinal infections. Surveys of Eskimo children indicate an inverse relationship of incidence of middle ear disease and breast feeding (Schaefer 1971; Timmermans and Gerson 1980). In the Boston study (Teele et al. manuscript in preparation), breast feeding was associated significantly with decreased risk of recurrent acute otitis media (three or more episodes) but only in the first year of life. Ever breast fed was as significantly associated with protection as was breast feeding for six months or longer.

Does breast feeding protect against respiratory infections or does bottle feeding promote infection? A number of hypotheses have been suggested:

1. Immunologic factors of value are provided in breast milk which prevent various bacterial and virus infections.

2. The facial musculature, including muscles which affect eustachian tube function, develop differently in breast and bottle fed infants.

3. Bottle fed infants need to produce high negative intraoral pressure, and fluids are aspirated into the middle ear during feeding.

4. Bottle fed infants are often placed in a reclining or horizon-

tal position that may result in reflux of milk into the middle ear whereas breast fed infants are held in a vertical or semivertical reclining position.

5. Allergy to one or more components in cow or formula milk may result in alteration of the mucosa of the eustachian tube and middle ear.

The Boston data that duration of breast feeding was a significant factor in protection against otitis media in the first year of life suggests that immune materials in breast milk provide durable anti-infective qualities. Breast milk contains various immunoglobulins, leukocytes, non-antibody factors such as interferon, lysozyme and various components of complement. The immune theory is further bolstered by recent data identifying protection against otitis media in children with cleft palate fed by bottle (plus special nipple) with breast milk rather than fed by bottle with formula or cow's milk (Paradise 1984).

## DAY CARE

The number of American children who receive care outside of the home is large and growing. Current estimates are that more than 11 million children receive full or part-time day care. More than 50 percent of mothers of children younger than six years of age work outside the home. Day care centers vary in size from small groups to large centers. Some facilities have adequate room and ventilation whereas others are crowded and stuffy. In the day care setting coughing and sneezing at close range is frequent and epidemics of respiratory disease are common.

Data from North Carolina (Henderson et al. 1982) and Scandinavia (Strangert 1977; Pukander et al. 1982) suggest that the incidence of otitis media is higher in children who attend day care but problems of bias are present that may account for all or part of the difference of incidence in children in day care or in home care. We need studies of appropriate design that observe in a comparable fashion the incidence and severity of otitis media in children who attend day care and children in home care.

## SUMMARY

Otitis media is most frequent during the first three years of life with a peak incidence between 6 and 18 months. Analysis of data from the Boston study and corroborated in other investigations reveals that certain factors are associated with recurrent middle ear infections: male sex; having a sibling with chronic ear disease; never having been breast fed; and onset of disease during the first year of life. Certain racial groups may have a predilection to ear disease based on anatomic or physiologic problems. Racial predilection may be difficult to dissect from confounding variables such as the effects of poverty including crowding, poor sanitation, poor hygiene and inadequate medical care. Studies of children in day care indicate that respiratory infections are frequent and spread readily but there are no data from studies of adequate design that have compared the incidence of otitis media in children in day care and children in home care. Analysis of risk factors for otitis media suggests children who should be managed aggressively and in whom programs of prevention by means of chemoprophylaxis (use of prolonged courses of antimicrobial agents), immunoprophylaxis (use of vaccines), or aggressive surgery (placement of ventilating tubes in children with recurrent disease or prolonged time spent with middle ear effusion) are warranted.

## REFERENCES

Beery, Q. C., Doyle, W. J., Cantekin, E. I., Bluestone, C. D., and Wiet, R. J. 1980. Eustachian tube function in an American Indian population. *Annals of Otology, Rhinology and Laryngology*. 89(68):28–33.

Bush, P. J., and Rabin, D. L. 1980. Racial differences in encounter rates for otitis media. *Pediatric Research*. 14:1115–1117.

Doyle, W. J. 1977. A functiono-anatomic description of Eustachian tube vector relations in four ethnic populations—an osteologic study. Ph.D. Dissertation.

Henderson, F. W., Collier, A. M., Sanyal, M., Watkins, J. M., Fairclough, D. L., Clyde, W. A., Jr., and Denny F. W. 1982. A longitudinal study of respiratory viruses and bacteria in the etiology of acute otitis media with effusion. *New England Journal of Medicine*. 306:1377–1383.

Kessner, D. M., Snow, C. K., and Singer, J. 1974. Assessment of Medical Care for Children, Vol. 3. Washington, D. C., Institute of Medicine, National Academy of Sciences.

Lous, J., and Fiellau-Nikolajsen, M. 1981. Epidemiology of middle ear effusion and tubal dysfunction: A one year prospective study comprising monthly tympanometry in 387 nonselected seven year old children. *International Journal of Pediatric Otorhinolaryngology*. 3:303–317

Paradise, J. L., and Elster, B. A. 1984. Breast milk protests against otitis media with effusion. *Pediatric Research*. 18:283A.

Prellner, K., Hallberg, T., Kalm, O., and Mansson, B. 1985. Recurrent otitis media: Genetic immunoglobulin markers in children and their parents. *International Journal of Pediatric Otorhinolaryngology*. 9:219–225.

Pukander, J., Luotonen, J., Sipila, M., Timonen, M., and Karma, P. 1982. Incidence of acute otitis media. *Acta Otolaryngologica*. 93:447–453.

Schaefer, O. 1971. Otitis media and bottle-feeding. An epidemiological study of infant feeding habits and incidence of recurrent and chronic middle ear diseases in Canadian Eskimos. *Canadian Journal of Public Health* 62:478–489.

Sly, R. M., Zambie, M. F., Fernandes, D. A., and Fraser, M. 1980. Tympanometry in kindergarten children. *Annals of Allergy*. 44:1–7.

Solomon, N. E., and Harris, L. J. 1976. Otitis Media in Children. Assessing the Quality of Medical Care Using Short-Term Outcome Measures. Quality of Medical Care Assessment Using Outcome Measures: Eight Disease-Specific Applications. Santa Monica, California, Rand Corp.

Spivey, G. H., and Hirschorn, N. 1977. A migrant study of adopted Apache children. *Johns Hopkins Medical Journal.* 140:43–46.

Strangert, K. 1977. Otitis media in young children in different types of day-care. *Scandinavian Journal of Infectious Diseases.* 9:119–123.

Teele, D. W., Klein, J. O., and Rosner, B. A. 1980. Epidemiology of otitis media in children. *Annals of Otology, Rhinology and Laryngology.* 89(68):5–6.

Timmermans, F. J., and Gerson, S. 1980. Chronic granulomatous otitis media in bottle-fed Inuit children. *Canadian Medical Association Journal.* 122:545–547.

# 5

# High Risk Populations for Otitis Media

*N. Wendell Todd*

## Overview of the Natural History of Otitis Media

Otitis media typically begins in infancy, is a bilateral phenomenon, and is associated with small mastoid pneumatization. The manifestations of otitis media are largely related to the age of the patient. Typically, recurring acute suppurative otitis media is a problem in infancy, middle ear effusion in early childhood, then atelectatic otitis media or perforation of the tympanic membrane in the teenage years; atelectatic and adhesive disease, perforation, and cholesteatoma are generally adult manifestations. These manifestations are the same in various racial groups. With better living and health care conditions, the otitis media rates apparently persist, but with less severe manifestations (Todd and Bowman 1985). Aeration of the middle ear to atmospheric pressure seems the major determinant of whether mastoid pneumatization develops normally. Mastoid development is essentially complete when skeletal maturation is complete (Tos, Strangerup, and Hvid 1984).

A change in the otitis media process seems to occur when the patient gets to age two or three years. Most children seem to "outgrow" the problem at this age (Howie and Schwartz 1983). Also, the usefulness of antibiotic prophylaxis seems less after that age transition (Varsano, Volovitz, and Mimouni 1985).

## Factors Associated with Otitis Media

Persons who have otitis media problems may belong to one or more otitis-prone groups (Table I). Some of these groups, for example

Table I

Groups at increased risk for having otitis media

| ACCEPTED* | CONTROVERSIAL* |
|---|---|
| INTRINSIC* | INTRINSIC* |
| craniofacial anomaly (Bluestone and Klein 1983) | male (Biles 1980; Bylander 1985; Casselbrant et al. 1985; Klein 1982; Pukander et al. 1985) |
| Down syndrome | bifid uvula |
| cleft palate | low birth weight |
| congenital velopharyngeal insufficiency | blood group A+ (Fiellau-Nikolajsen and Farkas 1985) |
| achondroplastic dwarf | first born |
| race: Indians, Eskimos, aborigines > whites > blacks | sinusitis |
| large adenoids (Maw 1985) | tonsillitis (Van Cauwenberge 1985) |
| family history | persistent middle ear mesenchyme |
| tumor (Berry 1985) | |
| immune abnormality | |
| congenital cilial abnormality immotile cilia syndrome Young's syndrome (Handelsman et al. 1984) | |
| | |
| EXTRINSIC* | EXTRINSIC* |
| winter season (Biles et al. 1980; Casselbrant et al. 1985; Pukander 1985) | amniotic fluid aspiration |
| | socioeconomic status (Shaw et al. 1981) |
| bottle feeding (Saarinen 1982) | geographic location |
| day care (Vinther 1984) | supine bottle feeding (Saarinen 1982) |
| upper respiratory infection (Casselbrant et al. 1985; Bylander 1984; Van Cauwenberge 1985) | nasal septal deformity (McNicoll 1983) |
| | food allergy |
| inhalant allergy (Todd and Feldman 1985) | antihistamine/decongestant abuse |
| passive smoking of tobacco (Black 1985a; Kraemer et al. 1983; Pukander et al. 1985 | |
| barotrauma (Randal 1971) | |

*The groups in the "Accepted" category have good supporting evidence for such a designation. The groups in the "Controversial" category have inconsistent or limited supporting evidence. The groups in the "Intrinsic" category have defects within the individual persons. In contrast, the groups in the "Extrinsic" category comprise persons who are exogenously affected.

cleft palate persons and Native Americans, have good substantiation for such an otitis proneness. Some groups have limited substantiation for being designated otitis media prone; an example is the group of people with congenitally bifid uvula. Recurring bacterial infections characterized by occurrence at the same anatomic site, as is typical for most persons with otitis media, is usually the result of a physical-anatomic defect rather than being the initial consequence of an immune disorder (Johnston 1984). The bacterial flora of the nasopharynx is the same in children with recurring otitis media as it is in children without otitis media (Prellner et al. 1984).

The winter seasonal exacerbation of both clinical encounters for otitis media and tympanometrically-detected middle ear abnormality in longitudinal studies seems well substantiated (Biles, Buffler, and O'Donell 1980; Casselbrant et al. 1985; Pukander et al. 1985; Tos, Holm-Jensen, and Sorensen 1981). The mechanism is probably through upper respiratory tract infection (Van Cauwenberge 1985). Black has recently reviewed the evidence regarding a number of presumptive contributors to "glue" ear and found much of the evidence inadequate (1985b). Findings in different populations and circumstances must be read critically (Greggs and Steele 1982). Ideally, of course, prospective life-long longitudinal studies, with multivariant analysis, using standard diagnostic criteria and involving various racial groups, would be available. Until such studies are done, or until we conceptualize the problem differently, we will continue to grope, exploring various facets of the problem; as a blind man palpating various parts of an elephant, we will not elucidate the overall picture.

There are racial differences in the following: fractions of the infant population that are "otitis media prone," risks of persistence of middle ear effusion after acute otitis media (Shurin et al. 1979), fractions of the school age populations with otitis media (Pearlman and Niles 1981), rates of surgery for otitis media (Griffith 1979), rates of clinical otitis media in adults (Titche et al. 1981; Wiet et al. 1980).

The racial variations in otitis media incidence (high in Native Americans and Australian aborigines, low in blacks) may be regarded, in a sense, as a form of familial predisposition (McCafferty et al. 1985; Ratnesar 1982). About 10 percent of Apache Indians at White River, Arizona, have clinical otitis media, a rate several times greater than the general population of the United States. Familial occurrence has been suggested for otitis media in infants and children (Fiellau-Nikolajsen and Farkas 1985; Klein 1982; Tos, Poulsen, and Borch 1979); however, a study by Black (1985a) did not substantiate a familial occurrence. A familial pattern, that was not multifactorial, was suggested ($p < .02$) in Apache Indians at Canyon Day, Arizona (Todd 1985b). There are clinical reports of a familial occurrence of mastoid size (Dahlberg and Diamant 1945) and cholesteatoma in adults (Plester 1980).

Nevertheless, the majority of persons troubled by otitis media cannot presently be included in any of these groups. That is, there is no good explanation why this common illness affects some children, and why some have life-long otitis media.

## Role of the Eustachian Tube

The pathogenic route of otitis media is usually ascribed to the eustachian tube, hematogenous and contiguous spread being other routes. The eustachian tube, which is derived from the first and second branchial pouches, connects the nasopharynx to the middle ear. The lumen of the eustachian tube is usually closed for air passage, but opens during swallowing, sniffing, and maneuvers used to open the tube transiently, e.g. the Valsalva, Politzer, Toynbee, and Frenzel maneuvers. Normally, the gas pressure in the middle ear and mastoid air system is within about 100mm water pressure of the ambient atmospheric pressure.

---

Frenzel maneuver: Named for a twentieth century German. Performed by increasing the pressure in the nasopharynx by contraction of the superior constrictor muscle of the pharynx and the muscles of the floor of the mouth and elevation of the base of the tongue while the palate is closed.

Politzer maneuver: Named for the Hungarian otologist Adam Politzer, 1835–1920. Performed by forcing air through the nose while the nasopharynx is closed. Closure is accomplished by having the patient either swallow or repeat the letter "K" several times. The air can be introduced from a rubber bulb or other pressurized source.

Toynbee maneuver: Named for the English otologist Joseph Toynbee, 1815–1866. Performed by pinching the nostrils closed and swallowing.

Valsalva maneuver: Named for the Italian anatomist Antonio Maria Valsalva, 1666–1723. Performed by holding shut both sides of the nose and mouth and blowing out the cheeks with forcible expiration.

---

The eustachian tube may be considered to have four functions (Table II). The most phylogenetically and ontogenetically ancient, and hence probably the most robust function for the human surviving embryogenesis, is that of mucociliary clearance. Indeed, the frog palate is commonly used for in vitro mucociliary transport studies of human mucin (Wetmore et al. 1983). Lesions arising early in embryogenesis usually have more drastic (i.e., lethal) effects since many more cells are involved. Remarkably, cystic fibrosis, a life-limiting congenital mucosal disease of the aerodigestive tract, is not associated with an increased occurrence of otitis media problems. In general, the mucus properties relating to viscoelasticity and surface tension are apparently not of clinical significance.

The eustachian tube's remaining three functions involve pressure and volume transmission through the lumen of the eustachian tube. These functions relate to the musculo-skeletal support derived from the branchial apparatus. The branchial apparatus is, compared to the mucociliary, phylogenetically and ontogenetically

Table II

| Functions of the eustachian tube |
| --- |

1. Ventilation of air from the nasopharynx into the middle ear, so that atmospheric pressure is maintained in the middle ear.
2. Mucociliary clearance, by the mucociliary escalator system, from the mastoid air cell system and middle ear, into the nasopharynx.
3. Protection of the middle ear from pressure fluctuations in the nasopharynx during sniffing.
4. Protection of the middle ear from aspiration of liquid from nasopharynx.

more recent, and hence is probably more commonly involved with malformations that do not affect the survivability of the embryo. The enthusiasm afforded tympanotomy-tubes for the past three decades may be considered support for the crucial importance of the ventilation function of the eustachian tube.

A guide to the etiologic classification of eustachian tube disorders is presented in Table III. Eustachian tube problems may generally be considered as being congenital (becoming apparent in infancy) or acquired, and as involving the mucociliary or musculoskeletal parts of the tube. Acquired eustachian tube problems, whether mucociliary or musculoskeletal, are usually unilateral. In contrast, the congenital problems, whether mucociliary or musculoskeletal, are bilateral.

A "different" eustachian tube is probably the prime etiologic factor for otitis media. The different eustachian tube manifests anatomically as having an abnormally large caliber at bougie assessment (Todd 1983, 1985a), and functionally as semi-patulous (Falk and Magnuson 1985; Jorgensen and Holmquist 1984). The different eustachian tube presumably accounts for the mechanisms of low pressurization of the middle ear, of inhalant allergens and irritants contributing to otitis media, and for reflux from nasopharynx into the middle ear. The different eustachian tube, which is probably genetically determined,

Table III

| | Guide to etiologic classification of eustachian tube disorders | |
| --- | --- | --- |
| | *MUSCULOSKELETAL* | *MUCOCILIARY* |
| *CONGENITAL* bilateral, infancy onset | cleft palate craniofacial syndromes achondroplastic dwarf Down syndrome "different" tube* | immotile cilia syndrome Young's syndrome |
| *ACQUIRED* unilateral | longitudinal temporal fracture tumor | tumor scarring after radiation or infection upper respiratory infection + inhalant irritant, allergen + |

*See text above.
+Factors probably operative clinically in persons having "different" eustachian tubes.

may be the crucial factor that allows potential insults to contribute to the occurrence of otitis media. With this conceptualization, perhaps the enigma of otitis media may be elucidated.

The mechanism by which the removal of large adenoids improves the otitis media patient is undetermined. Apparently the benefit is only in those with large adenoids, and in those who have already had otitis media. Perhaps the large adenoids narrow the nasopharyngeal airway so much that sniffing produces, by the venturi effect, tremendously negative air pressure in the nasopharynx, which is transmitted through the "different" eustachian tube to the middle ear.

INDICATIONS FOR TYMPANOTOMY-TUBE:

1. PERSISTENT MIDDLE EAR EFFUSION WITH COMMUNI-CATIVELY-SIGNIFICANT CONDUCTIVE HEARING LOSS

2. RETRACTED TYMPANIC MEMBRANE WITH RISKS OF CHOLESTEATOMA OR ADHESIVE OTITIS

REFERENCES

Berry, Q. C. 1985. Eustachian tube function and certain tumors of the head and neck. *Annals of Otology, Rhinology, & Laryngology.* Vol. 94, supplement 120, part 5. (eds. Bluestone, C. D. and Doyle, W. J.) 43–44.

Biles, R. W., Buffler, P. A., and O'Donell, A. A. 1980. Epidemiology of otitis media: A community study. *American Journal of Public Health* 70:593–598.

Black, N. 1985a. The aetiology of glue ear—a case-control study. *International Journal of Pediatric Otorhinolaryngology* 9:121–133.

Black, N. 1985b. Causes of glue ear: An historical review of theories and evidence. *Journal of Laryngology and Otology* 99:953–966.

Bluestone, C. D. and Klein, J. O. 1983. Otitis media with effusion, atelectasis, and eustachian tube dysfunction. *In* C. D. Bluestone and S. E. Stool (eds.). *Pediatric Otolaryngology.* pp. 356–512, Philadelphia: W. B. Saunders.

Bylander, A. 1984. Upper respiratory tract infection and eustachian tube function in children. *Acta Otolaryngologica (Stockholm)* 97:343–349.

Bylander, A. 1985. Influence of age, sex, and race on eustachian tube function. *Annals of Otology, Rhinology, & Laryngology* Vol. 94, supplement 120, part 5. (eds. Bluestone, C. D. and Doyle, W. J.) 28–29.

Casselbrant, M. L., Brostoff, L. M., Cantekin, E. I., Flaherty, M. R., Doyle, W. J., Bluestone, C. D., and Fria, T. J. 1985. Otitis media with effusion in preschool children. *Laryngoscope* 95:428–436.

Dahlberg, G. and Diamant, M. 1945. Hereditary character of the cellular system in the mastoid process. *Acta Otolaryngologica (Stockholm)* 33:378–389.

Falk, B. and Magnuson, B. 1985. Eustachian tube closing failure: Summary of experimental results. *Annals of Otology, Rhinology, & Laryngology* Vol. 94, supplement 120, part 5. (eds. Bluestone, C. D. and Doyle, W. J.) 40–41.

Fiellau-Nikolajsen, M. and Farkas, S. 1985. Hereditary factors in secretory otitis media: A prospective cohort study. Paper read at *International Symposium on Acute and Secretory Otitis Media,* 17–22 November 1985, at Jerusalem. Amsterdam: Kugler.

Gregg, J. B. and Steele, J. P. 1982. Mastoid development in ancient and modern populations: A longitudinal radiological study. *Journal of the American Medical Association* 248:459–464.

Griffith, T. E. 1979. Epidemiology of otitis media—an interracial study. *Laryngoscope* 89:22–30.

Handelsman, D. J., Conway, A. J., Boylan, L. M., and Turtle, J. R. 1984. Young's syndrome: Obstructive azoospermia and chronic sinopulmonary infections. *New England Journal of Medicine* 310:3–9.

Howie, V. M. and Schwartz, R. H. 1983. Acute otitis media: One year in general pediatric practice. *American Journal of Diseases of Children* 137:155–158.

Johnston, R. B., Jr. 1984. Recurrent bacterial infections in children: Current concepts. *New England Journal of Medicine* 310:1237–1243.

Jorgensen, F. and Holmquist, J. 1984. Toynbee phenomenon and middle ear disease. *American Journal Otology* 5(4):291–294.

Klein, J. O. 1982. Persistent middle ear effusions: Natural history and morbidity. *Pediatric Infectious Disease* 1 [supplement] S4-S10.

Kraemer, M. J., Richardson, M. A., Weiss, N. S., Furukawa, C. T., Shapiro, G. G., Pierson, W. E., and Bierman, C. W. 1983. Risk factors for persistent middle-ear effusions. *Journal of the American Medical Association* 249:1022–1025.

Maw, A. R. 1985. Factors affecting adenoidectomy for otitis media with effusion (glue ear). *Journal of the Royal Society of Medicine* 78:1014–1018.

McCafferty, G. J., Lewis, A. N., Coman, W. B., and Mills, C. 1985. A nine-year study of ear disease in Australian Aboriginal children. *Journal of Laryngology and Otology* 99:117–125.

McNicoll, W. D. 1983. Otitis media with effusion in children and its association with deformity of the vomero-ethmoid suture. *Journal of Laryngology and Otology* 97:203–212.

Pearlman, R. C., and Niles, L. A. 1981. The incidence of hearing disorders in the schoolchildren of Trinidad. *American Journal of Otolaryngology* 2:311–314.

Plester, D. 1980. Hereditary factors in chronic otitis with cholesteatoma. *Acta-Otorhinolaryngologica (Belgium)* 34:51–55.

Prellner, K., Christensen, P., Hovelius, B., and Rosen, C. 1984. Nasopharyngeal carriage of bacteria in otitis-prone and non-otitis-prone children in day-care centres. *Acta Otolaryngologica (Stockholm)* 98:343–350.

Pukander, J., Luotonen, J., Timonen, M. and Karma, P. 1985. Risk factors affecting the occurrence of acute otitis media among 2–3-year-old urban children. *Acta Otolaryngologica (Stockholm)* 100:260–265.

Randal, H. W. 1971. *Aerospace Medicine.* 2nd ed. p. 89. Baltimore: Williams and Wilkins.

Ratnesar, P. 1982. Ethnic origin: An important factor in the surgical management of chronic ear disease and cholesteatoma. In *Cholesteatoma and Mastoid Surgery*, Proceedings IInd International Conference, Tel Aviv, Israel, 22–27 March 1981, pp. 101–104. Amsterdam: Kugler.

Saarinen, U. M. 1982. Prolonged breast feeding as prophylaxis for recurrent otitis media. *Acta Pediatrica Scandinavia* 71:567–571.

Shaw, J. R., Todd, N. W., Goodwin, M. H., Jr., and Feldman, C. M. 1981. Observations on the relation of environmental and behavioral factors to occurrence of otitis media among Indian children. *Public Health Reports* 96:342–349.

Shurin, P. A., Pelton, S. I., Donner, A., and Klein, J. O. 1979. Persistence of middle-ear effusion after acute otitis media in children. *New England Journal of Medicine* 300:1121–1123.

Titche, L. L., Coulthard, S. W., Wachter, R. D., Thies, A. C., and Harris, L. L. 1981. Prevalence of mastoid infection in prehistoric Arizona Indians. *American Journal of Physical Anthropology* 56:269–273.

Todd, N. W. 1983. Otitis media and eustachian tube caliber. *Acta Otolaryngologica (Stockholm)* 404 (Suppl) 1–17.

Todd, N. W. 1985a. Inverse correlation of eustachian tube caliber and mastoid size: A cadaver study. Paper read at *International Symposium on Acute and Secretory Otitis Media*, 17–22 November 1985, at Jerusalem. Amsterdam: Kugler.

Todd, N. W. 1985b. Familial predisposition for otitis media in Apache Indians at Canyon Day, Arizona. Paper read at meeting of *Society for Ear, Nose, and Throat Advances in Children*, 5–8 December 1985, at Dallas, Texas.

Todd, N. W. and Bowman, C. A. 1985. Otitis media at Canyon Day, Arizona: A 16-year follow-up in Apache Indians. *Archives of Otolaryngology* 111:606–608.

Todd, N. W. and Feldman, C. M. 1985. Allergic airway disease and otitis media in children. *International Journal of Pediatric Otorhinolaryngology* 10:27–35.

Tos, M., Poulsen, G. and Borch, J. 1979. Etiologic factors in secretory otitis. *Archives of Otolaryngology* 106:582–588.

Tos, M., Holm-Jensen, S., and Sorensen, C. H. 1981. Changes in prevalence of secretory otitis from summer to winter in four year old children. *American Journal of Otology* 2:324–327.

Tos, M., Stangerup, S. E. and Hvid, G. 1984. Mastoid pneumatization: Evidence of the environmental theory. *Archives of Otolaryngology* 110:502–507.

Van Cauwenberge, P. 1985. Otitis media in relation to other upper respiratory tract infections. Paper read at *International Symposium on Acute and Secretory Otitis Media*, 17–22 November 1985, at Jerusalem. Amsterdam: Kugler.

Varsano, I., Volovitz, B. and Mimouni, F. 1985. Sulfisoxazole prophylaxis of middle ear effusion and recurrent acute otitis media. *American Journal of Diseases of Children* 139:632–635.

Vinther, B., Pedersen, C. B. and Elbrond, O. 1984. Otitis media in childhood. Sociomedical aspects with special reference to day-care conditions. *Clinical Otolaryngology* 9:3–8.

Wetmore, R. F., Brown, D. T., Litt, M., and Potsic, W. P. 1983. Human tracheal mucin: A preliminary study of physicochemical properties and mucociliary transport. *Otolaryngology, Head and Neck Surgery* 91:509–515.

Wiet, R. J., DeBlanc, G. B., Stewart, J., and Weider, D. J. 1980. Natural history of otitis media in the American native. *Annals of Otology, Rhinology & Laryngology* Vol. 89, supplement 68, part 2.

# 6

# Medical Aspects of Diagnosis and Prevention of Otitis Media

*Paul A. Shurin, Candice E. Johnson,* and *Dara L. Wegman*

Research has supported the thesis that those children who suffer greatest morbidity from chronic or recurrent otitis media (OM) have disease which begins in the early months of life. The relative incidence of otitis media with age was defined by research done in the 1960s and 70s by Virgil Howie in Huntsville, Alabama. Howie followed 488 children born into his practice for a total of 72 months, and 327 of them experienced one or more episodes of OM. He defined an "otitis-prone condition" (six or more diagnosed episodes) that existed in approximately 12 percent of his population (Table I). Klein (1985) and Freijd, Oxelius and Rynnel-Dagoo (1985) have also reported a 12 percent occurrence of chronic or recurrent otitis in the general pediatric population. Howie's findings (Howie, Ploussard, and Slayer 1975) further revealed that of this otitis-prone group, 90 percent had experienced the onset of disease in the first year of life.

A prospective study was performed in Cleveland by Marchant et al. (1984) to further define the high-risk group for chronic or recurrent OM. Seventy infants were followed for the first year of life, and pneumatic otoscopy was done at all well-child and illness visits. Working definitions of the various states of OM were established and used as follows: 1) acute OM–presence of effusion with some symptoms; 2) recurrent OM–three or more acute episodes and 3) bilateral chronic OM with effusion–the persistence of effusion in both ears for a period of at least three months.

Results from this prospective study showed that bilateral chronic otitis media with effusion eventually developed in eight of 24 (33%) infants with onset of the first epidsode of acute otitis media

Table I

Relationship of Otitis Proneness with Age at Time of
Initial Episode of Otitis Media*

| Number of Episodes | Age at Initial Episode, Months | |
| --- | --- | --- |
| | 0–11 | 12–72 |
| Less than 6 | 188 | 82 |
| 6 or more | 52 | 5 |
| Total | 240 | 87 |

*$X^2 = 10.2$, $p< .005$
(From Howie, V. M., Ploussard, J. H., Sloyer, J. 1975. The "otitis prone" condition. *American Journal of Diseases of Children* 129:676–678. Copyright 1975, American Medical Association.)

before age two months, compared to two of 30 (7%) with later onset ($p = 0.012$) (Table II, section A). If one looked only at the well-child visit at age two months, eight of 15 (53%) infants with bilateral middle ear effusion at age two months subsequently had bilateral chronic otitis media with effusion, compared to two of 55 (4%) infants without bilateral effusions at age two months ($p = 0.000007$) (Table II, Section B). An additional finding in this study was that 44 percent (31 of 70) of the initial episodes of OM presented asymptomatically, which suggests that careful otoscopic examinations should be performed at well-child visits.

Studies such as the preceding have indicated the value of accurate diagnostic procedures for proper management of otitis-prone children, with emphasis on procedures applicable to infants in the first few months of life. Currently, the most widely used diagnostic method

Table II

Outcome of Otitis Media in First Year of Life

| | Number of Infants | Infants with Recurrent Otitis Media | | Infants with Bilateral Chronic Otitis Media with Effusion | |
| --- | --- | --- | --- | --- | --- |
| | | N | % | N | % |
| A) Onset of otitis media | | | | | |
| Age ≤ 2 mo. | 24 | 10 | 42 | 8 | 33* |
| Age > 2 mo. | 30 | 15 | 50 | 2 | 7* |
| No otitis media | 16 | | | | |
| Total | 70 | | | | |
| B) Presence of otitis media at age 2 mo. | | | | | |
| Bilateral | 15 | 5 | 33 | 8 | 53** |
| Unilateral | 3 | 2 | 67 | | 0 |
| None | 52 | 18 | 35 | 2 | 4** |
| Total | 70 | 25 | 36 | 10 | 14 |

*$p = 0.012$
**$p = 0.000007$
(From Marchant, C. D., Shurin, P. A., Turczyk, V. A., Wasikowski, D. E., Tutihasi, M. A., and Kinney, S. E. 1984. Course and outcome of otitis media in early infancy: A prospective study. *Journal of Pediatrics* 104:826–831.)

is pneumatic otoscopy, which permits direct visualization of the movement of the entire tympanic membrane (TM) during insufflation, provided an airtight seal is achieved. (Figures 1 and 2). However, it is a very difficult diagnostic procedure, and its accuracy has never been demonstrated except by highly skilled researchers in the field. This technique is also a somewhat painful procedure, especially in young infants. Visualization of the entire TM may require a lengthy, tedious procedure of freeing the canal of wax and debris, and may include difficulties in tightly fitting the speculum into the canal to achieve an air-tight seal. These difficulties are present even when a highly skilled practitioner attempts examination, but pneumatic otoscopy, for now, remains the method of choice.

Alternative diagnostic procedures include tympanometry with acoustic reflex testing, reflectometry, and tympanocentesis. Tympanocentesis is employed only in clinical research and in selected clinical situations: infants under six weeks of age in whom unusual pathogens may occur; immunologically-suppressed children; symptomatic children who are failing antibiotic therapy; and severely ill children admitted to the hospital with effusions. The procedure is not

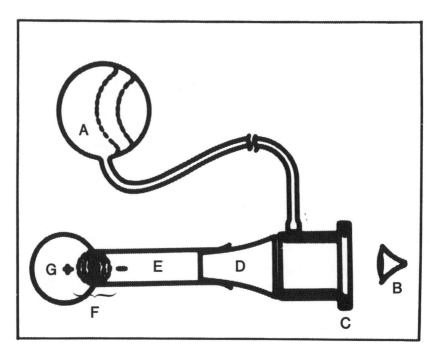

Figure 1. Diagram of pneumatic otoscope. The bulb (A) is squeezed or relaxed to produce either positive or negative pressure in the external ear canal (E). Observer (B) may directly view movement of the tympanic membrane (F) through the lens (C) and speculum (D). (G) designates the middle ear space.

| DEGREE OF TYMPANIC MOVEMENT ON PNEUMATIC OTOSCOPY | | | | | |
|---|---|---|---|---|---|
| | EXTERNAL CANAL PRESSURE | | | | MIDDLE EAR PRESSURE |
| TYMPANIC MEMBRANE POSITION | Low Positive | High Positive | Low Negative | High Negative | |
| 1 Neutral (normal) | + | ++ | + | ++ | Normal |
| 2 Neutral (hypermobile) | ++ | +++ | ++ | +++ | Normal |
| 3 Neutral (thickened) | 0 | + | 0 | + | Normal |
| 4 Retracted | 0 | 0 | + | ++ | Low negative |
| 5 Retracted | 0 | 0 | 0 | + | High negative |
| 6 Retracted | 0 | 0 | 0 | 0 | Very high negative or indeterminate |
| 7 Full | 0 | + | 0 | 0 | Positive or indeterminate |
| 8 Bulging | 0 | 0 | 0 | 0 | Positive or indeterminate |

Figure 2. The degree of tympanic membrane movement varies during insufflation in correlation to the presence or absence of middle ear effusion. (From Bluestone, C. D. and Shurin, P. A. 1974. Middle Ear Disease in Children. *Pediatrics Clinics in North America* 21(2):381.)

relevant to the detection of middle ear effusion in the general population.

Tympanometry and acoustic reflex testing deserve consideration since they are painless procedures without risk. In children over seven months of age, using the variance patterns defined by Paradise, Smith, and Bluestone (1976), Cantekin and his co-workers (1980) established the reliability of tympanometry performed at 220 Hz (Figure 3). However, Paradise et al. (1976) found that infants under seven months had an unacceptably high rate of false-negative studies in the presence of effusion using these patterns. Groothius et al. (1979), using the same instrument, found that tympanometry performed equally well in infants less than seven months of age compared to older infants and children. Shurin, Pelton, and Finkelstein (1977) tested both 220 Hz and 660 Hz and, using peak susceptance at 660 Hz, found that it was possible to distinguish normal ears from those with effusion for children four months of age and older. In this study the presence of effusion was verified by tympanocentesis if otoscopy indicated effusion. A peak susceptance of 0.16 mmho was found to best discriminate ears that were normal from those with effusion.

Because of the small number of young infants in Shurin, Pelton and Finkelstein's study, a second study of tympanometry in

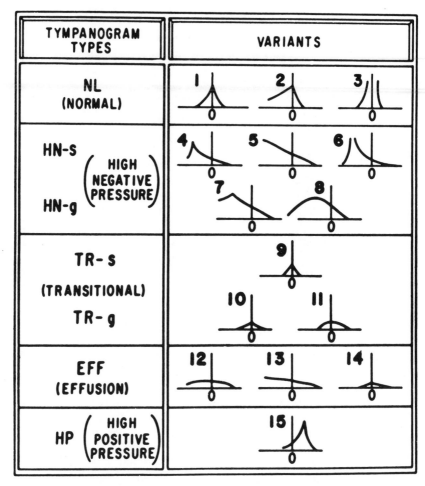

| TYMPANOGRAM TYPES | VARIANTS |
|---|---|
| NL (NORMAL) | |
| HN-s (HIGH NEGATIVE PRESSURE) HN-g | |
| TR-s (TRANSITIONAL) TR-g | |
| EFF (EFFUSION) | |
| HP (HIGH POSITIVE PRESSURE) | |

Figure 3. Tympanometric variants (at 220 Hz probe tone) are used to interpret test patterns which indicate presence or absence of middle ear effusion. (From Paradise, J. L., Smith, C. F., and Bluestone, C. D. 1976. Tympanometric detections of middle ear effusion in infants and children. *Pediatrics* 58:198–210. Reproduced by permission of *Pediatrics*.)

infants under five months of age was conducted. Marchant et al. (1985) studied 79 children with middle ear effusion and 82 normal children under the age of five months evaluating tympanometry, acoustic reflex measurements, and pneumatic otoscopy by two experienced otoscopists. Tympanograms that measured at 660 Hz probe tone were analyzed for both mean and peak susceptance; peak susceptance was found to be the more discriminating measurement for determination of middle ear status. Furthermore, an excellent agreement (Kappa 0.76 to 0.82) existed between susceptance tympanometry, ipsilateral acoustic reflex testing and pneumatic otoscopy. The sensitivity of peak susceptance was 0.89, and the specificity was 0.93 using the presence of any positive deflection as the decision criteria. Therefore, the 660 Hz peak susceptance tympanogram appears to be an accurate and effective procedure for evaluating the presence of middle ear effusion in very young infants. Drawbacks of tympanometry include the initial equipment costs and the time required to secure a good test. Tympanometry is atraumatic, does not require a thorough cleaning of the canal, and may be mastered readily by office assistants with practice. Tympanograms and reflexes are not applicable for use in diagnosing perforated or tympanostomy tube-bearing drums, or for evaluating extremely active or agitated children.

A final technique for evaluation of the middle ear is acoustic reflectometry. This quick, non-invasive procedure is attractive in that children need not be immobile or quiet while the test is performed. Like tympanometry, it is atraumatic and objective, but works on the principle of measuring sound reflected in the ear from an 80 dB source which varies from 2 to 4.5 Khz, over a 100 millisecond period. Published research findings for this relatively new device are scant, but Lampe and co-workers (1985) have evaluated reflectometry in children six months and older. On Teele and Teele's (1984) scale, high reflectivity (5-9 units) indicates effusion-filled ears and low reflectivity (0-4) indicates normal ears. Seventy-five children (141 ears) were tested prior to undergoing tympanocentesis or myringotomy for tube placement. Within this cohort, a specificity of 69.8 percent was seen, with an accompanying sensitivity of 86.7 percent. False-positive errors were usually found in association with thickened tympanic membranes. False-negative errors occurred in ears with air-fluid levels. Several ears, when tested and retested, exhibited inconsistent readings of 3, 4, or 5 depending upon the placement of the tip in the canal. It appears that reflectometry has its own set of drawbacks, and further research is needed to compare its accuracy with acoustic tympanometry. However, reflectometry requires less patient cooperation and offers a quick and mobile companion test to tympanometry.

All diagnostic methods have certain shortcomings, but by combining the above techniques we will enhance early detection of effusion. Enhancing our diagnostic abilities can improve our ability to identify, early in infancy, those children who will benefit from special preventive management. The most widely accepted prevention strategy in pediatrics is the chemoprophylaxis of OM with, most commonly, a sulfonamide such as sulfisoxazole. Perrin et al. (1974) studied 54 children, eleven months to eight years of age who had experienced at least three episodes of OM in the previous six months. Using a double-blind crossover design in which each child served as his own control, sulfisoxazole was compared to placebo for three months each. All children were placed on twice a day dosing. Results indicated a

Table III

| Sulfisoxazole Prophylaxis of Otitis Media | | |
|---|---|---|
| Attack Rate by Age | Sulfisoxazole | Placebo |
| 0–3 years | 0.09 | 1.82 |
| 4–5 years | 0.0 | 0.94 |
| 6–8 years | 0.35 | 0.43 |
| | $p<.01$ | |

(From Perrin, J. M., Charney, E., MacWhinney, Jr., J. B., McInerny, T. K., Miller, R. L., and Nazarian, L. F. 1974. Sulfisoxazole as chemoprophylaxis for recurrent otitis media. *New England Journal of Medicine.* 291:664–667. Reprinted by permission of the *New England Journal of Medicine.*)

20-fold reduction in the attack rate of acute OM (Table III). Only one child out of an initial 70 recruited dropped out, due to urticaria that developed while on the sulfonamide.

Other studies, employing slightly different strategies, have confirmed this result. Biedel (1978) supplied sulfonamides to high-risk children only when they were experiencing an upper respiratory infection, and found a 4-fold lowered rate of OM. Gray (1982) performed a double-blind year-long study of trimethoprim-sulfa in 50 high-risk infants; a 5-fold lower rate was observed in compliant infants, and no allergic reactions were observed. Chemoprophylaxis, however, carries the risk of allergic reactions to sulfonamides, including Stevens-Johnson syndrome. Antibiotic prophylaxis also requires parental compliance—a genuine problem in some families. Safer and more effective modalities for prevention of otitis are now being developed.

Vaccines have long been under study for prevention of OM, but the central problem remains the poor response of infants to polysaccharide capsular antigens. Several controlled trials have looked at the efficacy of pneumococcal vaccine in preventing OM in early childhood. Two trials using an octavalent vaccine showed no reduction in total episodes of OM, but showed a definite reduction in type-specific episodes (Sloyer, Ploussard, and Howie (1981); Teele et al. 1981). When data from the Huntsville study were further analyzed, a greater than 50 percent reduction in all episodes of OM was seen in black infants 6 to 11 months of age, but not in comparably aged white infants or older children of either race (Table IV) (Howie et al. 1984).

A study of 14-valent vaccine in Finland by Makela et al. (1981) showed a 15 percent reduction in all OM in the first six months after vaccination, but a 50 percent reduction in pneumococcal otitis. No protective effect was demonstrated with vaccination before seven months of age. In older children, two of three studies of vaccine (Douglas and Miles 1984; Makela et al. 1981; Rosen et al. 1984) have

Table IV

Episodes of Otitis Media (OM) Following Administration of
Pneumococcal Vaccine

| Race/Vaccine Status | No. of Patients | OM Episodes/Child Year Observed | |
| --- | --- | --- | --- |
| | | 1st Yr | 2nd Yr |
| White/vaccinated | 33 | 1.6 | .56 |
| White/control subjects | 34 | 1.7 | 1.0 |
| Black/vaccinated | 32 | .85 | .40 |
| Black/control subjects | 31 | 1.8 | .64 |

(From Howie, V. M., Ploussard, J. H., Sloyer, J., and Hill, J. C. 1984. Use of pneumococcal polysaccharide vaccine in preventing otitis media in infants: Different results
between racial groups. *Pediatrics* 73:79–82. Reproduced by permission of *Pediatrics*.)

shown significant reductions in total episodes of otitis media, ranging
from 12-20 percent. Just as in infants, there was a much larger effect on
vaccine-type pneumococcal disease (36-58 percent reduction).

In summary then, overall rates of otitis media will not be
reduced appreciably with pneumococcal vaccine, except perhaps in
black infants. This does not imply, however, that type-specific protection is not important, but rather that pneumococcal infections are
only a fraction of all otitis media.

A final method to be considered as a prevention strategy for
OM is immunoprophylaxis. As early as 1961, Diamant et al. evaluated
immune serum globulin (ISG) for prevention of OM in a non-blinded,
but randomly assigned, population of high-risk children. The controls
received no placebo; the treatment group received an injection of ISG
once a month for six months. Results showed two statistically significant findings: 1) the frequency of relapse in the ISG group was only
about one half that of the controls and (2) up to five recurrences were
seen in untreated controls, whereas no ISG-treated child experienced
more than two relapses in the fifteen-month course of study.

In 1983, Shurin et al. (in preparation) began a study of passive, immunoprophylaxis of OM in an animal model, in conjunction
with Giebink, of Minneapolis. In two separate experiments, using
double-blind random design, six chinchillas were given a human
bacterial polysaccharide immune globulin (HBPIG), and six chinchillas
received placebo injections of saline. The globulin was developed by
the Massachussetts Department of Health, the Dana Farber Cancer
Center, and the National Institute of Allergy and Infectious Disease.
HBPIG is a gammaglobulin made from the plasma of volunteers who
have received meningococcal, *H. influenzae,* and polyvalent pneumococcal vaccines.

In the experimental model, all right middle ears were inocu-
lated directly through the epitympanic bulla with 20 colony-forming

units of *S. pneumoniae* type 7F, three days after receiving HBPIG or placebo injections. Otoscopy, tympanometry, and blood cultures were performed regularly, and middle ear culture done when otoscopy or tympanometry yielded abnormal results. All six control animals developed pneumococcal OM within two days, and some of these animals had persistent effusions at sacrifice on day 31. The 12 HBPIG-treated chinchillas failed to develop pneumococcal OM. Approximately half of the controls developed sepsis or meningitis or died of infection, but none of the HBPIG treated animals did so.

With these encouraging results, in 1984 we began a clinical trial of the efficacy of HBPIG for prevention of otitis media in high risk infants, supported by the National Institute of Child Health and Human Development. The trial involves children 2 to 24 months of age with a history of one to three documented episodes of OM beginning in the first year of life. On a randomized double-blind basis, they receive an injection of either a saline placebo or one-half millimeter per kilogram of the globulin preparation; the same dose is repeated one month later. Enrollees are followed very carefully for four months, with acute attacks of OM documented by tympanocentesis and culture. To emphasize again the high-risk status of these children, prior to beginning the trial we predicted that one-third of our cohort would develop pneumococcal OM during the four month follow up period. This rate has actually been 50 percent higher than predicted. This trial is still in progress, but regardless of the efficacy of passive immunoprophylaxis, our findings will provide useful information on how immunoglobulin contributes to defense against bacterial otitis media and, potentially, the role of gammaglobulin in mucosal immune function.

In conclusion, diagnostic methods for otitis media must be applicable to very young infants if preventive strategies are to be useful. The otitis-prone condition develops in the first two months of life in the large majority of children, but may present as asymptomatic effusions. The ability to identify high-risk children early in life provides an opportunity for prevention strategies to be used before the critical period of language acquisition has ended. The prevention approaches now available will have only a limited effect on the public health problem of OM, but the development of new vaccines and immunoprophylactic measures holds promise for the future.

## REFERENCES

Biedel, C. W. 1978. Modification of recurrent otitis media by short-term sulfonamide therapy. *American Journal of Diseases of Children* 132:681–683.

Cantekin, E. I., Bluestone, C. D., Fria, T. J., Stool, S. E., Bury, Q. C., and Sabo, D. L.

1980. Identification of otitis media with effusion in children. *Annals of Otology, Rhinology and Laryngology* 89 (Suppl. 68):190–195.

Diamant, M., Ek, S., Kallós, P., and Rubensohn, G. 1961. Gammaglobulin treatment and protection against infections. *Acta Otolaryngologica* 53:317–327.

Douglas, R. M., and Miles, H. B. 1984. Vaccination against *Streptococcus pneumoniae* in childhood: Lack of demonstrable benefit in young Australian children. *The Journal of Infectious Disease* 149:861–869.

Freijd, A., Oxelius, V. A., and Rynnel-Dagoo, B. 1985. A prospective study demonstrating an association between plasma IgG2 concentrations and susceptibility to otitis media in children. *Scandinavian Journal of Infectious Disease* 17:115–120.

Gray, B. M. 1982. A controlled trial of sulfa-trimethoprim for the prevention of recurrent otitis media in young children. *In* P. Periti and G. G. Grassi (eds.). *Current Chemotherapy and Immunotherapy* Vol. II Washington: ASM Publishers.

Groothius, J. R., Sell, S. H. W., Wright, P. F., Thompson, J. M., and Altemeier, W. A. 1979. Otitis media in infancy: Tympanometric findings. *Pediatrics* 63:435–442.

Howie, V. M., Ploussard, J., Sloyer, J. L., and Hill, J. C. 1984. Use of pneumococcal polysaccharide vaccine in preventing otitis media in infants: Different results between racial groups. *Pediatrics* 73:79–82.

Howie, V. M., Ploussard, J. H., and Sloyer, J. 1975. The "otitis-prone" condition. *American Journal of Diseases of Children* 129:676–678.

Klein, J. O. 1985. Risk factors for otitis media. Presentation at Otitis Media and Child Development Conference of the National Institute of Child Health and Human Development, National Institutes of Health, September 1985, Bethesda, MD.

Lampe, R. M., Weir, M. R., Spier, J., and Rhodes, M. F. 1985. Acoustic reflectometry in the detection of middle ear effusion. *Pediatrics* 76:75–78.

Makela, P H., Leinonen, M., Pukander, J., and Karma, P. 1981. A study of the pneumococcal vaccine in prevention of clinically acute attacks of recurrent otitis media. *Review of Infectious Disease* 3:S124–5130.

Marchant, C. D., Shurin, P. A., Turczyk, V. A., Wasikowski, D. E., Tutihasi, M. A., and Kinney, S. E. 1984. Course and outcome of otitis media in early infancy: A prospective study. *Journal of Pediatrics* 104:826–831.

Marchant, C. D., McMillan, P. M., Shurin, P. A., Johnson, C. E., Turczyk, V. A., Feinstein, J. C., and Panek, D. M. Objective diagnosis of otitis media in early infancy by tympanometry and ipsilateral acoustic reflex thresholds. *Journal of Pediatrics* (In press).

Paradise, J. L., Smith, C. G., and Bluestone, C. D. 1976. Tympanometric detections of middle ear effusion in infants and children. *Pediatrics* 58:198–210.

Perrin, J. M., Charney, E., Mac Whinney, Jr., J. B., McInerny, T. K., Miller, R. L., and Nazarian, L. F. 1974. Sulfisoxazole as chemoprophylaxis for recurrent otitis media. *The New England Journal of Medicine* 291:664–667.

Rosen, C., Christensen, P., Henricksen, J., Hovelius, B., and Prellner, K. 1984. Beneficial effect of pneumococcal vaccination on otitis media in children over two years old. *International Journal of Pediatric Otorhinolaryngology* 7:239–246.

Shurin, P. A., Pelton, S. I., and Finkelstein, J. 1977. Tympanometry in the diagnosis of middle ear effusion. *The New England Journal of Medicine* 296:412–417.

Shurin, P. A., Giebink, G. S., Wegman, D. L. Ambrosino, D., Rholl, J., Overman, M., Bauer, T., and Siber, G. R. Circulating Immunoglobulin G in Mucosal Immunity: Prevention of Experimental Otitis Media with Human Bacterial Polysaccharide Immune Globulin (In preparation).

Sloyer, Jr., J. L., Ploussard, J. H., and Howie, V. M. 1981. Efficacy of pneumococcal polysaccharide vaccine in preventing acute otitis media in infants in Huntsville, Alabama. *Review of Infectious Disease* 3:S119–123.

Teele, D. W., Klein, J. O., and the Greater Boston Collaborative Otitis Media Group. 1981. Use of pneumococcal vaccine for prevention of recurrent acute otitis media in infants in Boston. *Review of Infectious Disease* 3:S113–118.

Teele, D. W., and Teele, J. 1984. Detection of middle ear effusion by acoustic reflectometry. *Journal of Pediatrics* 104:832–839.

# 7

# Audiometric Approaches Used in the Identification of Middle Ear Disease in Children

*Fred H. Bess*

There has been considerable emphasis placed on the possible deleterious effects of middle ear disease with effusion on speech, language, and the psychoeducational development of young children. Because of this potential for developmental complications, and since middle ear disease is one of the more prevalent health problems in childhood, great attention has been focused on improving the methods for identifying effusion in children. Those techniques most commonly used to assist in the detection of a middle ear problem include pure-tone and speech audiometry, electroacoustic immittance measurements, acoustic reflectometry and measurement of auditory brainstem responses.

## PURE-TONE AND SPEECH AUDIOMETRY

Although it has long been recognized that conventional pure-tone audiometry has distinct limitations for detecting middle ear disease (especially when used as a screening tool), this time-honored approach can contribute important supplementary information in the identification of an otitic complication. It is the presence and size of an audiometric air-bone gap that serves to confirm the suspicion of a middle ear disorder. In fact, prior to the widespread use of electroacoustic immittance a number of clinicians advocated an audiometric

Preparation of this report was supported in part by the Robert Wood Johnson Foundation air-bone gap screening technique as a means of detecting a fluid-filled ear (Lounsberry et al. 1965; Osborn 1970).

Perhaps the most valuable information offered by pure-tone audiometry in cases of middle ear disease with effusion is to determine whether hearing loss is present and, if so, the extent and nature of the hearing impairment. Interestingly, however, there is limited information available in this area. The natural history of hearing loss associated with middle ear disease is not clearly understood. It is recognized that hearing loss is the most common sequela of otitis media (Bess 1983). In addition, the hearing loss is usually conductive, but sensorineural involvement can also occur. In general, the prevalence rate of hearing loss is dependent on the criteria used to define an impairment. Too often there is limited information provided in prevalence studies about testing conditions, calibration of equipment, definition of hearing loss, and diagnosis of disease. Nevertheless, estimates of prevalence can be made by selecting data from some of the better-controlled investigations.

A typical audiometric profile accompanying otitis media with effusion is shown in Figure 1. The data for this figure, taken from

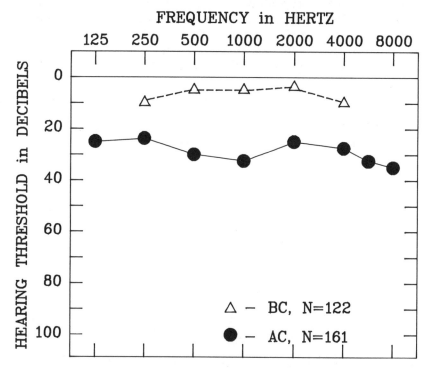

Figure 1. Audiometric profile accompanying otitis media with effusion. Mean air conduction (AC) values represent 161 ears, whereas mean bone conduction (BC) thresholds constitute 122 ears (adapted from Kokko 1974).

Kokko (1974), depict the mean air-conduction values for 161 ears and the mean bone-conduction thresholds for 122 ears. It is noted that air-conduction thresholds are relatively flat with a slight peaking at 2,000 Hz. The average degree of air-conduction loss through the speech frequency range (500, 1,000, 2,000 Hz) is 27.6 dB Hearing Level (HL) with a standard deviation of 12.8 dB HL. The bone conduction values averaged 3 dB HL through the speech frequencies, producing a mean air-bone gap of 24.6 dB HL.

Importantly, the degree of hearing loss varies considerably and can range from levels of normal sensitivity to hearing losses as great as 50 dB HL. A distribution of the expected hearing loss subsequent to otitis media with effusion is shown in Figure 2. These data, taken from three different studies and representing a total of 627 ears (Kokko 1974; Cohen and Sade 1972; Bluestone, Beery, and Paradise 1973), illustrate the number of ears falling within various hearing loss categories. Within the speech frequency range, fewer than 50 ears (7.7 percent) showed an average loss of 10 dB HL or less, and only five ears showed losses of 50 dB HL or more. The vast majority of ears exhibited losses between 16 and 40 dB HL with 21–30 dB HL representing the hearing loss category with the most ears. If hearing loss is defined as average at 500, 1000, and 2000 Hz of 21 dB HL or more, then the prevalence rate for this sample is 55 percent. If the criterion is an average loss greater than 30 dB HL, then the prevalence is 26 percent. In another study employing 762 subjects (Fria, Cantekin, and Eichler

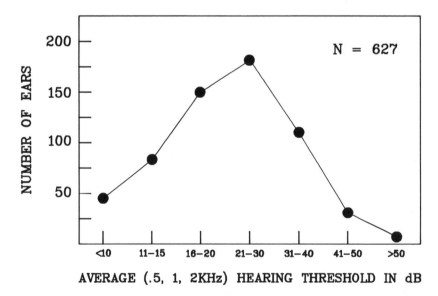

Figure 2. Distribution of hearing loss (500, 1000, and 2000 Hz) accompanying otitis media with effusion (627 ears).

1985), it was reported that 50 percent had pure-tone averages poorer than 23 dB HL and 20 percent were poorer than 35 dB HL. These prevalence values are similar to those observed in Figure 2.

The variability of air-conduction thresholds seen among cases of middle ear disease with effusion is thought to be related, to some extent, to the presence or absence of air-fluid level or bubbles in the middle ear. The influence that the type of fluid can have on the degree of hearing loss is shown in Figure 3. These data (Fria et al. 1984) represent the relative frequency distribution of average air-conduction hearing loss (500, 1000, 2000, 4000 Hz) observed in four groups of children: those who displayed no otitis media with effusion (OME) and also showed a normal tympanogram; those who had no OME but showed an abnormal tympanogram; those who had OME plus either a visible fluid level or visible air-filled bubbles; and those who had OME with no fluid level or bubbles visible. Several points are pertinent to this discussion. First, it is noted that hearing loss can occur in a sample of children when there is no effusion and a normal tympanogram is present. Second, there is a shift in the distribution toward greater hearing loss when there is no effusion but an abnormal tympanogram is present. Finally, in those cases of effusion, ears that have no visible fluid levels or bubbles exhibit a much flatter distribution with a relatively large percentage of ears having hearing loss in excess of 30 dB HL.

Two additional findings by Fria and co-workers (1985) are worthy of comment here. First, children with bilateral diseases had

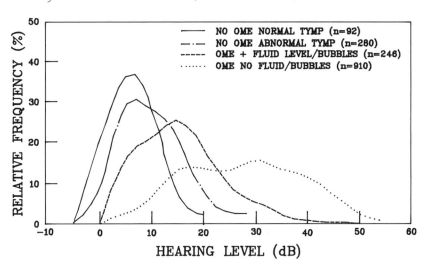

Figure 3. Frequency distribution of average hearing loss (500, 1000, 2000, and 4000 Hz) in four groups of children exhibiting different tympanometric and/or otoscopic conditions (adapted from Fria, Cantekin, Eichler, Mandel, and Bluestone 1984).

markedly poorer hearing than children with unilateral disease (on the order of 10 to 15 dB poorer). Second, hearing levels could not be predicted accurately on the basis of middle ear pressure or the shape of the tympanogram.

Speech audiometry is an approach used to determine hearing thresholds for age-appropriate speech materials and to assess speech understanding when the stimuli are presented at comfortable levels of loudness. Once again, there is a paucity of data concerned with the application of this technique in the assessment of children with OME. Thresholds for speech serve as an excellent check against the pure-tone data and provide the examiner with a more realistic estimate of the effect of the loss on speech recognition. Interestingly, it has been shown that hearing for simple speech material is somewhat less impaired than for pure-tone stimuli averaged across the speech frequency range—a finding which may suggest that we tend to over-estimate the degree of hearing impairment when using pure-tones (Fria, Cantekin, and Eichler 1985).

It appears that some children with recurrent otitis media are delayed in developing speech recognition skills under adverse listening conditions. Jerger and co-workers (1983) reported that children with otitis media between the ages of 24 and 39 months exhibited considerably greater problems in speech recognition in the presence of a competing message than did a matched control group. Although the otitis children had trouble understanding both words and sentences, more difficulty was realized with monosyllabic materials. Jerger and colleagues concluded that middle ear disease can temporarily delay the development of word recognition in competition for some children.

The techniques used to measure hearing sensitivity for pure-tones and speech will vary depending upon the age of the child. For the younger infant, aged two months to about two years, visual reinforcement audiometry (VRA) is the test of choice; whereas, for children two to five years of age, conditioned play audiometry or tangible reinforcement operant conditioning audiometry (TROCA) is more appropriate (Bess and McConnell 1981).

Indeed, although pure-tone and speech audiometry can afford valuable information about hearing levels and speech-understanding difficulties associated with middle ear disease, a number of important questions remain. The answers to these questions could provide valuable insight into the influence of middle ear disease with effusion on child development. Most importantly, we need to better understand the fluctuating nature of hearing loss associated with middle ear disease. It would also be of value to know more about the effects of these mild impairments on more complex auditory perceptual tasks, such as those in the study reported by Jerger et al. (1983).

## ELECTROACOUSTIC IMMITTANCE

There are few who would question the significant contribution that acoustic immittance has made to the identification of middle ear complications. Since 1970, when Jerger detailed the clinical application of this technique with a variety of disorders and populations, immittance has become a standard component of the audiologic test battery. It was, in fact, the Jerger publication which established the ABC classification system that is commonly used in the interpretation of typanometric results. Despite the universal application of the ABC system for classifying tympanograms, this scheme was not developed by correlating the immittance test findings with either otoscopy or surgical outcome.

Since the initial work of Jerger (1970), there has been a plethora of studies that have examined the effectiveness of immittance in the detection of middle ear disease with effusion. As noted by Schwartz (1986), however, few such studies have verified the tympanometric data using a validated otoscopist or findings at surgery.

Perhaps one of the earliest attempts to correlate tympanometric findings with surgical data was by Bluestone and co-workers (1973), who compared the tympanometric results of 87 ears to surgical outcome. Although test sensitivity was an impressive 100 percent, test specificity was only 55 percent, yielding a false-positive rate of 45 percent. Bluestone and colleagues concluded that when tympanometry and pure-tone audiometry are combined they are quite effective in the identification of otitis media.

One year following the study by the Bluestone group, Mc-Candless and Thomas (1974) compared tympanometric findings with pneumatic otoscopy in a sample of 730 children. Once again, test sensitivity was found to be high at 89 percent. In contrast to the Bluestone study, however, test specificity was also high at 98 percent.

Since these original investigations there have been numerous subsequent studies that have examined the effectiveness of this diagnostic tool in a wide range of populations and age groups. Recently, Schwartz (1986) analyzed the operating characteristics of tympanometry in nine studies that were conducted since 1976. The retrospective analysis was performed on data obtained from a sample of more than 2500 children. Test sensitivity for tympanometry averaged 94 percent across the nine studies. Test specificity, however, was an unacceptably low 57 percent. Furthermore, it was found that for those studies that incorporated an acoustic reflex there was no apparent improvement in the sensitivity-specificity characteristics of the test. Interestingly, Schwartz also reported that all of the studies reported in his analysis utilized a Madsen diagnostic instrument and that there was essentially no data to show the operating characteristics of the other instruments currently available on the market. This appears to be a particularly relevant point given the multitude of commercially available screening instruments that receive widespread usage in public school and public health programs.

It thus seems clear that acoustic immittance offers excellent test sensitivity and relatively low test specificity. This is somewhat disconcerting when one considers the universal acceptance of impedance as a diagnostic tool and a screening tool for large numbers of children.

The general question of whether to advocate immittance screening on a nationwide basis continues to be a controversial issue. Even though this controversy began almost ten years ago there has been painfully slow progress towards reaching a resolution. Research concerned with the use and effectiveness of existing guidelines is almost nonexistent. There continues to be a lack of data pertaining to the validity of immittance screening with different populations and instruments. Additionally, the issue of whether the middle ear disease is treatable once identified compounds the controversy. Nevertheless, widespread use of immittance screening is evidenced in local educational agencies, day-care centers, head start programs, and well-baby clinics. In fact, a recent survey of state school screening programs revealed that two states mandate screening in all educational programs and 16 others incorporate some form of immittance screening as a supplement to pure-tone audiometry (Bess and Kenworthy 1986).

A study by Hallett (1982) offered some interesting data that has important implications for immittance screening programs. A cohort of 553 five-year-old children from three schools received tympanometry, pure-tone screening, and pneumatic otoscopy on four separate occasions (March, April, May, November). In support of recent epidemiological research which suggests that many effusions will resolve spontaneously with no significant residual effects, Hallett found that tympanogram type varied markedly from one test occasion to the next. Persistently flat tympanograms (type B) were found for the same ear in nine children and flat tympanograms bilaterally occurred on all occasions in only four children. Only 19 of 553 children exhibited repeating tympanometric evidence of middle ear disease in either one or both ears. Some of the data from this study are summarized in Table I. This table illustrates the tympanometric changes that can occur in a single cohort of children present for all tests. Types I or V in this table would be typically classified as Jerger's Type A and Types II or III represent the standard classification of B or C. Note that of those who cleared the first test, 29 percent changed to a failed category by next test, and a further 45 percent changed from pass to fail by the third test. It thus appears that a single tympanometric screening or even a double

Table I

Tympanometric changes occurring in both ears over four
different visits (March, April, May, and November) in a
single cohort of children (from Hallett 1982).

| | Types I or V | | Types II or III | |
| --- | --- | --- | --- | --- |
| | Children | % Change | Children | % Change |
| 1st Visit | 31 | — | 40 | — |
| 2nd Visit | 22 | 29%* | 23 | 42% |
| 3rd Visit | 12 | 45% | 17 | 26% |
| 4th Visit | 12 | 0% | 9 | 47% |

*Percent change calculated as follows, $\frac{(31\text{-}22)}{31} \times 100 = 29\%$

This means that 29% of those children with Type I or V tympanograms in both ears had changed to Types II or II tympanograms in both ears at second visit.

test on a given cohort of children will not identify those children with persistent asymptomatic disease and will no doubt produce numerous over-referrals.

## ACOUSTIC REFLECTOMETRY

A relatively new and simple approach for detecting middle ear disease with effusion has been proffered by Teele and Teele (1984). This technique, known as acoustic reflectometry or the acoustic otoscopy, represents a non-invasive objective method that requires no hermetic seal and can reportedly be useful even if a child is crying or when there is partial obstruction of the canal (Schwartz 1986).

The instrument generates a multifrequency 80 dB SPL probe tone beginning at a frequency below 2000 Hz and sweeping linearly to just below 4500 Hz within 100 milliseconds. The associated microphone measures the combined amplitude of the probe tone and any sound waves reflected off the lateral plane of the tympanic membrane. (See Figure 4.) The principle of operation is based on the consideration of ¼-wavelength resonances. Briefly, an acoustic wave traveling in a tube will be completely reflected when it impinges upon the closed end of that tube. The reflected wave will completely cancel the original one at a distance ¼-wavelength away from the closed end of the tube resulting in zero sound amplitude at this point. Accordingly, the level of reflected sound is inversely proportional to the total sound; greater reflection produces a reduced sound level at the microphone and suggests that middle ear impedance is high, as in OME. The degree of reflectivity is numerically displayed on the otoscope—hence, a reflectivity reading of 0–2 represents a clear ear and a reflectivity of

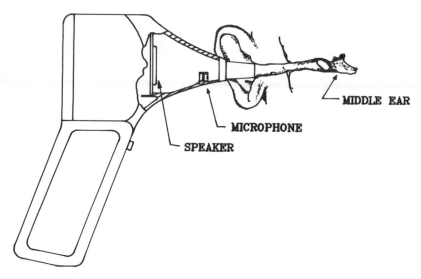

Figure 4. Schematic of the acoustic otoscope.

greater than 5 suggest an ear with effusion. Teele and Teele (1984) compared the findings of reflectometry, pneumatic otoscopy, and immittance measures in 290 ears. Test sensitivity for the acoustic otoscope was 94.4 percent and test specificity was 79.2 percent.

Recently, Schwartz and co-workers (Schwartz, Schwartz, and Daly 1984) compared reflectometry data in a group of 256 children (511 ears) with pneumatic otoscopy. Some of the findings are shown in Figure 5. These data illustrate the Receiver Operator Characteristics (ROC's) of the Acoustic Otoscope using various pass/fail criteria. Also provided, for comparison purposes, are the ROC curves for a perfect test and a useless test. The function depicted by solid squares represents the perfect screening instrument. Its value of 1-specificity is 0 at different sensitivity levels, whereas its sensitivity remains 100 percent for different levels of 1-specificity. In contrast, the values of sensitivity and 1-specificity for the useless test are identical at each point. The ROC performance for the acoustic otoscope reveals that a cut-off criterion of 5 yields a test sensitivity value of 89 percent with an acceptably low false-positive rate of 17 percent; a cut-off of 6 on the other hand maintains a high sensitivity and yet reduces a false alarm rate to only 6 percent.

The data of Schwartz et al. are most impressive and suggest that within the sample studied the test shows good efficiency. Interestingly, tympanometry obtained on a subsample of children in this same study showed test sensitivity similar to acoustic reflectometry and a specificity rate that was somewhat higher.

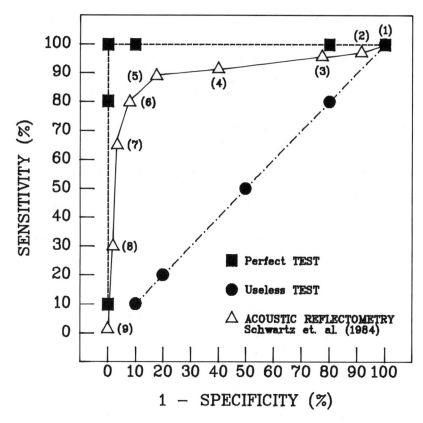

Figure 5. Receiver operating characteristics of the acoustic otoscope. Data for a perfect test and a useless test are also provided for comparison.

Unfortunately, Buhrer, Wall, and Schuster (1985) did not find the acoustic reflectometry to be so promising. In fact, when test results for reflectometry were compared to pure-tones, immittance, and otologic examination, reflectometry was reported to be the least sensitive and the least specific.

Hence, although the acoustic otoscope appears to have potential as an adjunct to the available methods currently used to detect middle ear disease with effusion, there is need for additional data before it can be used with confidence in the clinical setting. If this tool is as effective as suggested by the study of Schwartz et al., it would be most valuable for the primary-care physician. In a recent survey, it was suggested that only 25 percent of primary-care physicians used pneumatic otoscopy. In another survey, it was found that 15 percent of those who use otoscopy had instruments in which the illumination was insufficient to visualize properly the tympanic membrane (Schwartz 1986).

## AUDITORY BRAINSTEM RESPONSE (ABR)

The auditory brainstem response (ABR) has gained wide-spread acceptance as a tool for estimating hearing sensitivity and for detecting retrocochlear lesions. Normal results of an ABR test consist of five-to-seven waves that occur in the first ten milliseconds following presentation of an abrupt acoustic stimulus (click). Evidence suggests that Waves I through V of the ABR represent activity in or around the eighth cranial nerve, cochlear nucleus, superior olivary complex, lateral lemniscus, and inferior colliculus (Fria and Sabo 1980). Typically, Wave V is the most robust component of the ABR and historically it has been the focus of the majority of the studies in clinical assessment.

The ABR response is age-dependent for younger children. That is, Wave I latency approximates normal adult values by 6 to 8 weeks of age; while Wave V latency matures by 18 to 24 months of age (Finitzo-Hieber and Friel-Patti 1985).

Distinctions can be made between the normal and hearing-impaired ear by examining the ABR Wave-V latency as a function of stimulus intensity. An example of a latency-intensity function for Wave V for a normal ear and an ear with conductive hearing loss is shown in Figure 6. With a conductive impairment the amount of stimulus energy that reaches the cochlea is reduced. This results in a Wave-V latency-intensity function that parallels that of the normal ear but is displaced by an amount that is consistent with the degree of conductive hearing loss. It has been suggested that such data can provide us with one means to estimate the amount of hearing impairment. As shown in Figure 6, a horizontal line is drawn to illustrate the amount of horizontal shift of the latency-intensity function from the conductively impaired ear. The conductively impaired ear consistently requires a 25 dB greater sound level than normal hearers to produce the same Wave V latency. This decibel difference between the two functions represents the predicted amount of conductive hearing loss for a given test ear. Fria and Sabo (1980) have suggested that the use of Wave I, as opposed to Wave V, is preferable in making such an assessment. Hence, the ABR not only is useful in the detection of a conductive component, but also can be used to make gross predictions of the degree of conductive loss at higher audiometric frequencies. Despite the apparent potential for this particular technique, however, the cost of the equipment precludes its widespread clinical application. In addition, the ABR is most sensitive to high-frequency hearing loss ($\geq$ 2000 Hz). This limits its application to more advanced conductive impairments producing flat configurations.

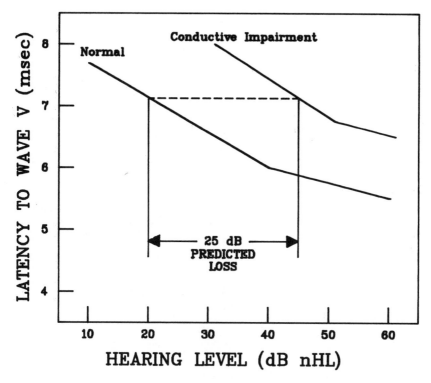

Figure 6. A method used in predicting conductive hearing loss from the wave V-latency-intensity function.

## AFTERWORD

To summarize, the audiometric approaches used most commonly in the identification and assessment of otitis media with effusion have been reviewed. Pure-tone and speech audiometry, while not considered a diagnostic procedure for the detection of effusion, offers valuable information, particularly when one is attempting to speculate as to whether the hearing impairment can affect linguistic competency. Immittance measurements probably represent the most popular means of detecting effusion. It should be apparent, however, that we need to learn more about the operating characteristics of this technique, especially as it applies to screening. In addition, the acoustic otoscope appears to have considerable potential for use in primary-care practices and public health and education facilities. Finally, the use of ABR may also prove useful in providing insight into the presence and extent of a conductive hearing impairment. This tool may be especially useful with the difficult-to-test populations.

## REFERENCES

Bess, F. H. 1983. Hearing loss associated with middle ear effusion. *In* Workshop on effects of otitis media on the child. *Pediatrics* 71:639–652.

Bess, F. H. and Kenworthy, O. T. (1986). The current status of impedance screening in the United States. *In* Workshop on controversies in screening for middle ear disease and hearing loss in children. *Pediatrics* 77: 57–70.

Bess, F. H. and McConnell, F. E. 1981. *Audiology, Education and the Hearing-Impaired Child.* St. Louis: C. V. Mosy Co.

Bluestone, C. Beery, Q., and Paradise, J. 1973. Audiometry and tympanometry in relation to middle ear effusions in children. *Laryngoscope* 83:594–604.

Buhrer, K., Wall, L. G., and Schuster, L. 1985. The acoustic reflectometer as a screening device: A comparison. *Ear and Hearing* 6:307–314.

Cohen, D. and Sade, J. 1972. Hearing in secretory otitis media. *Canadian Journal of Otolaryngology* 1:27–29.

Finitzo-Hieber, T. and Friel-Patti, S. 1985. Conductive hearing loss and the ABR. *In* J. T. Jacobson (ed.) *The Auditory Brainstem Response.* San Diego: College Hill Press.

Fria, T. J., Cantekin, E. I. and Eichler, J. A. 1985. Hearing acuity of children with effusion. *Archives of Otolaryngology* 111:10–16.

Fria, T. J., Cantekin, E. I., Eichler, J. A., Mandel, E. M., and Bluestone, C. D. 1984. The effect of otitis media with effusion ("secretory" otitis media ) on hearing sensitivity in children. *In* D. J. Lim, C. D. Bluestone, J. O. Klein and J. D. Nelson (eds.) *Recent Advances in Otitis Media with Effusion.* Philadelphia: B. C. Decker, Inc.

Fria, T. J. and Sabo, D. L. 1980. Auditory brainstem responses in children with otitis media with effusion. *Annals of Otology, Rhinology and Laryngology* 89:200–206.

Hallett, C. P. 1982. The screening and epidemiology of middle-ear disease in a population of primary school entrants. *The Journal of Laryngology and Otology* 96:899–914.

Jerger, J. 1970. Clinical experience with impedance audiometry. *Archives of Otolaryngology* 92:311–324.

Jerger, S., Jerger, J., Alford, B. R. and Abrams, S. 1983. Development of speech intelligibility in children with recurrent otitis media. *Ear and Hearing* 4:138–145.

Kokko, E. 1974. Chronic secretory otitis media in children. *Acta Otolaryngologica* 372 (Suppl):7–44.

Lounsberry, E. W., Osborn, C. D., Schuneman, J. W. and Viscomi, G. J. 1965. Air-bone gap measurements in identification audiometry. Lansing, Michigan Department of Public Health.

McCandless, G. A. and Thomas, G. K. 1974. Impedance Audiometry as a screening procedure for middle ear disease. *Trans American Academy of Ophthalmology and Otolaryngology* 78:2.

Osborn, C. D. 1970. Air-bone gap measurements in identification audiometry. *Marco Audiological Library Series* 9, Report 2.

Schwartz, D. M. 1986. Current status of techniques for screening and diagnosis of middle ear disease in children. *In* Workshop on controversies in screening for hearing loss and middle ear disease. *Pediatrics* 77:57–70.

Schwartz, D. M. and Schwartz, R. H. 1984. Efficacy of a new method for detecting middle ear fluid in children. Presented at Audiology Update 1984: Pediatric Audiology, Newport.

Schwartz, D. M., Schwartz, R. H. and Daly, N. J. 1984. Efficacy of acoustic reflectometry in detecting middle ear fluid. Presented at the Annual Meeting of the American Speech-Language Hearing Association, San Francisco.

Teele, D. W. and Teele, J. 1984. Detection of middle ear effusion by acoustic reflectometry. *Pediatrics* 104:832–838.

# 8

# Predicting
# Speech and Language Problems
# with Persistent Otitis Media

*Paula Menyuk*

## INTRODUCTION

The title of this paper should be a question and not a statement; that is, "Can one predict speech and hearing problems with persistent otitis media?" A controversy exists in the literature as to whether or not early otitis media should, theoretically, have any effect on the speech and language development of children. The position that it should not is based on the fact that these children usually suffer only mild to moderate hearing losses during episodes of the disease (that is, approximately, from 10 to 40 dB losses) and their hearing threshold presumably returns to normal after the episode.

Given data on children with mild to moderate hearing losses, one might predict some effect on speech and language development from even these losses (Nober and Nober 1977). However, these effects could be overcome by the normal hearing these children experience between episodes and by the fact that the frequency of episodes of otitis media, even in those children who do have frequent episodes during the early years of life, decreases dramatically after age three.

The other side of the theoretical argument, that early persistent otitis media should have an effect, is based on the assumption that fluctuating hearing loss during the early years of life presents the child with a speech signal that is difficult to process. Such an unstable signal might, in fact, create more problems in establishing speech and language categories than would the stably diminished signal produced by a mild or moderate hearing loss. It may be especially crucial to have a steady signal during the first three years of life when speech and language categories are first being established (Menyuk 1980).

There are few data available on the effect of early persistent otitis media on later speech and language development and what data have been collected leave a confused picture. These data do not provide the answer to the question of whether or not there is a lasting effect on speech and language development of early persistent otitis media, nor do they indicate those factors that might lead to a lasting effect. Some of the reasons for the confused picture become evident when we examine some of the studies that have been carried out.

Most studies that have examined the question have been retrospective. Given this fact, it is very difficult to determine the frequency or extent of fluctuating hearing losses experienced by the experimental subjects or to control for other factors that might affect speech and language development. Some studies have found that speech and language problems are more prevalent in children with histories of persistent otitis media than in children without such histories while other studies have found no differences or "catch up" in children with persistent otitis media.

Holm and Kunze (1969) found that children, aged five to nine years, with histories of otitis media and fluctuating hearing loss were significantly delayed in language perception and production when compared to children of those ages without such histories. Sak and Ruben (1982) found that eight- to eleven-year-old children with such histories were significantly poorer in verbal production, auditory decoding, and spelling than their siblings without early otitis media. Masters and Marsh (1978) found that there was a greater incidence of middle ear disease in learning disabled children than in their classroom peers. Bennett, Ruuska and Sherman (1980) found that learning disabled children, compared to their school age peers, had had more frequent episodes of otitis media with effusion and exhibited significantly more middle ear problems.

Although the above cited studies point to the possibility of there being long-lasting speech and language problems due to the early effects of persistent otitis media, other studies indicate no such effects. Needleman (1977) found that children with early histories of otitis media were different from their age peers in speech and language processing at three to five years but were catching up by age six. Hoffman-Lawless, Keith and Cotton (1981) found no differences in the auditory processing abilities of seven- and nine-year-old children with and without middle ear disease histories.

The reasons for the differences in the findings concerning long-term speech and language effects of otitis media may be due to variations within the populations of children being used to examine the effect. Some studies have used only middle class children while others have used only children from lower income families. Environmental factors are known to have an effect on speech and language development. Given the fact that the studies are, for the most part, retrospective it is possible that the incidence of otitis media and of effusion suffered by the children labelled as having early histories of otitis media significantly varies, as does the amount of hearing loss they experience. Thus, the differences in findings may be a result of important variations in the experiences of the children examined. Finally, the age at which the behavior is sampled and the way it is sampled might also have a differential effect. To examine more fairly the question of the effect of early otitis media with effusion it is important to attempt to control for some of this variability.

In this paper an attempt will be made to do two things. First, a logical argument will be presented to support, theoretically, the notion that fluctuating hearing loss during the first three years of life can have an effect on speech and language development. Second, some data obtained in a longitudinal study of the speech and language development of children with and without persistent otitis will be discussed.[1] These data will be used to argue for a more precise determination of those factors that might account for and predict speech and language problems in children with persistent otitis media at varying ages.

## REASONS FOR SPEECH AND LANGUAGE PROBLEMS

It is during the first three years of life that the most frequent episodes of otitis media occur and it is also during these first three years that the most dramatic developments in language acquisition occur. It is during this period that the infant moves from being a communicator to being a competent (although not fully competent) user of the speech and language categories of the language. These developments are highly dependent on the acoustic information that the hearing baby is receiving.

### THE FIRST YEAR—LEXICAL AND COMMUNICATIVE DEVELOPMENT

During the first year of life, as Strange (this volume) points out, the infant is able to discriminate between the sounds of the

[1]The research reported here was supported in part by a grant from the National Institute of Allergy and Infectious Diseases (A1 5253). All members of the Greater Boston Otitis Media Study Group and, in particular, Jerome O. Klein M.D. and David Teele M.D., played crucial roles in the design of the study and the collection of the data.

language on the basis of certain acoustic differences. It is also during this period that the infant becomes an excellent communicator. Before the baby becomes mobile, face to face communication interaction between caregiver and baby is frequent and this interaction is dependent on the use of surface structure or acoustic aspects of the speech signal produced, i.e., the pitch, intonation, and stress. The facial expressions and gestures used by the caregiver and the baby are also important in communication. The caregiver signals that the baby should take a turn in the conversation by rising intonation, pause, and particular facial expression (Menyuk 1985).

Clearly, if the baby is having difficulty in interpretating sound, then communication between caregiver and baby may be partially affected. In addition, there is evidence that the frequency with which caregivers provide opportunities for babies to take a turn affects the rate at which they become conversational participants (Liebergott et al. 1984) Other factors such as illness, pain, and irritability that may accompany episodes of otitis media can also, of course, affect this interaction.

At about twelve months of life a shift in the basis upon which the infant processes the speech signal apparently occurs. There is evidence that at about this time the infant begins to comprehend the meaning of familiar words and not just the supra-segmental aspects (pause, intonation, and stress) of the signal (Menyuk and Menn 1979). Further, a word need not be used in a particular context in order to be understood. To comprehend words the infant must be able to segment the stream of speech heard in order to isolate the words in it. Although the caregiver sometimes does this for the infant, the lion's share of the task is the infant's. The child must also be able to recognize that a particular sequence of speech sounds refers to a particular object or event. This latter competence must be based on the ability to detect the invariable parameters of these particular speech sequences. This must be done despite the fact that different caregivers produce acoustically different versions of the same word and the same caregiver can produce different versions of the same word on different occasions.

During this period the child begins to produce words. The version of a particular word produced by an infant is variable and based on the child's interpretation of the words heard and the constraints of a child's speech production mechanism. Thus, while the child's comprehension of the relation between words and references is becoming more stable, the child's production of these same words is much less so. Further, word production seems to be governed by some universal constraints on the developing speech mechanism. Therefore, language-specific speech gestures occur some time after language-specific speech sound discriminations occur.

SEMANTIC AND SYNTACTIC DEVELOPMENT

This sequence of speech and language perception preceding speech and language production holds throughout the first three years of life, although the time gap between the two processes, comprehension and production, appears to be small during these early years. When, between 18 and 24 months, two-part relations such as "see daddy," "go car," and "baby kiss" are understood the child will probably still be producing single words or jargon phrases. When, at 24 to 30 months, the child is producing three-part relations such as "daddy be car," "that big boat," and "what he doing" the formally correct versions of these sentences ("Daddy is in the car," "That is a big boat," "What is he doing?") are understood. Shortly after producing three-part relations the child begins producing sentence structures according to the rules of his or her language. In essence, productive categorizations are based on perceptual categorizations which in turn, are based on developments in the processing of the speech signal.

By the age of three years the child has developed a great deal of knowledge of both the structures of language and how to use these structures in many communication situations. The comparison of what the child knows about language at twelve and at thirty-six months indicates how rapid the process of language acquisition is. However, each of the developments cited is dependent on previous developments. It was suggested that children with fluctuating hearing loss might have difficulty in determining the stable speech sound characteristics of a word. If this is the case there might be some delay in vocabulary acquisition. If there is such a delay then the other steps in development might also be delayed.

In addition to the possibility of delay, each step in development has its own processing requirements. Although caregivers may speak in special ways to their children, which may make the task easier, the child is still confronted with the task of segmenting the stream of speech heard into meaningful words and learning that they can be combined in multiple but fixed or rule-governed ways.

There are cues in the signal the child hears that are helpful in segmenting the stream of speech. Word boundary markers (special qualities of final sounds in words), morphophonological markers of, for example, tense (*walks*) and plural (*boys*), phrase markers such as articles (*a* and *the*) and prepositions (*at, to*), and so on. Such markers and words rarely are stressed in an utterance and, therefore, provide a weak signal. Further, they may be made up of speech sounds that are difficult to hear such as /s/, /z/ and /t/, or introduce subtle changes such as lengthening the vowel before final + voice consonants. Children with fluctuating hearing losses may not be able to establish the categories of cues that help in segmenting the stream of speech at the same rate as normally hearing children. In turn, they may be delayed in using these categories in their own utterances.

A child who may have developed fuzzy speech and language categories and may be delayed in vocabulary acquisition, and morphological and syntactic development would certainly be at a disadvantage on entrance to school. One source of difficulty is a crowded and possibly noisy classroom in which complex auditory information ("Sit down and pick up your pencil. Draw a circle around all the red ones.") is being presented. Another source of difficulty might be learning to read. This task requires awareness of speech sound, word, and syntactic categories in the language (Menyuk and Flood 1981). Awareness, in turn, requires well learned categories of speech and language (Menyuk 1983).

The above is a summary of the problems that might be encountered by children with early persistent otitis media in speech and language development and in academic performance. However, as indicated initially, early persistent otitis apparently does not always lead to speech and language delay or school difficulties. The question is, why are there differences in outcome findings? The next section of the paper will discuss the data obtained in a longitudinal study of children with and without early otitis. These data will be used to speculate about reasons for differences in findings and to suggest some factors that might be predictive of delay and difficulties.

## A LONGITUDINAL STUDY

The subjects for this study were selected from a population of children who had been followed from birth. Between July 1975 and August 1977, pediatricians working in five medical-care facilities in urban and suburban communities enrolled 2568 consecutively born children for a study of middle ear disease. All children were seen initially before the age of three months. At every visit, regardless of its primary purpose, the pediatrician examined the ears and completed a form with information relevant to middle ear disease.

Each participating pediatrician was trained in the use of the otoscope to increase uniformity of diagnosis. Each time a diagnosis of acute otitis media was made, the child was considered to have had 29 days of effusion, unless the period of effusion was documented as being shorter. This figure was based on what pediatricians have observed as being the average period of effusion. Seventy percent of the children in this population still had fluid in the middle ear at two weeks, 40 percent at one month, 20 percent at two months, and 10 percent at three months after initial diagnosis. A cumulative total of days with middle ear effusion during the first seven years of life was recorded for the entire sample of 2568 children.

The study's design afforded a careful monitoring of middle ear disease episodes in all the children over the first seven years of life. In addition, the study included children from low income and middle income families so that the role of this factor in conjunction with middle ear disease could be examined. A Hollingshead two-factor index, education and occupation of head of household, was used to determine the socioeconomic status (SES) of each subject (Hollingshead and Redlich 1958). This analysis indicated that eighty percent of the children from suburban practices came from households that were above the median score for the entire sample while eighty percent of the children from the large urban center came from families that scored below the median. All subjects were Caucasian.

The sample was divided into three groups: those who had experienced 32 days of effusion, those who had experienced 32 to 108 days of effusion, and those who had experienced more than 108 days of effusion during each of the first three years of life. This was done to examine the effect of early effusion on later speech and language development. Two time periods were sampled, age three (Teele, Klein, and Rosner 1984) and age seven years (Menyuk and Chase 1985). The results of both samplings are presented below.

THE CHILDREN AT THREE YEARS

At three years children were selected for testing from lists prepared by computer that displayed age, sex, race, number of episodes of acute otitis media, and number of siblings in the family. The children consecutively selected from the list and who agreed to participate in the follow-up study included children who had had at least three episodes of acute otitis media and those who had had no more than one episode by two years. The study sample consisted of 205 children. These children's primary language was English and they had no history of developmental delay, cleft palate, or seizures.

The tests of speech and language administered were the Peabody Picture Vocabulary Test (Dunn and Dunn 1981), the Preschool Language Scale (Zimmerman, Steiner, and Pond 1979), and a Test of Articulation (Goldman and Fristoe 1970). In addition, a language sample was obtained from each child and analyzed for structural complexity and mean length of utterance. At the time of testing all children's hearing was screened and no child with a loss greater than 25 dB at 125, 250, 1000, 2000, and 4000 KHz was tested.

One analysis of the data, amongst others, was t-test comparisons of the scores on each of the above measures for the group with the least amount of effusion (less than 30 days) with the group with the middle amount of effusion (30 to 129 days) and this latter group with the group with the greatest amount of effusion (130 or more days). For the entire population (children from both suburban and urban practices) differences between effusion groups were found only for performance on the PPVT, a test of word comprehension. When the performances of suburban children and urban children were examined separately it was found that the above difference could largely be accounted for by the presence of middle SES children with varying degrees of effusion. It was only within this group of children that significant differences on the PPVT between the lowest effusion group as compared to the middle effusion group, and the middle effusion group as compared to the highest effusion group occurred. Within this group significant differences among effusion groups also occurred on the auditory comprehension and verbal ability quotient scores of the Pre-school Language Scale. These data are presented in Table I.

The fact that the only significant differences that were found in speech and language measures in this comparison were in the middle SES group was somewhat surprising. One might hypothesize that the possible effects of persistent otitis media might be mitigated by the experiences of the middle SES group. However, a possible reason for this finding is that, perhaps, during the third year of life the comparatively otitis-free middle SES children were showing the normal rapid spurt in language development and leaving their otitis-prone peers behind, whereas no such general spurt was occurring at that time with the low SES children. This is somewhat supported by the range of mean scores obtained on each of these measures by

Table I

| Measures | Effusion Groups | | | | |
| --- | --- | --- | --- | --- | --- |
| | Low | p value | Mid | p value | High |
| Middle SES Children | | | | | |
| PPVT Mean Scores | 113.5 | N.S. | 108.5 | .01 | 104.2 |
| Auditory Comprehension Quotient Mean | 135.0 | .07 | 126.6 | .003 | 120.4 |
| Verbal Ability Quotient Mean | 130.0 | .02 | 114.4 | .004 | 112.4 |
| Low SES Children | | | | | |
| PPVT Mean Scores | 92.2 | N.S. | 94.0 | N.S. | 92.8 |
| Auditory Comprehension Quotient Mean | 111.6 | N.S. | 113.2 | N.S. | 116.9 |
| Verbal Ability Quotient Mean | 108.8 | N.S. | 114.1 | N.S. | 115.8 |

Language Differences at Three Years with Effusion

effusion groups in the two SES groups of children. PPVT scores ranged from 92.2 to 94.0 for the low SES children as compared to 104.2 to 113.5 for the middle SES children. The auditory comprehension quotient and verbal ability quotient scores on the Pre-school Language Scale ranged from 111.6 to 116.9 and from 108.8 to 115.8 for the low SES children as compared to ranges of 120.4 to 135.0 and 112.4 to 130.0 for the middle SES children.

These findings indicated that, at least for a normally developing middle SES group of children, there were differences in word comprehension and in language comprehension and production that might be attributed to the amount of time these children spent with depressed hearing over the first three years of life. The results of the next sampling of the speech and language development of this population sheds light on the question of whether there are effects of early persistent otitis media that are present in the early school years.

THE CHILDREN AT SEVEN YEARS

Since difficulty in processing the speech signal might possibly affect all aspects of language, the speech and language measures designed to assess the children's language processing at age seven examined all structural aspects of language: speech sound discrimination and production, comprehension and production of morphological endings, comprehension and production of lexical items, comprehension of complex sentences, and production of complex sentences in connected discourse.

To examine speech sound articulation and discrimination, a sub-sample of items on the Goldman-Fristoe (Goldman and Fristoe 1970) and the Goldman-Fristoe-Woodcock (Goldman, Fristoe, and Woodcock 1970) tests were used. The items selected were those found in previous studies to be most difficult for children with slight hearing impairments. In the articulation test, the production of sibilants, plosives, nasals, and glides was examined in all positions (initial, medial, and final) in words. In the discrimination test, the discrimination of all +/− voice plosives, +/− voice continuants and nasals were examined.

The so-called "WUG" test (Berko-Gleason 1958) was used to test the children's ability to produce morphological endings of number, tense, possession, and derivation for nonsense stems (such as "wug"). The same items were adapted for use in a test of perception and identification of appropriate endings. An experimenter-generated list of sentences which contained target stems and morphological endings (for example, "The green box fell down." and "He kicks the ball hard.") were given to the children for repetition to assess further the children's ability to identify and produce morphological endings.

Vocabulary or lexical comprehension was assessed by giving the children the PPVT; their lexical production was assessed with the Boston Naming Test (Kaplan, Goodglass, and Weintraub 1983). Comprehension of complex sentences was examined by giving the children an experimenter-generated list of sentences containing complex structures and asking them questions about each sentence. For example, after hearing the sentence, "The boy promised the girl who was there to clean the fish tank." they were asked, "Who cleaned the fish tank?" The number correct for each of these speech sound, morphological, vocabulary, and complex sentence measures was coded for each child. To examine complex sentence production they were given a set of pictures and asked to tell a story about these pictures. The language sample obtained was analyzed for the proportion of varying sentence structures used and the type/token ratio of the lexical items used in the sample.

Again, one way analysis of variance was used to assess the differences in the speech and language behaviors of the three effusion groups—highest, middle, and lowest. Amount of effusion over the first three years of life was used to create the three groups. Effusion over the next four years did not significantly change the results. Thus, the data obtained and to be discussed directly address the question of whether or not there are long term effects on speech and language behavior of early persistent otitis media.

Comparisons of the three groups on varying speech and language measures at age seven indicate that amount of effusion (and, therefore, presumably, amount of time during which hearing is depressed) has very specific effects at age seven. They also indicate that there is, probably, little long lasting effect of one to four episodes of otitis but marked effect with four or more episodes. There were, in most instances no significant differences between low and middle and middle and high effusion groups. Table II lists those speech and language measures for which significant differences were found between the lowest and highest effusion groups and, in two instances, between the middle and highest effusion groups.

As can be seen in Table II, lexical production as measured by the Boston Naming Test is significantly better in children with one or no episode of effusion as compared to those with the most effusion. Lexical comprehension, however, is not significantly different. The ability to produce and reproduce certain morphological endings is also significantly different between low and high effusion groups but perception of morphological differences is not. Proportion of production of sentences with prepositional phrases significantly differs between high and low effusion groups, and proportion of use of complex and coordinate sentences differs between middle and high effusion groups. The comprehension of relations in complex sentences, how-

Table II

Significant Speech and Language Differences at Seven Years With Effusion

| Measures | Effusion Groups | | | |
| | Low | Mid | High | |
| | | Mean Scores | | |
| | | | | p Value |
| Vocabulary | | | | |
| Boston Naming | 42.8 | | 37.9 | .05 |
| Morphology | | | | |
| Plural Possessive | 2.9 | | 2.3 | .05 |
| Past | 2.9 | | 2.5 | .04 |
| Reproduction | 18.2 | | 17.5 | .01 |
| Speech Production | | | | |
| Initial Sib. | 8.6 | | 8.1 | .01 |
| Medial Sib. | 8.7 | | 8.1 | .01 |
| Final Sib. | 7.7 | | 7.1 | .01 |
| Speech Perception | | | | |
| Initial + voice plos. | 12.9 | | 12.6 | .03 |
| Final + voice plos. | 10.9 | | 10.6 | .02 |
| Initial − voice plos. | 8.7 | | 8.3 | .02 |
| Medial − voice plos. | 7.8 | | 7.4 | .01 |
| Final − voice plos. | 7.7 | | 7.4 | .05 |
| − Voice Continuants | 5.9 | | 5.7 | .05 |
| Syntax | | | | |
| Complex Utterances | | 16.7 | 11.5 | .02 |
| Conjunctions | | 8.9 | 6.5 | .02 |
| Prepositions | 20.9 | | 17.1 | .04 |

ever, does not differ among effusion groups. It is only in processing speech sounds that one observes differences in both perception and production.

These results indicate several important things about the speech and language sequelae of early persistent otitis. First, there *do* continue to be effects of early persistent otitis on the speech and language of school age children. That is, there is no across the board catch-up in this population by school age, as has been suggested by other studies that find no differences at six to nine years. Further, the differences found make sense in terms of what aspects of language might be affected by early periodic depressed hearing. Some continued difficulty in perception and production of speech sounds that are difficult to process because of their particular acoustic characteristics and difficulty in production of morphological markers that consist of these speech sounds seems to be directly related to the possible development of fuzzy speech sound categories. Delay in lexical production and in production of more elaborate sentence structures might be directly related to difficulties in categorization of speech sounds and morphological markers.

Second, almost all the differences found were in the production of language. The only exception was in speech sound processing where the child is given little higher order information to discriminate between events. The important implication of this finding is that early persistent otitis delays development but does not seriously distort it. Because of this, different aspects of language processing are affected at different ages by persistent otitis in a developmentally logical fashion. Since language perception precedes production, this would account for the differences in lexical comprehension, over-all comprehension and production of language found, at least in the middle SES children, in the three year sampling of these children's language knowledge. By age seven, differences are only seen in lexical production, the production of morphological markers, and in the production of more elaborate sentence structures; in other words, in later aspects of language development. It is important, however, to note that these aspects of development are crucial for successful performance in academic tasks.

The final implication of these findings is that most of the differences observed at seven years are, apparently, due to differences in the performance of children with one or no episode of effusion as compared to those with four or more episodes. This suggests that a certain critical level of information processing distortion has to occur before there are consequences for the acquisition of language. This makes sense in light of what is known about development in general and language development in particular. Children are capable of compensating for a great deal of variability up to a certain point. Where this point is exceeded can, of course, vary depending on both physiological and experiential factors.

## CAN SPEECH AND LANGUAGE PROBLEMS BE PREDICTED?

The data obtained in the longitudinal study discussed indicate that prediction of speech and language problems in children with otitis media is possible. Further they indicate what aspects of speech and language processing should be examined early on, and in which children.

First, the data indicate that children with one to four episodes of otitis during the first three years of life probably will not end up with speech and language difficulties at age seven. If one assumes that it is the amount of depressed hearing that a child suffers during the early years of life that make the difference then this makes sense. To attempt to predict later speech and language difficulties one should compare the early language development of two groups of children, those with less than four episodes of otitis and those with more than four episodes.

There are confounding factors that might exacerbate the effect of less than four episodes. These factors are probably both physiological (such as cleft palate or retardation) and experiential. There were significant differences in the lexical and morphological production of the low SES as compared to the middle SES children at age seven as well as age three. Those children with the greatest amounts of effusion within the low SES population performed significantly more poorly than the children with the least amounts of effusion in lexical and morphological production. This places the low SES children with the greatest amount of effusion at greater risk for academic problems than their middle SES peers with the greatest amount of effusion. Therefore, the amount of distortion of information that these children can compensate for might be less than can be tolerated by middle SES children.

Finally, the developmental findings of the study indicate that, in looking for behaviors during the early years that might predict later speech and language development, researchers should concentrate on measures of discrimination and comprehension of the categories of language rather than on production of such categories. It is in discrimination and comprehension of language categories that the effects of persistent otitis media should be seen during the first two years of life. If such differences are found suggestions can be made to help caregivers provide the kinds of additional information that are needed to help compensate for the childs' processing difficulties.

## REFERENCES

Bennett, F., Ruuska, S., and Sherman, R. 1980. Middle ear function in learning-disabled children. *Pediatrics* 65:254–260.

Berko-Gleason, J. 1958. The child's learning of English morphology. *Word* 14:150–157.

Dunn, L., and Dunn, L. 1981. *Peabody Picture Vocabulary Test.* Circle Pines, MN.: American Guidance Service Inc.

Goldman, R., and Fristoe, M. 1970. *Test of Articulation.* Circle Pines, MN.: American Guidance Service Inc.

Goldman, R., Fristoe, M., and Woodcock, R. 1970. *Test of Auditory Discrimination.* Circle Pines, MN.: American Guidance Service Inc.

Hoffman-Lawless, K., Keith, R., and Cotton, R. 1981. Auditory processing abilities in children with previous middle-ear effusion. *Annals of Otology, Rhinology and Laryngology* 90:543–545.

Hollingshead, A., and Redlich, F. 1958. *Social Class and Mental Illness.* New York: John Wiley and Sons.

Holm, V., and Kunze, L. 1969. Effects of chronic otitis media on language and speech development. *Pediatrics* 43:833–839.

Kaplan, E., Goodglass, H., and Weintraub, S. 1983. *Boston Naming Test.* Philadelphia: Lea and Febiger.

Liebergott, J., Menyuk, P., Schultz, M., Chesnik, M., and Thomas, S. 1984. Individual variation and mechanisms of interaction. Paper read at 8th Biennial Southeastern Conference on Human Development, April 1984, Atlanta.

Masters, L., and Marsh, G. 1978. Middle ear pathology as a factor in learning disabilities. *Journal of Learning Disabilities* 11:103–106.

Menyuk, P. 1985. Early communication and language behavior. *In* J. Rosenblith and J. Simms-Knight (eds.) *In the Beginning: Development in the First Two Years of Life.* Monterey, CA.: Brooks Cole.

Menyuk, P. 1983. Language development and reading. *In* T. Gallagher and C. Prutting (eds.) *Pragmatic Issues: Assessment and Intervention.* San Diego: College Hill Press.

Menyuk, P. 1980. Effect of persistent otitis media on language development. *Annals of Otology, Rhinology and Laryngology* 89:257–263.

Menyuk, P., and Chase, C. 1985. Otitis media with effusion before three years: Linguistic and cognitive sequelae at seven years. Submitted to *Child Development.*

Menyuk, P., and Flood, J. 1981. Linguistic competence, reading and writing problems and remediation. *Bulletin of The Orton Society* 31:13–28.

Menyuk, P., and Menn, L. 1979. Early strategies for the perception and production of words and sounds. *In* P. Fletcher and M. Garman (eds.) *Studies in Language Acquisition.* Cambridge: Cambridge University Press.

Needleman, H. 1977. Effect of hearing loss from early recurrent otitis media on speech and language development. *In* B. Jaffe (ed.) *Hearing Loss in Children.* Baltimore: University Park Press.

Nober, E., and Nober, L. 1977. Effects of hearing loss on speech and language in the post babbling stage. *In* B. Jaffe (ed.) *Hearing Loss in Children.* Baltimore: University Park Press.

Sak, R., and Ruben, R. 1982. Effects of middle ear effusion in preschool years on language and learning. *Developmental and Behavioral Pediatrics* 3:7–11.

Teele, D., Klein, J., and Rosner, B. 1984. Otitis media with effusion during the first three years of life and development of speech and language. *Pediatrics* 74:282–287.

Zimmerman, I., Steiner, V., and Pond, R. 1979. *Preschool Language Scale.* Columbus, OH.: Charles E. Merrill Publishing Co.

# The Effect of a Temporary Mild Hearing Loss During the First Three Years of Life on Later Child Development

# 9

# Is There a Relationship between Otitis Media and Learning Disorders?

*Alan Leviton* and *David Bellinger*

## INTRODUCTION

A number of recent publications describe meta-analysis, the procedure of reviewing multiple reports about a relationship between an antecedent (or a therapy) and an outcome (Glass 1976; Rosenthal 1978; Goldsmith and Beeser 1984; Hedges and Olkin 1984; Louis, Fineberg, and Mosteller 1985; Light and Pillemer 1985). In an attempt to compare the findings of the different studies, a universal measure has been sought. One candidate, "effect size," is a measure of the difference in the outcome between two groups that differ only in terms of an exposure that could conceivably influence the outcome. Usually this is expressed as a fraction or percent of the standard deviation.

Initially we planned a meta-analysis of those studies that evaluate the relationship between early otitis media and later language and reading handicaps. We encountered studies that varied so widely in design and quality that we considered meta-analysis inappropriate. Instead of effect size we prefer to emphasize data quality. This reflects our appreciation of the distortions of associations due to problems in measuring exposure and in measuring the outcome (Sackett 1979).

## IDEAL STUDY

We begin by going through the simple exercise taught to graduate students in epidemiology—that of designing the ideal study. Perhaps in this way we will have a benchmark against which to compare published studies.

The ideal study is often prohibitively expensive and logistically difficult to carry out. We feel, however, that only those studies that achieve feasibility with minimal loss in data quality should be conducted and considered for meta-analysis.

What follows is a discussion of characteristics of ideal studies, and how reports published or first presented in 1984 and 1985 approximated or deviated from the ideal. This emphasis on recent studies is intended to document that previous discussions of design limitations have, by and large, not yet achieved their goal of improving future studies (Kudrjavcev and Schoenberg 1979; Leviton 1980; Paradise 1981; Bluestone et al. 1983).

## COMPONENTS OF THE "IDEAL STUDY"

TESTABLE HYPOTHESIS.

Although at first thought it would seem that a testable hypothesis should be evident in each study, such has not been the case. To give you a sense of the complexity of the problem we list a number of testable hypotheses that have been considered, or could readily be considered to assess the topic at hand.

*Hypothesis 1.* Frequently recurring (or persistent) "mild" hearing impairment (defined as . . . ) between the ages of x and y is associated with auditory processing or language impairment (as defined . . . ) at age z (Lous and Fiellau-Nikolajsen 1984; Klein 1984; Hutton 1984; Teele, Klein, and Rosner 1984; Schlieper et al. 1985; Fischler, Todd, and Feldman 1985; Feagans et al. 1985).

*Hypothesis 2.* The more persistent (or severe) the hearing impairment between ages x and y the greater the risk of, or the more severe will be, the auditory processing deficit, language impairment, or reading handicap at age z (Teele, Klein, and Rosner 1984; Feagans et al. 1985).

*Hypothesis 3.* In children at high risk of otitis media, tube insertion before age x is associated with a reduced risk of hearing loss, auditory processing deficit, language impairment, or reading handicap at age y (Hubbard et al. 1985).

SAMPLE

The sample for each study should be based on the design chosen. The least expensive and quickest-to-complete study design is what epidemiologists call a case-control study. The first step is to identify a group of children with the outcome of interest. This group might include children with a single, or a small number of relatively homogeneous language handicaps, or a group of children with relatively homogeneous auditory processing deficits. The major problems posed in identifying cases are those related to homogeneity and selection. The homogeneity aspect refers to the similarity of the handicap in each of the children, and the selection refers to the bias that might be introduced by including only those children who come to a highly specialized educational or medical center (Sackett 1979).

Once the cases are selected, a comparable group of controls needs to be identified. Issues that must be addressed include the following: On what variables should controls be matched to cases? Should controls be randomly selected from people who do, or do not come to the same center as cases? (McKinlay 1977; Rosenbaum and Rubin 1984)

The cohort or longitudinal design identifies a group of children at the time of exposure and follows these children until they might be expected to have developed or manifested the outcome. All four of the recent studies cited in this review are of the longitudinal type. With low prevalence outcomes large samples are needed (v.i. "power"). In addition, because language and auditory processing handicaps might not be readily detected until age four or so, this may mean that babies need to be followed for three, four, or even five years. Obviously, most children will not begin to master reading skills until seven to nine years. Thus, cohort studies that evaluate the relationship between otitis media and reading handicap will require almost ten years for data collection and analysis. The likelihood is small that any study section of the National Institutes of Health will provide any group of investigators with a promise of ten years funding. One alternative is to design a five year study that will gather sufficient information by the end of the fourth year, enabling the investigators to prepare a strong proposal to continue for another five years. Another alternative is to seek foundation or other non-federal support.

To keep costs down the sample selected for the cohort study can be restricted to those children who are at high risk of the exposure (or the outcome) (Hubbard et al. 1985). Although this is economical, it limits the ability to generalize the findings. The most generalizable sample for a cohort study might be those children who are attending a health maintenance organization of one form or another (Fischler et al. 1985; Feagans et al. 1985).

Children in a cohort study cannot be classified by a single episode of otitis. Thus, it is probably prudent to follow a large sample of children even before any episode of otitis has occurred. This is especially important because some children might have only one episode of otitis in their lives, whereas others may have many. The most careful investigator is unlikely to tell with any degree of assurance who will be in each category.

## EXPOSURE

A basic characteristic of the case-control design is that information about exposures is obtained retrospectively. This usually involves asking the parent how many ear infections the child had, or at what ages tubes were inserted. Because many investigators are concerned about recall bias and uniformity of exposure data, it has been suggested that objective measures of exposure be obtained. These might include review of medical care records for documentation of episodes of otitis media, telephone calls about suspected otitis, medication recommendations, results of tympanic membrane examination, and hospitalization summaries when a child had been admitted for surgical therapies. The limitations of this approach have been emphasized recently (Marchant et al. 1984; Hayden and Schwartz 1985).

For prospective studies, uniformly high quality data are more readily available. In designing a cohort study, the investigators need to consider what to measure, how to measure it, and how often to make the measurements. Several recent studies are flawed by classifying children based on audiometry or otoscopic examination at such "late" ages as three years (Lous and Fiellau-Nikolajsen 1984; Schlieper et al. 1985). Inferences about the results of another study were based on such tenuous assumptions as: a) middle ear disease had "invariably" been present up to the time of initial myringotomy, and b) middle ear disease was resolved by myringotomy (Hubbard et al. 1985).

Teele and his colleagues (1984) examined children frequently and in a standardized fashion, but only when brought to medical attention. Although they wisely considered total number of days of middle ear effusion (or diminished ear drum mobility) as one measure of exposure, they could only make assumptions about the duration of each episode of otitis.

Lynne Feagans and her colleagues at Chapel Hill had children attending a day-care center examined every day whenever an ear infection was considered and until it had resolved completely (Feagans et al. 1985). We consider this as close to the ideal as practicable.

## OUTCOME

Unfortunately, physicians and epidemiologists have tended not to select the most appropriate outcome measures. For example, one recent study used the verbal subtest of the WISC-R (Hubbard et al. 1985). Speech and language clinicians should be able to come to some consensus about what are the best measures (see the papers in this volume written by Friel-Patti et al. and by Menyuk).

Epidemiologists by and large tend to use the medical model

and thus dichotomize their sample into those with the undesired outcome and those without the undesired outcome. Reasonable people might argue about where to draw the line between normality and a disorder of language or auditory processing. Zadeh has coined a term, "the fuzzy set," to describe the uncertain boundary between what is normal and what is not (Zadeh 1969). Perhaps it is time for epidemiologists to welcome outcomes that are continuous, and can be transformed so that the distribution is normal.

## COVARIATES

Confounding is the distortion of the apparent relationship between exposure and outcome (Last 1983). A true confounder is a variable associated with both the exposure and the outcome. Much of epidemiologists' thinking concerns ways of minimizing the effects of potential confounders.

Oliver Cromwell is reported to have said, "I beseech you in the bowels of Christ consider that you might be wrong" (1650). Many epidemiologists assume a Cromwellian posture when evaluating claims that an exposure is associated with an outcome.

Possible confounders include socioeconomic status and its correlates, congenital anomalies, medical disorders that increase the risk of otitis, sepsis, meningitis, and medical disorders that are associated with recurrent hospitalization (Teele, Klein, and Rosner 1984; Portoian-Shuhaiber and Cullinan 1984). Indeed, Teele and his colleagues (1984) found a relationship between the number of days with a middle ear effusion during the first year and later vocabulary and auditory comprehension tests, but only in the upper socioeconomic group. One way to avoid the distortion these covariates might produce is to exclude children who have them (Fischler, Todd, and Feldman 1985).

## ANALYTIC STRATEGIES

We do not necessarily advise one statistical technique in preference to all others. Rather, we feel that no substitute exists for "getting a feel for the data." No less an authority than Tukey (1977) has entitled one of his books "Exploratory Data Analysis," which in essence, strongly advocates "getting a feel for the data." Our own experience emphasizes this point.

In our study of the association between prenatal lead exposure and early infant development, children from families in the higher socioeconomic groups had slightly higher lead levels than did children from lower socioeconomic groups (Bellinger et al. 1984; Bellinger et al. 1985). Without taking into consideration socioeconomic status and its correlates, we would have failed to identify a relationship between prenatal lead exposure and Bayley Mental Development Index scores. This example deserves consideration in any study of a relationship between early minor hearing impairment and later language and auditory processing function or reading.

Mathematical modeling procedures for handling covariates appear to be gaining recognition. Indeed, a number of people are devoting their energies to improving models that might be most suitable for longitudinal studies (Nesselroade and Baltes 1979; Waternaux et al. 1985).

Although they have many advantages multivariate techniques are not necessary. Without using such techniques, Teele, Klein, and Rosner (1984) were able to parcel out an effect of number of days of middle ear effusion during the first year not evident in subsequent years.

## SAMPLE SIZE

Power has been defined as the "relative frequency with which a true difference of specified size between populations would be detected by the proposed experiment or test" (Last 1983). A power of .9 indicates that if the study were repeated 10 times the anticipated difference should be evident in 9 of those trials. One recent study claimed to have a power of .9 to perceive a verbal-subtest IQ's difference of 10 points with a one-tailed test of significance (Hubbard et al. 1985). We know of no exposure that would reduce the IQ in a sample by 10 points without devastating the brain. With a standard deviation of 15 points, we feel a 10 point difference, or .66 standard deviation is highly unlikely to occur. Much more realistic is a .33 standard deviation difference (i.e., 5 IQ points).

It is conceivable, although unlikely, that any potential adversity might improve a child's language or auditory processing function. Thus, we consider it appropriate to use a two-tailed test, rather than a one-tailed test.

The study that claimed to have a .9 power turns out to have a power of .21 if the difference between the two samples is only 5 IQ points, and the test of statistical significance is two-tailed (Leviton and Bellinger 1985).

This point about power and the consequences of inadequate attention to it are especially important when claims are made that there is no association between an exposure and an outcome (Freiman et al. 1978; Beaumont and Breslow 1981). The ideal study should have a power approximating .9 for a small difference in function between the two samples when a two-tailed test is used.

## CONCLUSION

Only two of the five recent studies are deemed adequate tests of the hypothesis suggested by our title. Interestingly, they are the ones that showed a convincing association between early and persistent otitis media and later reduction in language function as measured by paraphrase quality. This underscores our view that any future meta-analysis of the otitis media/learning or language handicap relationship be limited to the highest quality studies.

## REFERENCES

Beaumont, J. J., and Breslow, N. E. 1981. Power considerations in epidemiologic studies of vinyl chloride workers. *American Journal of Epidemiology* 114:725–34.

Bellinger, D. C., Leviton, A., Waternaux, C., and Allred, E. 1985. Methodologic issues in modelling the relationship between low-level lead exposure and infant development: Examples from the Boston Lead Study. *Environmental Research*, in press.

Bellinger, D. C., Needleman, H. L., Leviton, A., Waternaux, C., Rabinowitz, M. B., and Nichols, M. L. 1984. Early sensory-motor development and prenatal exposure to lead. *Neurobehavioral Toxicology and Teratology* 6:387–402.

Bluestone, C. D., Klein, J. O., Paradise, J. L., Eichenwald, H., Bess, F. H., Downs, M. P., Green, M., Berko-Gleason, J., Ventry, I. M., Gray, S. W., McWilliams, B. J., and Gates, G. A. 1983. Workshop on effects of otitis media on the child. *Pediatrics* 71:639.

Cromwell, O. 1650. Letter to the general assembly of the C. Church of Scotland, August 3. 1650. In *Familiar Quotations*, 15th ed. Bartlett, J. (ed. E. M. Beck), p, 272. Boston: Little Brown & Co.

Feagans, L., Sanyal, M., Henderson, E., and Collier, A. 1985. Middle ear disease in early childhood and later language skills. Presented at the Society for Research in Child Development, April 1985.

Fischler, R. S., Todd, N. W., and Feldman, C. M. 1985. Otitis media and language performance in a cohort of Apache Indian children. *American Journal of Diseases of Children* 139:355–60.

Freiman, J. A., Chalmers, T. C., Smith, Jr. H, and Kuebler, R. R. 1978. The importance of beta, the type II error and sample size in the design and interpretation of the randomized control trial: Survey of 71 "negative" trials. *New England Journal of Medicine* 299:690–4.

Glass, G. V. 1976. Primary, secondary, and meta-analysis of research. *Educational Researcher* 5:3–8.

Glass, G. V., McGaw, B., and Smith, M. L. 1981. *Meta-Analysis in Social Research* Beverly Hills: Sage.

Goldsmith, J. R., and Beeser, S. 1984. Strategies for pooling data in occupational epidemiological studies. *Annals of the Academy of Medicine* 13:297–307.

Hayden, G. F., and Schwartz, R. H. 1985. Characteristics of earache among children with acute otitis media. *American Journal of Diseases of Children* 139:721–23.

Hedges, L. V., and Olkin, I. 1984. *Statistical Methodology for Meta Analysis*. New York: Academic. In press.

Hubbard, T. W., Paradise, J. L., McWilliams, B. J., Elster, B. A., and Taylor, F. H. 1985. Consequences of unremitting middle-ear disease in early life: Otologic, audiologic, and developmental findings in children with cleft palate. *New England Journal of Medicine* 312:1529–34.

Hutton, J. B. 1984. Incidence of learning problems among children with middle ear pathology. *Journal of Learning Disabilities* 17:41–2.

Klein, J. O. 1984. Otitis media and the development of speech and language. *Pediatric Infectious Diseases* 3:389–91.

Kudrjavcev, T., and Schoenberg, B. S. 1979. Otitis media and developmental disability: Epidemiologic considerations. *Annals of Otology, Rhinology and Laryngology* 88:88–98.

Last, J. M. (ed.) 1983. *A Dictionary of Epidemiology*. New York: Oxford University Press.

Leviton, A., and Bellinger, D. C. 1985. Letter to the editor. *New England Journal of Medicine*, in press.

Leviton, A. 1980. Otitis media and learning disorders. *Developmental and Behavioral Pediatrics* 1:58–63.

Light, R. J., and Pillemer, D. B. 1985. *SUMMING UP: The Science of Reviewing Research*. Cambridge, MA and London: Harvard University Press.

Louis, T. A., Fineburg, H. V., and Mosteller, F. 1985. Findings for public health from meta-analysis. *Annual Review of Public Health* 6:1–20.

Lous, J., and Fiellau-Nikolajsen, M. 1984. A 5-year prospective case-control study of the influence of early otitis media with effusion on reading achievement. *International Journal of Pediatric Otorhinolaryngology* 8:19–30.

Marchant, C. D., Shurin, P. A., Turczyk, V. A., Wasikowski, D. E., Tutihasi, M. A., and Kinney, S. E. 1984. Course and outcome of otitis media in early infancy: A prospective study. *Journal of Pediatrics* 104:826–31.

McKinlay, S. A. 1977. Pair-matching—A reappraisal of a popular technique. *Biometrics* 33:725–35.

Nesselroade, J. R., and Baltes, P. B. (eds.). 1979. *Longitudinal Research in the Study of Behavior and Development*. New York and London: Academic Press.

Paradise, J. L. 1981. Otitis media during early life: How hazardous to development? A critical review of the evidence. *Pediatrics* 68:869.

Portoian-Shuhaiber, S., and Cullinan, T. R. 1984. Middle ear disease assessed by impedance in primary school children in south London. *Lancet* 1:1111–13.

Rosenbaum, P. R., and Rubin, D. B. 1985. Constructing a control group using multivariate matched sampling methods that incorporate the propensity score. *American Statistician* 1:1–18.

Rosenthal, R. 1978. Combining results from independent studies. *Psychological Bulletin* 85:185–93.

Rosenthal, R. 1979. The "file drawer problem" and tolerance for null results. *Psychological Bulletin* 86:638–41.

Rosenthal, R., ed. 1980. *Quantitative Assessment of Research Domains*. San Francisco: Jossey-Bass.

Sackett, D. 1979. Bias in analytic research. *Journal of Chronic Diseases* 32:51–63.

Schlieper, A., Kisilevsky, H., Mattingly, S., and Yorke, L. 1985. Mild conductive hearing loss and language development: A one year follow-up study. *Journal of Developmental and Behavioral Pediatrics* 6:65–8.

Teele, D. W., Klein, J. O., and Rosner, B. A. 1984. Otitis media with effusion during the first three years of life and development of speech and language. *Pediatrics* 74:282–287.

Teele, D. W., and Teele, J. 1984. Detection of middle ear effusion by acoustic reflectometry. *Journal of Pediatrics* 104:832.

Tukey, J. W. 1977. *Exploratory Data Analysis*. Reading, MA and London: Addison-Wesley Publishing Company.

Waternaux, C., Laird, N. M., and Ware, J. H. 1985. Methods for analysis of longitudinal data: Blood lead concentrations and cognitive development. Submitted for publication.

Zadeh, L. A. 1969. Biological application of the theory of fuzzy sets and systems. The proceedings of an international symposium on Biocybernetics of the Central Nervous System. L. D. Proctor, (ed.). Boston: Little Brown & Co.

# 10

# Perceptual and Academic Deficits Related to Early Chronic Otitis Media

*Peter W. Zinkus*

Developmental language disorders and potential subsequent learning disabilities are multifaceted problems having a myriad of descriptive labels reflecting etiological concepts based on neurological deficit theories, perceptual handicaps, delayed maturation, developmental dyslexia, emotional disorders, and teacher disability. The variability in definition and identification methods has led to a multitude of treatment procedures, many of which are of questionable value. Little attention has been paid to the prevention of what are predominantly language-based disorders, that is, disruptions in the child's basic communication skills, especially the receptive components. The child's ability to understand verbal communication is limited by deficits in auditory memory, the ability to follow directions, and the ability to communicate effectively.

A particularly common and very disruptive type of language disorder is the auditory processing deficit. Central auditory processing disturbances included under the category of Specific Learning Disabilities include impairments of auditory attention, sequential memory, discrimination, sound blending, and closure skills. Although the child's cognitive functions remain intact, the processing of auditory input is deficient. Frequently disturbances in central auditory processing interfere with the ability to develop reading, spelling, and mathematical proficiency despite average or above average intelligence. Identification, interpretation, and organization of sensory data received through the ear appear to be basic functions necessary to all auditory learning. Children with auditory processing disorders frequently show difficulties in following sequences of directions as well as retaining verbal material in the classroom. Short-term memory decay is often quite rapid. These children may learn auditory material, such as spelling from dictation, but be unable to pass a spelling test the next day on the same words.

Figure-ground difficulties are also prevalent. Children with this type of difficulty are often highly susceptible to auditory distraction, yet when evaluated in a quiet examining room are found to have excellent attention span and normal auditory acuity. Their limited ability to separate the main auditory stimulus from the background noise often leads to the misdiagnosis of attention deficit disorder and hyperactivity. These children simply cannot filter background noises and select the main auditory stimulus which, in the case of a classroom setting, is the teacher's voice. Learning the basic phonetic approaches to reading as well as acquiring and retaining such auditory material as multiplication tables may prove difficult.

Many subjects with auditory processing disorders had serious ear disease in early childhood. In one study (Gottlieb, Zinkus, and Thompson 1979) a group of children with auditory processing disorders had a 46 percent occurrence of significant ear disease during the first three years of life. When a similar group of children with visual processing disorders were studied, only 22 percent were found to have a similar history of ear disease. The question arose as to whether there was a relationship between chronic otitis media during the first three years of life and subsequent disorders in auditory processing. Since all subjects with auditory processing disorders do not manifest a history of early ear disease it has been further assumed that the link may be significantly more complex than a simple one-to-one relationship.

Concern over the child's history of ear disease in the first three years of life relates to the fact that critical periods of speech and language development occur during this period of time. During the first three years of life the child progresses from the use of single words at about 12 months of age to more complex communication skills involving meaningful combinations of words at about 20 to 24 months of age. During these formative years of language development, also, the child is most susceptible to chronic middle ear infections. It is hypothesized that intermittent hearing loss and distortion of auditory signals secondary to chronic ear disease during the early years of language acquisition could be associated with development of auditory processing disturbances and subsequent deficiencies in academic performance.

## HEARING AND DEVELOPMENT

Children with acute otitis media may continue to have significant middle ear effusion for an extended period of time and therefore impaired hearing may occur in a relatively asymptomatic child. Shurin and his colleagues (1979) found that 44 of 62 patients with acute otitis media had persistent middle ear effusion up to 13 weeks after the initial acute episode. With this in mind it is interesting to speculate on the developmental sequelae in some children who may have lengthy periods of auditory deprivation or distortion of auditory signals resulting in delays in the development of basic language and auditory processing skills.

There does seem to be a close relationship between hearing impairment and delayed language development with potential subsequent impaired learning. Subjects with hearing loss typically show lower verbal intelligence skills when compared to normal hearing subjects. When hearing impaired subjects are compared on the basis of non-verbal tests, their performances are often similar to normal hearing subjects. Therefore, hearing loss appears to have a prominent effect on the development of overall verbal capabilities. Omer (1972) studied children with hearing loss on a series of speech discrimination tests and compared these results with mental age scores. The results indicated that hearing loss, as measured by deficits in auditory discrimination, has a profound effect on mental age measures. Lower mental age scores were obtained by subjects with the poorest discrimination scores. Hamilton and Orwid (1974) further demonstrated that hearing impaired subjects are often comparable to normal hearing counterparts on tests of non-verbal intelligence. On language-based tests, the hearing impaired subjects show a significant deficit in verbal intelligence as well as overall language development. The evidence suggests that the acquisition of normal receptive language skills and verbal intelligence depends greatly on the ability to receive auditory input accurately. Chronic middle ear effusion would prevent many of the auditory messages from accurately reaching the nervous system. This transient fluctuation in auditory acuity could actually be more disruptive to some listening skills than a consistent hearing loss.

## MIDDLE EAR DISEASE AND DEVELOPMENT

The relationship of conductive hearing loss to potential organic changes provides an intriguing theoretical basis for the development of auditory processing disorders in children. Studies by Webster and Webster (1977) demonstrated that a conductive hearing loss during critical periods of brain maturation may lead to morphological changes in certain neurons of the brain stem auditory nuclei in laboratory rats. Webster and Webster note that the auditory system is dependent upon environmental input and may suffer significant structural change as a result of chronic conductive hearing loss in early life. In a series of studies, they demonstrated that conductive hearing loss during critical post-natal periods led to anatomical and physiological alterations of the auditory brain stem nuclei. The morphological changes resulting from conductive hearing loss in the laboratory animals may well be a model for the types of dysfunction occurring in children with chronic hearing disorders. It appears that a significant set of data from non-human studies support the hypothesis that a critical period of development is present during which adequate sound stimulation is necessary for the development and increasing sophistication of central auditory processing skills.

Human studies have been carried out with greater frequency over the past few years. Primitive populations have been studied to determine the effect of chronic middle ear disease on the development of basic language skills. Kaplan and his colleagues (1973) completed a study of 489 Eskimo children who were followed over a ten year period. The attainment of developmental milestones was assessed, and there appeared to be no difference in children with chronic middle ear disease compared with normal children in the age at which basic motor skills develop. A significant difference, however, was found in the acquisition of both words and sentences compared to normal hearing subjects. The children with chronic middle ear effusions were much slower in attaining these basic language milestones. Healthy children were also found to have a much higher verbal I.Q. in comparison to children with chronic middle ear effusion although there was no difference between the subjects on non-verbal I.Q. measures. From an academic standpoint the group of children who suffered middle ear effusion prior to two years of age were worse off academically than those whose ear disease began after two years of age, and the overall language development in the group with chronic middle ear effusion was 25 months behind the group who developed ear disease later than two years of age. Studies by Lewis (1976) indicated similar results to the Kaplan study although the numbers of subjects in these studies were very small. Lewis compared children with chronic middle ear disease to normal controls. Again, verbal I.Q. was much lower among subjects with a history of chronic middle ear disease although there was no difference in non-verbal I.Q. In addition, auditory discrimination, as well as reading ability was impaired.

Holm and Kunze (1969) studied groups of children with a history of chronic otitis media. These children had severe ear disease early in childhood and were studied when they were of school age. Significant differences were found on numerous tests of auditory processing skills, language development, and articulation between this group and the group with no history of ear disease. The group with no history of ear disease was found to be vastly superior to the chronic otitis media group on most measures of auditory processing and language development.

Howie (1979) studied a number of children who had otitis media during the first year of life compared with a group who had no ear disease during that period of time. When the groups were matched by age, sex, school attended, and socioeconomic class, it was found that children who had no otitis media had significantly higher scores on the California Achievement Test than the ear disease group. Howie further studied groups of children who had three or more episodes of otitis media during the first 18 months of life. These children were compared with a group of subjects who had no history of otitis media during the same period. Again, the achievement test scores on tests administered in the third and sixth grades were significantly better in the group that was free of early middle ear disease.

When groups of learning-disabled children are studied, there appears to be a higher frequency of middle ear disease among these subjects. Freeman and Parkins (1979) studied a group of 50 children who were defined educationally as learning-disabled. These subjects were given an extensive battery of audiometric, tympanometric, and medical examinations. Subjects were matched on the basis of intelligence and compared to a group of school children who had no history of school difficulty. Screening audiograms showed six to eight times as many failures at 20 to 25 decibels in the learning-disabled group as in the control group; 24 percent of the learning-disabled children had abnormal tympanometry as compared to 8 percent in the normal group; 20 percent of the learning-disabled children had abnormal otological examinations versus 10 percent of the normal group. Masters and Marsh (1978) also found that their groups of learning-disabled subjects had almost twice as much middle ear pathology as normal children.

Sak and Ruben (1982) studied eight to eleven year old children with normal hearing and histories of recurrent middle ear effusion before the age of five years. These children were evaluated with a battery of audiological, psychological, language, and achievement tests. Each child was compared to his sibling who did not suffer from middle ear effusion during the first five years of life. None of the children were diagnosed as learning-disabled, and both groups tested in the bright-normal range of intelligence. Comparison of the sibling data revealed that subjects with histories of middle ear effusion had deficits in verbal ability, auditory decoding, and spelling skills compared with control subjects. It was also noted that the subjects with a history of middle ear effusion had developed strengths in visual sequential memory beyond those of their siblings, a factor that the investigators suggest is evidence of a compensation developing as the result of these subjects having auditory processing deficits. A recent Danish investigation (Lous and Fiellan-Nikolajsen 1984) was a five year prospective case-control study of the influence of early otitis media with effusion on reading achievement. These investigators found no effect on reading related to the presence of chronic middle ear disease. Their subjects, however, were studied beginning at the age of three years, and no consideration was given to the presence of ear disease during the first three years of life, often considered a critical period of language development. In addition, the testing for basic reading skills was done on an entirely visual test with no requirement for the child to deal with auditory input. In spite of the lack of data prior to three years of age, the prospective nature of the study adds merit to a consideration of the results.

The effects of middle ear pathology in auditory perception and academic achievement have been studied in more recent investigations. These studies have demonstrated a disruption in auditory processing skills as well as a greater need for special education services among children with histories of chronic middle ear disease (Brandes and Ehinger 1981). In addition, it has been shown that recurrent middle ear problems place children at a greater risk for language delay and potential academic deficits (Schlieper et al. 1985). In a large scale prospective study following children with chronic middle ear disease, Teele and his colleagues (1984) consistently demonstrated a poorer performance across a wide range of language measures in the group of children with chronic otitis media and effusion.

Other studies (Zinkus, Gottlieb, and Schapiro 1978, Gottlieb et al. 1979, Zinkus and Gottlieb 1980) compared children with histories of chronic otitis media during the first three years of life with a control population having no such history. Subjects with a history of prenatal, perinatal, and postnatal neurological disease or injury were excluded from the study. Subjects with severe behavioral or emotional disorders were also excluded. A confirmed history of recurrent otitis media during the first three years of life was required for experimental subjects. Confirmation of history was established by medical records from the child's pediatrician and from parent interviews detailing the symptomatology, frequency, and severity of episodes of middle ear disease. The results of these studies indicated a significant difference between the groups with and without a history of middle ear disease during the language formative years. In terms of development, the subjects did not differ on the age of acquisition of motor skills such as walking. However, in the age of acquisition of single word vocabulary, the subjects differed significantly with the chronic otitis media group being much slower in the development of this skill. Even more significant was the difference in the development of three-word phrases with the onset of this developmental skill being much later in the group with the history of early ear disease. Comparison of intellectual factors consistently indicated a lower verbal I.Q. in groups with early history of chronic otitis media. Analysis of subtests indicated selective depression of those tests requiring auditory memory skills, whereas basic cognitive functions seemed to remain untouched. Visual processing skills were comparable between the two groups although visual tasks that were language-based or had a language component showed some impairment in the group with early ear disease. Auditory processing skills were also impaired in the group with the history of chronic otitis media during the first three years of life. Compared to their normal counterparts this group had difficulties with auditory memory, auditory discrimination, and basic skills in the analysis of auditory material. In comparing subjects with auditory processing deficits and with a history of ear disease during the first three years of life with others who had no such history, the auditory processing deficit group with a history of early ear disease was significantly more impaired than the group without the disease.

The previous studies have been criticized for a number of design problems as well as for selection bias in choosing subjects, and many have been criticized because of their retrospective nature. The question still remains: Is there a difference between children with chronic otitis media during the first three years of life and disease-free children and, if this difference exists, what are the manifestations in terms of the child's basic language development? In assessing the potential academic effects of chronic otitis media, numerous variables present experimental and design difficulties. Three levels of measurement are involved.

At the first level hearing must be assessed. No studies have consistently measured the variable of intensity and duration of chronic middle ear effusion throughout the entire course of the disease. Even with frequent otological and auditory acuity measurements, extensive periods of time between these examinations render an exact measurement of hearing loss impossible. The question that arises in longitudinal studies is: At what point do you treat the child rather than study him? To deny treatment to someone for an extended period of time with the idea that it would be harmless to the child is highly questionable. In addition, critical periods may or may not exist in terms of the effects of chronic otitis media.

At the second level, measurements related to the effects of transient hearing loss secondary to chronic otitis media on the development of auditory processing, language, and speech is again problematic. Faced with measuring the intensity of a deficit as well as its duration is complicated by a myriad of environmental, intellectual, and socioeconomic variables.

At the third level measuring the educational effects becomes extremely difficult. Reading is one example. A number of influences such as basic intellectual abilities, teaching approach, and family influences, in addition to basic auditory processing skills, determine how well a child can read. The tests used can often best be termed "tests of convenience." Many tests are used simply because they have always been used, not necessarily because of any particular usefulness or sensitivity. The validity and reliability of many of the tests are questionable, and the results are often too global to capture the essence of the deficit that the child is experiencing. Many basically academic tests yield nothing but grade level scores and fail to evaluate information on significant error patterns which would differentiate a particular type of disorder. In this respect, there are types of errors made by children who have language or auditory processing difficulties that are often different from those made by children who have poor reading skills for other reasons. For example, if the child is given the word "mother" to spell and then spells "m-u-t-h-r," this would represent a good phonetic representation of the word "mother." If, on the other hand, the spelling is "m-o-t-r" or some variation that is not phonetically correct, the question arises as to whether the child has problems with the processing of auditory sequences. Again, both errors would be minus one point on many achievement tests, but the reasons for those errors may be vastly different. The significance of these pathological error patterns might be lost in a simple grade level score.

## CONCLUSION

The question remains as to whether ear disease is a necessary or sufficient condition to develop language-based disorders or is a coincidental condition. Some children with chronic middle ear effusion develop no obvious deficits. This, however, may be related to the global testing procedures that are used and that frequently mask the presence of a disability. In some children with chronic middle ear effusion, speech difficulties develop and in others auditory processing problems emerge. The question of what places these children at risk is one of great importance. My studies in progress indicate that the effects of chronic middle ear effusion may not be the same for all children. While these studies are not yet complete, they are based on the hypothesis that in some children language disorders as well as auditory processing deficits may be inherited conditions with no other known etiology available to explain the presence of the disorder. A further assumption states that while a child may be at risk because of the presence of this recessive trait, the presence of chronic middle ear effusion during the first three years of life may well lead to expression of the disorder. While the data are incomplete, trends indicate that children who had chronic middle ear effusion during the first three years of life and who had siblings with auditory processing disorders appeared to be much more at risk for developing auditory processing disturbances than children with no history of middle ear effusion but who had siblings with an auditory processing disorder. These data may indicate that a simple one-to-one relationship between chronic middle ear disease and auditory processing deficits does not exist and that a host of other variables, such as being at risk for the development of auditory processing deficits based upon family history of such disorders, may well interact with chronic middle ear effusion to produce such deficits.

There is growing evidence (American Academy of Pediatrics 1984) demonstrating the correlation between middle ear disease and hearing impairment with delays in development of speech, language, and cognitive skills. The 1984 policy statement of the American Academy of Pediatrics states that any child whose parent expresses concern about whether the child hears correctly should be considered for referral for audiometric studies without delay.

Risk factors are difficult to specify. Children with chronic middle ear effusion need to be assessed carefully, especially in areas of basic language development (Zinkus 1982). Two factors become important. The child's use of words in isolation is often a misleading marker for basic language development. The assessment of language development should involve the child's communication skills and the use of phrases and sentences as well as proper syntax, grammar, and articulation. The child who is using single words at 12 months of age should also be using three and four word phrases and sentences by two years of age and have an extensive vocabulary including the ability to express himself in multiple word sentences by age three. The importance of these communication skills is often ignored in children with chronic middle ear effusion. In addition, a family history of language delay or auditory-based learning disabilities should be considered as a risk factor with chronic middle ear effusion. Early intervention in speech and language difficulties may well prevent subsequent academic deficits.

As the child approaches the beginning of his school years high risk factors include a history of chronic middle ear effusion in early childhood in combination with a delay in the acquisition of words and sentences and a family history of language-based learning difficulties. Children with this history should be monitored closely for possible academic difficulties and early intervention should be made available in the form of special education or remedial efforts. Educational jeopardy resulting from deficits in auditory processing may be preventable in some children. If a defined association between auditory processing disorders and chronic middle ear disease can be demonstrated in future research, a significant step in the prevention, detection, and therapeutic intervention of learning disabilities can be undertaken.

## REFERENCES

American Academy of Pediatrics Policy Statement 1984. Middle Ear Disease and Language Development. *Pediatrics* 74:9.

Brandes, P., and Ehinger, D. 1981. The effects of early middle ear pathology on auditory perception and academic achievement. *Journal of Speech and Hearing Disorders* 22:301–307.

Freeman, B., and Parkins, C. 1979. Prevalence of middle ear disease among learning impaired children. *Clinical Pediatrics* 18:205–212.

Gottlieb, M., Zinkus, P., and Thompson, C. 1979. Chronic middle ear disease and auditory perceptual deficits. *Clinical Pediatrics* 18:725–732.

Hamilton, P., and Orwid, H. 1974. Comparisons of hearing impairment and sociocultural disadvantage in relation to verbal retardation. *British Journal of Audiology* 8:27–35.

Holm, V., and Kunze, L. 1969. Effect of chronic otitis media on language and speech development. *Pediatrics* 43:833–839.

Howie, V. 1979. Developmental sequelae of chronic otitis media: The effect of early onset of otitis media on educational achievement. *International Journal of Pediatric Otorhinolaryngology* 1:151–168.

Kaplan, G., Fleshman, J., Bender, T., Baum, C., and Clark, P. 1973. Long term effects of otitis media: A 10 year cohort study of Alaska Eskimo children. *Pediatrics* 52:577–584.

Lewis, N. 1976. Otitis media and linguistic incompetence. *Archives of Otolaryngology* 102:387–390.

Lous, J., and Fiellan-Nikolajsen, M. 1984. A 5-year prospective case-control study of the influence of early otitis media with effusion on reading achievement. *International Journal of Pediatric Otorhinolaryngology* 8:19–30.

Masters, L., and Marsh, G. 1978. Middle ear pathology as a factor in learning disabilities. *Journal of Learning Disabilities* 11:54–57.

Omer, J. 1972. The incidence of hearing impairment in students identified as learning disabled. *Language, Speech and Hearing Services in Schools* 3:34–45.

Sak, R., and Ruben, R. 1982. Effects of recurrent middle ear effusion in preschool years on language and learning. *Journal of Developmental and Behavioral Pediatrics* 3:7–12.

Schlieper, A., Kisilevsky, H., Mattingly, S., and Yorke, L. 1985. Mild conductive hearing loss and language development: A one year follow-up study. *Developmental and Behavioral Pediatrics* 6:65–68.

Shurin, P., Pelton, S., Donner, A., and Klein, J. 1979. Persistence of middle ear effusion after acute otitis media in children. *New England Journal of Medicine* 300:1121–1135.

Teele, D., Klein, J., and Rosner, B. 1984. Otitis media with effusion during the first three years of life and development of speech and language. *Pediatrics* 74:282–287.

Webster, D., and Webster, M. 1977. Neonatal sound deprivation affects brain stem auditory nuclei. *Archives of Otolaryngology* 103:392–406.

Zinkus, P., Gottlieb, M., and Schapiro, M. 1978. Developmental and psychoeducational sequelae of chronic otitis media. *American Journal of Diseases of Children* 132:1100–1104.

Zinkus, P., and Gottlieb, M. 1980. Patterns of perceptual and academic deficits related to early chronic otitis media. *Pediatrics* 66:246–253.

Zinkus, P. 1982. Psychoeducational sequelae of chronic otitis media. *Seminars in Speech, Language and Hearing* 3:305–312.

# 11

# Cognitive Development and Strategies of Assessment in Young Children

*Jerome Kagan*

Although the intriguing questions that surround varied consequences of chronic otitis media are being addressed with imagination, I suspect that the deepest answers will require a battery of new procedures that are derived from a view of human cognition that emphasizes a number of very separate and specific talents. The invention of new procedures to evaluate coherences in nature is guided simultaneously by the premises of the investigator and by pragmatic constraints, with the first usually the more powerful of the two. The evaluation of individual differences in cognitive functions in children and adults has, until recently, been influenced by the conviction that the construct of general intelligence was theoretically useful. Because this assumption has obvious pragmatic advantages, there have been few competitors to the omnibus tests of mental ability, or of developmental level, whether the instrument is the Wechsler Intelligence Scale for Children, the Stanford-Binet, or the Bayley Developmental Scale for Infants. The attraction to the idea of general mental or academic ability is not unique among European and American social scientists. Sister concepts such as level of moral development, sexual identity, extraversion, emotionality, and psychopathy also are conceived of as universals, the assumption being that humans may be placed along a continuum of some highly abstract characteristic that is indifferent to the context in which it is actualized. However, such a Platonic conception of the component parts of human nature is not universal. Many

Preparation of this paper was supported by a grant from the Robert Wood Johnson Foundation.

societies, especially those of China and Japan, favor a more detailed parsing of human characteristics that acknowledges the critical role of the specific target of a person's action and the specific class of information that is being processed and manipulated.

However, the enthusiasm for intelligence and IQ scores is beginning to falter after almost three quarters of a century because of historical events and new empirical facts. The historical events are familiar to all of us. Most Americans are either egalitarian or wish to be so, and the complaint by spokespeople for minority groups that the IQ test is unfair and gives a biased evaluation of the mental abilities of black or Hispanic children has motivated a receptive audience to search for substitute assessment procedures, However, the complaint against omnibus tests requires facts and, in the end, empirical fact is the matador that will slay the concept of general intelligence. Three facts are relevant to this claim.

First, the child's language development, that is, the rate of mastery of syntax and vocabulary, is not highly correlated with the rate of development of other important cognitive talents, including recall memory, symbolic attitude, perceptual analysis, or inference, when these are measured in contexts that do not require linguistic ability. This fact is embarrassing to the idea that children differ in general intelligence, for surely language and memory ability are two critical components of mental functioning. If these two competences are relatively independent in their rate of growth, it is difficult to defend the idea of general intellectual ability (Kagan 1981).

A second fact is that many studies of school age children who were given broad batteries of tests find statistical independence among varied types of cognitive performance. Even when recall memory is the function measured one can find correlations as low as 0.2 between recall memory for sentences from stories and recognition memory of pictures from scenes. Surely if there were a general intellectual ability a child with a good memory for a story should also have a good memory for his or her perceptual experiences in a forest. Of course, we have known that some of the subscales of the Wechsler Intelligence Scale for Children, digit recall and coding for example, had low correlations with the vocabulary and arithmetic scales. But because a factor analysis always yielded a first factor with a large portion of variance these low correlations were suppressed from critical consciousness. It is only because the professional community is now ideologically prepared to question the idea of general intelligence that a low correlation among cognitive skills is brooded upon and taken to be an important fact. The contemporary willingness to replace general intelligence with a conception of mind that is composed of many separate abilities is illustrated by the wide reception of Gardner's (1983) book *Frames of Mind*. Although J.P. Guilford proposed a very similar conception over 20 years ago, the community was not yet ready for Guilford's (1967) message.

A third fact: research on the relations between the functioning of the central nervous system and cognitive performances have provided a serious critique of general intelligence. The products of this research suggest that the brain is partially modular and does not, as Lashley believed, act as a unit. One of the most publicized examples of this principle is the work on left and right brain functions, which implies that verbal and nonverbal processes are elaborated differentially in the two hemispheres. This finding confronts, in a direct way, the validity of the idea of general intelligence, or degree of competence in an abstract cognitive ability, and replaces it with the notion of qualitatively different types of cognitive abilities. A quantity has been replaced with several qualities. That substitution does not mean that genetic differences among children have less influence on cognitive functioning. Indeed, I believe that the work on the relation between brain and cognition will create an even stronger prejudice, one that states that the differences in cognitive characteristics among children are influenced in a major way by inherent biological processes. The data presented at this meeting suggest that some children who show cognitive retardation as a result of chronic otitis media were born with qualities that made them biologically vulnerable to chronic otitis media.

## WHAT ARE THE BEST CONSTRUCTS?

Deciding that the hypothesis of multiple abilities is a better premise than general intellectual ability is much easier than selecting the theoretically best set of talents. The current strategy among psychologists and educators, in the absence of strong theoretical guidance, is to select constructs that are the least likely to be seriously incorrect. Thus they classify mental abilities on the basis of relatively obvious and intuitively appealing concrete performances that can be observed. Some of the more popular abilities include verbal, spatial, mathematical, and musical, and the ability to get along with others. William of Ockham, the fourteenth-century Oxford skeptic, was of similar mind for he divided all words into three unusually concrete categories: those that are written, those that are spoken, and those that occur in our minds. This phenotypic categorization of words resembles Francis Bacon's binary classification of all substances in the world into fiery and non-fiery, a dimension that probably appeared reasonable to colleagues and friends because this was a time when there was neither central heating and nor electric stoves.

But the history of natural science, especially biology, chemistry, and physics, implies that constructs based on intuitively reasonable concrete observables, although usually the first phase in theory construction, rarely turn out to be the most powerful set of categories. These sciences, which began with concrete ideas, have replaced them with hypothetical terms that are invisible but much more powerful. For example, pre-Darwinian biological classifications involved morphological characteristics of plants and animals that one could see and touch; contemporary biologists use similarities and differences in proteins. Seventeenth-century alchemists used similarities in color, texture, and weight to classify inorganic substances. Modern chemists use similarities and differences in atomic structure inferred from the output of a linear accelerator.

I believe that theoretical analyses of human cognition must begin to move away from the obvious concrete qualities seen in the performances of children and move toward hypothetical, basic cognitive processes. The remainder of this presentation is an attempt, albeit speculative, to suggest what some of these processes might be. I admit without embarrassment that 25 years from now the next generation of psychologists will smile at the crudity of the suggestions to be made in this paper. But they are the best I can do. This is not a weak defense, for Lagerqvist had God reply to a dead man who asked him why He had made life so difficult with, "I did the best I could."

## MEMORIAL FUNCTIONS

I interpret contemporary research on cognitive functioning in both animals and children as indicating that the length of time a representation of experience persists on the stage of short-term memory is a fundamental competence that increases with phylogeny as well as ontogeny. Hence, in infants and young children of a particular age this ability might be a sensitive sign of one aspect of the integrity of cognitive functioning. These memory functions are assessed by using recognition memory with infants under seven or eight months of age and recall memory with children over eight months. Research by many psychologists has shown that by eight weeks of age infants will, after being familiarized on a given visual or auditory stimulus, attend more to a novel or discrepant event when both old and new are present or, if habituated on a particular event, show increased attention to a new event (Kagan 1972; Quinn and Siqueland 1985). This phenomenon is so robust it can be seen in newborns and many investigators use this phenomenon as a way to measure the child's discriminative capacities.

In an easy procedural actualization of this function, the examiner lets a four-month-old infant play with a green rattle for ten seconds, takes a toy away gently, and then presents, after some delay, the green rattle along with a blue top. If the delay is less than ten seconds most infants will look longer at the novel blue top. However, the delay between the removal of the first toy and the presentation of the pair does influence the tendency to fixate the novel event. I believe that an effective test of the integrity of this memorial function in the infant is a test series of about 12 items. For four items the delay might be 3 seconds, for four other items the delay might be 10 seconds, and for a final set of four items the delay might be 30 or 60 seconds in duration. The tendency to attend to the novel toy should decrease as the delay increases. But by 12 to 18 months of age all infants should tolerate delays as long as one minute. Fagan and McGrath (1981) are so convinced of the sensitivity of the infant's preference for novelty they are promoting a version of this idea as a predictive test of the child's future intelligence. And Rose and Wallace (1985) have reported that the administration of Fagan's stimuli to six-month-olds reveals that infants who show greater attention to a novel member of a pair following a brief familiarization on each of four pairs of identical stimuli (faces or designs) have a higher IQ score at three-and-a-half and six years of age (correlations from .4 to .5). Although the attention to novelty was not correlated with social class, both class and a preference for novelty made equal contributions to the IQ score at six years, and accounted for about 50 percent of the variance in IQ score.

Thus, if a four to six month old infant does not look longer at a novel stimulus when faced with an old and new event over eight to ten different stimulus items one should question the integrity of memorial functioning in that infant, and assess, in other ways, the integrity of selected parts of the central nervous system and/or the quality of home rearing. It would not be inappropriate for a physician to administer such a procedure to a six-month-old with otitis media who is suspected of cognitive retardation.

After eight months, when children will retrieve an object that they have watched being hidden, a more sensitive index of memorial function is recall memory for the location of a hidden object. A useful procedure for children between eight and twelve months involves two covers and an attractive toy. The toy is hidden under one of the covers, a screen is raised for delays of one, five, or ten seconds, after which the screen is removed and the infant is permitted to search for the toy. There is a linear increase with age in the probability of reaching correctly across the varied delays in infants between 8 and 15 months of age (Kagan, Kearsley, and Zelazo 1978). Almost all 15-month-old children with no evidence of central nervous system insult are able to find the toy after the longest delay. We have used this fact to construct a procedure that we call *Memory for Locations*. This test is most relevant for children between one and three years of age. After age three the test is too easy but it could be made more difficult for the older child by using two objects or more receptacles. In the procedure the examiner hides an attractive object under two, four, or six identical cups using delays of one, five, ten, or fifteen seconds with a screen between the child and the cups during the varying delays. The child is first tested with two cups at all delays, then four cups at all delays, and finally six cups at all delays. The proportion of children solving this problem increases linearly with age (Kagan 1981). This procedure has been tried with children from different cultural settings, including children growing up on isolated atolls in the Fiji chain, Vietnamese refugee children living in northern California, and children from New England. This procedure is also being administered to several hundred children as part of the Robert Wood Johnson collaborative project on communicative delay, and to several thousand children who are subjects in a national longitudinal study. I believe that any two-year-old who cannot successfully find a toy that was placed under one of two cups with a five-second delay after several motivated attempts is probably at risk for a serious cognitive disability and urge clinicians to consider such a procedure for children with chronic otitis media who are displaying signs of disturbances in attention.

After age three or four the examiner can also use recall memory for words and for visual sequences, as well as recognition memory for pictures. The average four-year-old can recognize at least 80 percent of a series of 24 unrelated pictures when first shown 24 pictures and then shown 12 new and 12 old ones. Any four-year-old who could not be better than 50 percent correct recognition, despite motivation, is at risk for memorial deficit due to organic or environmental reasons. The reader will notice that these procedures do not require language and are, therefore, useful for hard of hearing children or children who have language delay due to otitis media or other environmental conditions.

The fact that assessments of recall memory, like remembering the location of a toy, cannot be assessed before eight months is probably due to the maturation of the central nervous system. Patricia Goldman-Rakic told a conference that her research group at Yale has found that the growth function for density of synapses in all areas of the rhesus monkey cortex is the same and reaches a peak at about two months of age. Two months in rhesus is comparable to about eight months in the human infant. It is likely that the appearance of recall memory is due, in part, to structural changes in pre-frontal cortex. This interesting fact also implies that cognitive assessments of infants under eight months of age should be more ambiguous in their diagnostic significance than assessments made after that age.

## CATEGORICAL FUNCTIONING: CATEGORIES

The creation of a schema or cognitive representation of a dimension (or set of dimensions) that is shared by different events is also a fundamental human competence. But unlike persistence of a representation in short-term memory, it is more difficult to measure. Although most psychologists use habituation-dishabituation procedures with infants, we have found in several extensive studies that failure of dishabituation to the presentation of a member of a new category, following habituation on a different category, cannot be treated as evidence of failure to extract the familiarized category or failure to possess the category. I believe that the habituation-dishabituation method is a little more sensitive during the familiarization if one shows a pair of nonidentical exemplars of that category, provides continuous presentation until the child habituates to the category (rather than a fixed number of trials), tests the child with a pair of stimuli, and holds the intertrial intervals short (about two seconds) in order to keep the child aroused and alert. However, it is rare for a child to show no dishabituation to a half dozen different categories. Hence, a one- to two-year-old child who failed to show dishabituation to at least one or two categories in a battery of six (when the categories included people, animals, vehicles, food, or furniture) is probably at risk for a defect in a vital cognitive function; namely, the ability to extract similarities in events. Because this talent is central to language development, there is potential utility to using such a procedure to evaluate the growth of comprehension and expressive vocabulary in children with otitis media.

A useful method for assessing possession of categories in children one to three years old is to place a set of 12 to 16 objects in front of the child. The objects might comprise four different categories, let us say foods, clothing, vehicles, and animals. The normal child will group spontaneously the objects that belong to the same category, or at least will touch in sequence the objects that belong to the same category. Completely random behavior with the objects would be diagnostic of a "deficit" in cognitive functioning.

A third method that shows promise for children one to three years old is to place in front of the child two pictures from two different categories, say an animal and a food, with a two-inch space between them. The examiner then presents pictures, one at a time, some are illustrations of animals, some of foods, and some belong to neither category, and asks the child to put the picture on the correct pile— "Where does it go?" The child should place most of the pictures correctly and show signs of conflict to a picture that belongs to neither category.

## Amodal Schema

A cognitive function that is closely related to category inference and also inherent in human functioning is present in subtle form by one year of age and in clear form by two to three years of age. Some psychologists claim this ability can be observed much earlier, but their data are still controversial. The ability is the competence to extract a dimension from events in two different sensory modalities and to create an amodal schema for that dimension. One of the most compelling examples of this ability is Bushnell's (1985) demonstration that one-year-olds who are looking at a toy block with a furry surface, but exploring with their hands a hidden cube that has a smooth surface (to which the child does not have visual access) will show obvious signs of surprise. The child could only show surprise if he/she recognized that the feeling of smoothness was inconsistent with the visually given surface. This fact means that the infant understands *smoothness* in an abstract way.

In a second demonstration Bahrick (1983) first showed an infant a pair of color films side by side. One film illustrated a pair of hands wearing blue gloves banging together two yellow blocks. The second film showed the same pair of hands squeezing two yellow sponges together. For the first 90 seconds of the film the infant heard the sound track of one of the events (the blocks or the sponges) while for the second 90 seconds the infant heard the other sound track. Following a short break, the two films were shown again (right-left position was reversed) but this time there was no continuous sound track. On an irregular schedule the silent films were interrupted by a five-second segment of sound track from one of the films. When this event happened the infants were likely to look at the film that corresponded to the sound track. This reliable result suggests that the infant had, during the prior phase, learned to associate the correct sounds and sights by extracting similarity in either energy profile, rhythm, or synchrony between the sound of the two blocks coming together and the sight of that event. Similar demonstrations have been reported by others. The infant was able to recognize the similarity between an abrupt sound and an abrupt sight.

We know that infants as young as three years of age are able to say that loud sounds are heavier than light ones, or that a red cube is hotter than a blue one. And synesthesia is common in older children and adults. I suspect that the ability to extract schemata for an abstract dimension present in events from two different modalities is a basic human competence that emerges sometime during the first year. Therefore, we should develop procedures to evaluate this competence in children who are between one and three years of age. The studies by Bahrick, Bushnell, and others could serve as a basis for developing psychometrically sound instruments. I suspect that two-year-olds who show no evidence of this ability, despite attentiveness to the tasks, may lack a fundamental cognitive talent that is vital to language and to the ability to understand and generate analogy and metaphor.

## LANGUAGE

The critical importance of language makes it mandatory to assess its comprehension as early as possible. One problem has been that one could not administer recognition vocabulary tests like the Peabody Picture Vocabulary Test to most children until they are at least three years old because of the child's inability to understand the procedure. My colleague, J. Steven Reznick, has verified, however, that one procedure is remarkably effective with one- to two-year-old children. The child is first shown a pair of pictures (usually slides on a screen) for about six seconds (for example, a slide of a *key* and a *ball*). An observer codes the duration of time the infant fixates each of the two pictures. The slide is then removed and a few seconds later the same pair of slides appears, but this time the mother has been cued to ask the child to attend to only one of the pictures. The mother may say, "Where is the key?" or "Show me the ball." Under these conditions most one- to two-year-olds will look longer at the object requested, if they know the word and will not do so if the word is unfamiliar. I believe that this test is ready for standardization and offers the promise of assessing vocabulary knowledge in the critical two year interval when no other sensitive procedure is available. It should be especially valuable for diagnosis of language delay in children with chronic otitis media.

## INFERENCE

The ability to infer an event from presentation of its component parts or to infer a category from verbal descriptions of its features is also a vital cognitive function. Although I do not have confidence in procedures that test this ability in children under two to three years, after age three it is possible to evaluate these functions. In one procedure, the child is shown schematic line drawings that are only suggestive of familiar objects (a table, a cup, a car) and the child is asked to name the objects that might be represented by the parts. In the linguistic mode the examiner names two or three qualities and asks the child to guess the proper object (for example, "What tastes sweet and you can eat it?" "What has fur and barks?"). Development and standardization of testing procedures for these two competences would be important in evaluations of cognitive functioning.

## REFLECTION-IMPULSIVITY

The tendency to be reflective or impulsive in cognitive situations cannot be measured effectively until the child is at least five or six years old. But at that age investigators can give either an embedded figures task or one in which the child is shown pairs of either identical pictures or pictures that are different in a subtle way and ask the child to decide whether the pictures are the same or different. Some children decide quickly with latencies under 5 or 6 seconds and usually make an error. Such children are called impulsive. Other children take longer than 10 to 15 seconds to make their decision and are usually correct. They are called reflective.

The tendency to be reflective or impulsive is influenced both by socialization and biology. Most children who have been socialized to avoid error will be reflective. This is, of course, an adaptive strategy in school. Among the impulsive group there are two very different types of children. One type is poorly motivated to do well or has hostility to the tester or the testing situation as a result of socialization experiences in the home. The other group, which is small in number, is composed of temperamentally inhibited and fearful children. These children have high excitability in the stress circuits that link the hypothalamus to the pituitary-adrenal axis, the reticular activating system, and the sympathetic nervous system. These children are easily aroused and can be very impulsive. They are also likely at four or five years of age to be fearful and shy. Thus, the combination of being fearful and shy as well as impulsive implies that the impulsivity may have a biological contribution. If, on the other hand, an impulsive child is sociable, talkative, and fearless, the impulsivity is apt to be due to socialization and/or motivation.

## SUMMARY

I appreciate that these theoretical suggestions and proposals for new test procedures are too preliminary to command general acceptance. But I also appreciate the inertia that opposes the development of new procedures. Our progress in understanding the cognitive growth of all children will be enhanced if we develop new assessment methods. In an issue of *Scientific American* devoted to the molecules of life, Robert Weinberg (1985) states that the amazing advances in molecular biology are due first to the invention of methods—electron microscopy, paper chromatography, enzymes that snip or repair pieces of DNA, and the cloning of genes. New theories came after new facts were revealed by these procedures. One psychological example is the use of high amplitude sucking, a relatively simple procedure, to make elegant inferences about speech perception in infants (Eimas and Miller 1980).

Psychologists, both developmental and educational, often have not been enthusiastic over investing a great deal of time and money in the development of new procedures. A psychologist will accept a grant for a half-million dollars for a major study of children and then go to the standard shelf of mental tests and questionnaires, without spending a penny on the creation of a new instrument. Many psychologists believe that if a child has a particular cognitive quality it will appear on one of the standardized tests that they choose. Hence, it does not seem wise to invest effort and money in developing new instruments. But I believe this conclusion is flawed. Our current terms for cognitive competences are not essences that are present in the child's mind waiting to be discovered with the proper test. Terms like "impaired communicative skills," "poor short-term memory," and "learning disability" are specific to the evidence revealed by the instruments used. Consider the following finding as illustrative. Patients who have bilateral occipitotemporal lesions cannot recognize photographs of familiar faces when the examiner shows them a series of photographs and asks, "Do you know who this is?" "Do you recognize this person?" But the same patient will show a galvanic skin response to the familiar, but not to the unfamiliar, photographs (Tranel and Damasio 1985). Thus, the diagnostic classification "impaired recognition memory for faces of people" is not an essence; rather, it is a label for a person's performance with a very specific procedure; namely, being asked to respond *yes* or *no* with respect to the sense of familiarity of a photograph. This diagnostic label is inaccurate when the evidence comes from a procedure in which galvanic skin responses are measured.

I believe that if behavioral scientists begin to develop new procedures for memory, language comprehension, inference, and categorization—among others—and collect data on large numbers of children, normal and at risk, the resulting data will produce major insights, some surprising, and will have a major impact on the diagnostic testing of children with otitis media as well as those with other physical and psychological problems. As a consequence, we eventually will be able to make more accurate diagnoses of those children with anomalous cognitive development or those who are at risk for future academic failure and associated problems of adaptation.

## REFERENCES

Bahrick, L. E. 1983. Infants' perception of substance and temporal synchrony in multi-modal events. *Infant Behavior and Development* 6:429-451.
Bushnell, E. W. 1985, in press. The basis of infant visual tactual functioning—amodal

dimensions or multi-modal compounds? *In* L. P. Lipsitt and C. K. Rovee-Collier (eds.). *Advances in Infancy Research.*

Eimas, P. D., and Miller, J. L. 1980. Contextual effects in infant speech perception. *Science* 209:1140-1141.

Fagan, J. F., and McGrath, S. K. 1981. Infant recognition memory and later intelligence. *Intelligence* 5:121-130.

Gardner, H. 1983. *Frames of Mind.* New York: Basic Books.

Guilford, J. P. 1967. *The Nature of Human Intelligence.* New York: McGraw-Hill.

Kagan, J. 1971. *Change and Continuity in Infancy.* New York: John Wiley.

Kagan, J. 1981. *The Second Year.* Cambridge: Harvard University Press.

Kagan, J., Kearsley, R. B., and Zelazo, P. R. 1978. *Infancy: Its Place in Human Development.* Cambridge: Harvard University Press.

Quinn, P. C., and Siqueland, E. R. 1985. Delayed recognition memory for orientation by human infants. *Journal of Experimental Child Psychology.* 40:293-303.

Rose, S. A., and Wallace, I. F. 1985. Visual recognition memory: A predictor of later cognitive functioning in preterms. *Child Development* 56:843-852.

Tranel, D., and Damasio, A. R. 1985. Knowledge without awareness. *Science* 228:1453-1454.

Weinberg, R. A. 1985. The molecules of life. *Scientific American* 253:48-57.

# 12

# Speech-Language Learning and Early Middle Ear Disease: A Procedural Report

*Sandy Friel-Patti, Terese Finitzo, William L. Meyerhoff, and J. Patrick Hieber*

Otitis media, an inflammatory condition of the middle ear, is the second most common infectious disease affecting children under six years of age. In a preliminary analysis of the Greater Boston Collaborative Otitis Media Program, designed to follow 2,565 children prospectively from birth, Teele, Klein, and Rosner (1980) report that 71 percent of the children enrolled in the study had one or more episodes of acute otitis media before their third birthday. Further, 33 percent experienced three or more episodes. Persistence of the middle ear effusion (MEE) was frequent: after the first episode of otitis media, 70 percent of the children had MEE at a two-week check-up, 40 percent had MEE which persisted for one month, 20 percent had MEE lasting two months and 10 percent had MEE three months after the onset of the episode.

In spite of intensive research in the area of otitis media, many important questions persist (Ventry 1980). The developmental and psychoeducational sequelae have not been well documented and remain controversial. While many authors have expressed concern

The preliminary work reported in this paper was funded by a grant from the American Hearing Research Foundation. The current investigation is funded by the National Institute of Neurological and Communicative Disorders and Stroke (1 RO1 NS19675-01A1). The authors wish to acknowledge the contributions of Peter Roland, M.D., Ellen Formby, M.A., Karen Clinton Brown, M.S., Denise Dunlap, M.S., H.S. Gopal, M.S., and A. Syrdal, Ph.D. to the study.

about the deleterious effects of mild, fluctuating, conductive hearing loss on language development, auditory perception, and subsequent educational achievement (Zinkus, Gottlieb, and Schapiro 1978; Katz 1978; Gottlieb, Zinkus, and Thompson 1979), design problems have often confounded data interpretation. Contributing to the inherent difficulty of establishing a methodologically sound research plan is the fact that otitis media is a disease on a continuum. That is, the disease symptoms change from day to day making monitoring the disease process an extremely complex task.

Conceptually, the hypothesis that there is a link between chronic conductive hearing impairment and normal language development is tenable. It is well-known, for example, that the phonological system is dependent in part upon the child's repeated experience with spoken language (Menyuk 1979; Rapin 1979). The presence of fluctuating changes in hearing means that the young child must deal with conflicting or inconsistent information on which to base language learning. Indeed, one would expect that a chronic conductive hearing loss during the period of oral language learning would pervade all aspects of rule acquisition.

Stillman (1980) speculates that central auditory abilities, in addition to sound localization, might be affected by the absence of normal binaural input during critical periods. One could anticipate physiological and perceptual changes, as a result of abnormal auditory input caused by early middle ear pathology, which may persist even after treatment of the disorder. Studying children on whom there is documented early asymmetrical or unilateral impairments will address the question of whether binaural input is critical to normal development of brainstem neural mechanisms and to higher level neural organization, particularly to hemispheric specialization related to speech and language.

It is important to evaluate the perception of speech sounds apart from higher-level linguistic variables in order to detect subtle deficits in auditory/phonetic processing of the kind observed in dyslexic children by Godfrey et al. (1981). The ability to perceive speech sounds should be tested in a way that precludes use of linguistic redundancy, contextual cues, or visual aids, focusing specifically on the child's capacity to recognize essential acoustic cues to particular phonetic distinctions. Redundancy of language also interferes with the ability to identify subtle language learning disorders. The traditional assessment procedures and materials used are sufficiently redundant to enable the child to perform adequately in spite of some deficits (Sloan 1980). Sloan (1980) suggests that these subtle problems missed in early childhood may well present themselves in later years as learning and reading disabilities.

PRELIMINARY STUDY

In an earlier study, we reported preliminary findings on language delay associated with fluctuating conductive hearing loss for 28 infants evaluated longitudinally. The infants were selected from a larger study of auditory development in the first two years of life using the auditory brainstem response (ABR), along with immittance measurements and behavioral audiometry (Friel-Patti et al. 1982). Because ABR has been reported to be sensitive to the presence of otitis media in infants and young children, it was the primary determinant of the degree of hearing loss (Finitzo-Hieber and Friel-Patti 1985; Mendelson et al. 1979; Fria and Sabo 1980). Tympanometry was utilized as an adjunct to the otoscopic examination in infants six months or older. This population was therefore unique in that there was confirmed evidence of a hearing impairment and middle ear pathology using three independent measures: 1) auditory brainstem responses, 2) immittance measures, and 3) a pediatrician's otoscopic examination.

The majority of the 28 infants were premature but all were judged to be developing normally at their first birthday. Families of these children represented a low socioeconomic population and included those who received a score of 3 or less on the Four Factor Index of Social Status (Hollingshead 1975). Additionally, all infants were similar on the following variables: mother's level of education (mean = 10th grade, SD = 1.8, range = 8th grade to 2 years post high school) and mother's age at delivery (mean = 20 years, SD = 4.9, range = 15 to 34 years).

At least one auditory brainstem response (ABR) was completed on each infant prior to discharge from the hospital nursery. The children were re-evaluated at the Callier Center for Communication Disorders. All follow-up examinations were based on corrected chronological age (age post-term) rather than on the child's birthdate and consisted of an ABR at 6 weeks and ABR, immittance, and behavioral audiometry using a visual reinforcement paradigm at 6 months, 12 months, and 18 months.

The 28 infants were evaluated by a speech-language pathologist who was kept unaware of their hearing status. Mothers were prompted not to discuss this aspect of the child's history in order to minimize examiner bias. However, the infants with histories of repeated middle ear infections were occasionally recognizable because of either overt signs or behavioral manifestations of illness such as rhinitis, mouth breathing, congestion, and irritability. Again, in an effort to minimize examiner bias, the results of the language testing were not made available to the audiologist until the conclusion of the study.

Language development was assessed using two standardized

measures administered in conjunction with a detailed interview. The format for the interview was the same for all families. The two language measures were the Receptive-Expressive Emergent Language Scale (REEL) (Bzoch and League 1971) and the Sequenced Inventory of Communication Development (SICD) (Hedrick, Prather, and Tobin 1975). The REEL was selected because it relies on parental report of the child's abilities thus permitting evaluation of behaviors not readily tapped in an unfamiliar, clinical environment. The SICD provides a detailed profile of the child's communicative development, including comprehension, production, and discrimination. The test combines an interview format relying on parental report of the child's typical performance with the direct observation and assessment of the child by the examiner. The REEL was administered at 12, 18, and 24 months and the SICD was scored at 18 and 24 months.

The results of this double-blind study revealed a remarkable correspondence between the degree of hearing loss in the better ear over time and the severity of the language delay. A correlation of $-.59$ ($p < .001$) was obtained between the mean hearing loss and the language test performance. Furthermore, receptive language skills correlated more highly (r = $-.65$) with hearing loss than expressive language skills (r = $-.52$; $p < .001$). That the long-term degree of conductive hearing loss accounted for 42 percent of the variance in the receptive language performance is a strong incentive to pursue an investigation of the auditory perception of speech in these children.

The generalizability of these preliminary findings is limited by two factors. The major limitation is that the children were drawn exclusively from a lower socioeconomic group. Secondly, the possible contamination resulting from the premature neonatal status of the subjects cannot be overlooked. However, the results were sufficiently strong to prompt the larger study reported below in which these factors are controlled.

## CURRENT INVESTIGATION

### MAIN STUDY QUESTIONS

The current ongoing investigation began in December, 1984 as a prospective study of a large group of healthy middle class newborns. The study is designed to address four main research questions:
1. Is the degree of hearing loss associated with otitis media with effusion (OME) over time predictive of language delay?
2. Assuming the answer to 1 is yes, is the time of occurrence of OME predictive of language delay?

3. Is the amount and time of hearing loss associated with OME predictive of delay in speech production and perception?
4. Is recurrent OME predictive of the overall development of children?

Based on our estimates of means and standard deviations from the preliminary investigation, we projected a sample size of 31 in the chronic otitis group for a clinically significant difference to reach statistical significance with a confidence (power) level of .80 or better. From estimates of occurrence of otitis media and withdrawal from the pediatric practice, we calculated the necessary subject size of 250 children. The study is designed to follow this group of full-term infants enrolled before their six month well-baby evaluation until their third birthday.

The subjects are all drawn from one private pediatric practice in Dallas, Texas and all of the families are mid- to high-middle (scores of 4 or greater) on the Hollingshead Scale (1975). In addition, they have all met the following inclusion criteria:
1. normal newborn examination
2. apgar at least 7/8
3. birthweight greater than 2400 grams
4. pregnancy 37 weeks or greater
5. English as the only language in the home
6. attendance at all well-baby checks
7. normally developing at time of enrollment (i.e. no noted neurological problems nor major physical defects)
8. no multiple births

The audiometric battery includes ABR testing at six months in addition to regular otoscopic examinations and immittance measures. Behavioral audiometry evaluations begin at 12 months. The infants are seen at the Callier Center for Communication Disorders every six months beginning with the six month evaluation. At the time of the first Callier visit, the ABR is obtained. An otoscopic examination is performed by an otologist and immittance measures are taken. In the event that the ABR is abnormal at six months, a re-test is scheduled for the 12 month Callier visit.

The ABR is elicited by a .1 millisecond rarefaction click transduced by a TDH 49 earphone. Stimuli are presented at 20, 30, and 60 dB normal Hearing Level (nHL) at a repetition rate of 37.7 per second and at 80 dB at a rate of 21.1 per second. The nHL value is referenced to the average threshold of normal young observers in our laboratory. Peak equivalent SPL of the 0 dB nHL (psychological click threshold) signal is 30 dB re: .0002 dynes per centimeter squared. If the Wave V response is absent at 30 dB, additional testing is undertaken to obtain threshold response. Each infant is tested in natural or sedated sleep in a double-walled sound booth. A stimulus intensity trial consists of two independently summed waveforms, each averaged about 2048 presentations and replicated within .24 milliseconds. Peak latencies and amplitudes are obtained from the composite response to 4096 stimulus trials. Wave I and V latencies are obtained, along with the Wave V to Wave I interpeak latencies at 80 dB nHL. A Wave V to Wave I amplitude ratio is obtained at 60 dB nHL and Wave V latencies are measured at all other intensities tested.

Behavioral audiometric evaluations beginning at 12 months of age are obtained using a visual reinforcement paradigm based on Moore and Wilson (1978). At 12 months, the evaluation consists of sound field warble tone measurements at 500 and 2000 Hz and provides a measure of hearing in the better ear. Additionally, an ascending response to speech and a Speech Awareness Threshold (SAT) are recorded. At 18, 24, and 30 months, additional warble tone measures at 1000 and 4000 Hz are added. Beginning at 30 months, pure tone testing under earphones will be begun.

Immittance measures are taken following enrollment at the time of all well-baby check ups (regularly scheduled at 6, 9, 12, 18, 24, and 36 months) in the pediatrician's office by a study representative. A study representative is present in the pediatrician's office whenever the office is open, including the pediatrician's day off and weekends, so that immittance measures can be obtained whenever a study baby is brought in for a sick-baby visit.

Home and/or day care center visits are made by a study representative when the children are 8, 11, 13, 15, 17, 21, 28, and 33 months old. In this way, during the first year and a half, the children have some contact with a study representative at least every 8 weeks. After 18 months, the lapse between contact may be up to 12 weeks. Obviously, the contact is more frequent for those children who are sick and report to the pediatrician for sick-baby visits. The scheduled home visits are also intended to increase the likelihood that asymptomatic episodes of OME will be discovered and documented.

There are four types of contact with each subject: well-baby visits, sick-baby visits, home/day care center visits, and the Callier Center Visits. The types of contact, the examiners, and measures taken at each visit are summarized in Table 1. The schedule of the visits is presented in Table 2.

Table 1

Types of Contact

| Type of Visit | Examiners | Measures |
|---|---|---|
| Well baby | pediatrician, audiologist, or speech pathologist | immittance otoscopy |
| Sick baby | pediatrician, audiologist, or speech pathologist | immittance otoscopy |
| Home/Day Care | audiologist or speech pathologist | immittance language |
| Callier | otolaryngologist, audiologist, and/or speech pathologist | immittance otoscopy ABR language behavioral audio eval speech perception |

LANGUAGE AND SPEECH PRODUCTION MEASURES

Beginning at the 12 months Callier visit, the language speech production measures include the Receptive-Expressive Emergent Language Scale (Bzoch and League 1971) and the Sequenced Inventory of Communication Development (Hedrick, Prather, and Tobin 1975). These are repeated at 18, 24, 30, and 36 months of age. The Goldman-Fristoe Test of Articulation (Goldman and Fristoe 1969) will be scored beginning at the 18 month visit. In addition, spontaneous language samples will be collected at each evaluation. The production samples will form the data base for a variety of structural and semantic analyses. Dialogue analyses will be done on samples collected when the children are 24 and 36 months old. The procedures for the dialogue analyses will be similar to those described in Friel-Patti and Conti-Ramsden (1984) and Conti-Ramsden and Friel-Patti (1983, 1984). At the conclusion of the study, the Peabody Picture Vocabulary Test—Revised (Dunn and Dunn 1981) and the Test of Early Language Development (Hresko, Reid, and Hammill 1981) will also be administered.

Table 2

Schedule of Visits

| Type of Visit | Subject's Age in Months |
|---|---|
| Well baby | 6, 9, 12, 18, 24, 36 |
| Home/Day Care | 8, 11, 13, 15, 17, 21, 28, 33 |
| Callier | 6, 12, 18, 24, 30, 36 |

High quality recordings will be made of two repetitions of the children's productions on the Goldman-Fristoe Test of Articulation and will be analyzed acoustically. Other acoustic analyses will include selected minimal pairs sampling vowel and consonant contrasts. Vowel contrasts include: /i,ɪ/, /a,ʌ/, /u,ʊ/ to compare place of articulation and tensity distinctions. Consonant contrasts to be sampled are stops differing by place (e.g., /ba/-/da/, /da/-/ga/) and stops differing by voicing (e.g., /pa/-/ba/, /ta/-/da/). In addition, liquids differing by place (e.g., /r/-/l/), voiceless fricatives differing by place (e.g., /s/-/ʃ/) and voiceless fricative-affricate contrasts (e.g., /ʃ/-/tʃ/).

The recordings will provide samples of standard consonant and vowel segments, spoken by every child, to be analyzed acoustically. Fundamental frequency, the first four format frequencies as estimated by linear prediction techniques, and durations of target segments will be measured. The frequency values will also be transformed into an auditory scale developed by Syrdal (1982a; 1982b, 1984, 1985) and Syrdal and Gopal (1986) for the purposes of normalization, classification, and evaluation. In this way, acoustic-phonetic aspects of the children's vocal productions can be specified, compared, and related to their perceptual performance with similar materials, and to adult productions.

SPEECH PERCEPTION MEASURES

Speech perception measures include tests of perceptual judgments of phonetic distinctions chosen to represent a variety of spectral and temporal information important for speech. These phonetic distinctions will cover a range of difficulty in the order in which they characteristically appear in the speech of normal children.

OTHER MEASURES

The Vineland Social Maturity Scale—Revised (Sparrow, Balla, and Cicchetti 1984) is administered at 12, 24, and 36 months. This scale permits evaluation of social development through a parental interview format as well as through observation and natural interaction with the examiner. The Arthur Adaptation of the Leiter International Performance Scale, (Leiter 1979) a standardized nonverbal test of intelligence, will be given to each subject at 36 months.

# SUMMARY

There is a need for longitudinal research to explore the possible causal relationships among chronic conductive hearing loss during the first years of life, auditory/phonetic perceptual problems, and persistant language and speech production deficits. Based on the results of our preliminary work, we have initiated a prospective, longitudinal study of a group of 250 children in order to examine the relationship between speech-language learning and early middle ear disease. The design of the current study is once again double-blind: the audiologists are not aware of the child's performance on the speech and language development measures and the speech-language pathologists are similarly unaware of the child's hearing test results and/or history of middle ear disease.

We have hypothesized that chronic conductive hearing loss during the first three years of life may have serious long-term effects on the child's auditory perception in addition to his receptive and expressive speech and language skills. We have begun a longitudinal study of a hierarchy of behaviors in order to examine their interrelationships and to relate them to the well-documented degree and type of auditory abnormality associated with chronic middle ear disease. Recognizing that the problem is complex, we have assembled a multidisciplinary team of investigators who in turn developed a set of procedures for gathering measures to document hearing, the status of the middle ear, speech-language production, speech perception and social and intellectual development.

## REFERENCES

Bzoch, K., and League, R. 1971. *Receptive—Expressive Emergent Language Scale.* Baltimore: University Park Press.

Conti-Ramsden, G., and Friel-Patti, S. 1984. Mother-child dialogues: A comparison of normal and language impaired children. *Journal of Communication Disorders* 17:19–35.

Conti-Ramsden, G., and Friel-Patti, S. 1983. Mothers' discourse adjustments to language-impaired and non-language-impaired children. *Journal of Speech and Hearing Disorders* 48:360–367.

Dunn, L., and Dunn, L. 1981. *Peabody Picture Vocabulary Test—Revised.* Circle Pines, Minnesota: American Guidance Service.

Finitzo-Hieber, T., and Friel-Patti, S. 1985. Conductive hearing loss and the ABR. *In* J. Jacobson (ed.). *The Auditory Brainstem Response.* San Diego: College-Hill Press.

Fria, T. J., and Sabo, D. L. 1980. Auditory brainstem responses in children with otitis media with effusion. *Annals of Otology, Rhinology, and Laryngology* 68:220–206.

Friel-Patti, S., and Conti-Ramsden, G. 1984. Discourse development in atypical language learners. *In* S. Kuczaj (ed.). *Discourse Development.* New York: Springer-Verlag.

Friel-Patti, S., Finitzo-Hieber, T., Conti, G., and Brown, K. 1982. Language delay in infants associated with middle ear disease and mild, fluctuating hearing impairment. *Pediatric Infectious Disease* 1:104–109.

Godfrey, J. J., Syrdal-Lasky, A. K., Millay, K. K., and Knox, C. M. 1981. Performance of dyslexic children on speech perception tests. *Journal of Experimental Child Psychology* 32:401–424.

Goldman, R., and Fristoe, M. 1969. *The Goldman-Fristoe Test of Articulation.* Circle Pines, Minnesota: American Guidance Service.

Gottlieb, M. I., Zinkus, P., and Thompson, A. 1979. Chronic middle ear disease and auditory perceptual deficits. *Clinical Pediatrics* 18:725.

Hedrick, D. L., Prather, E. M., and Tobin, A. R. 1975. *Sequenced Inventory of Communication Development.* Seattle: University of Washington Press.

Hollingshead, A. 1975. *Four Factor Index of Social Status.* Working paper available from Department of Sociology, Yale University.

Hresko, W., Reid, K., and Hammill, D. 1981. *Test of Early Language Development.* Austin: Pro-Ed.

Katz, J. 1978. The effects of conductive hearing loss on auditory function. *ASHA,* 20:879–886.

Leiter, R. G. 1979. *Leiter International Performance Scale.* Chicago, Illinois: Stoelting Co.

Mendelson, T., Salamy, A., Lenoir, M., and McKeon, C. 1979. Brainstem evoked potential findings in children with otitis media. *Archives of Otolaryngology* 105:17–20.

Menyuk P. 1979. Design factors in the assessment of language development in children with otitis media. *Annals of Otology, Rhinology, and Laryngology* 88:78–87.

Moore, J. M., and Wilson, W. R. 1978. Visual reinforcement audiometry (VRA) with infants. *In* S. E. Gerber and G. T. Mencher (eds.). *Early Diagnosis of Hearing Loss.* New York: Grune and Stratton, Inc.

Rapin, I. 1979. Conductive hearing loss effects on children's language and scholastic skills. *Annals of Otology, Rhinology and Laryngology* 88:3–12.

Sloan, C. 1980. Auditory processing disorders and language development. *In* P. J. Levinson and C. Sloan (eds.). *Auditory Processing and Language: Clinical and Research Perspectives.* New York: Grune and Stratton.

Sparrow, S. S., Balla, D. A., and Cicchetti, D. V. 1984. *Vineland Adaptive Behavior Scales.* Circle Pines, Minnesota: American Guidance Service.

Stillman, R. 1980. Auditory brain mechanisms. *In* P. J. Levinson and C. Sloan (eds.). *Auditory Processing and Language: Clinical and Research Perspectives.* New York: Grune and Stratton.

Syrdal, A. K. 1982a. Frequency analyses of American English vowels. *Journal of the Acoustical Society of America* 71:S106(A).

Syrdal, A. K. 1982b. Frequency analyses of syllable initial and final liquids spoken by American English talkers. *Journal of the Acoustical Society of America* 71:S105(A).

Syrdal, A. K. 1984. Aspects of an auditory representation of American English vowels. Speech Commun. Group, Res. Lab. Electron. MIT, Workshop papers 4:27–41.

Syrdal, A. K. 1985. Aspects of a model of the auditory representation of American English vowels. *Speech Communication* 4:121–135.

Syrdal, A. K., and Gopal, H. S. 1986. A perceptual model of vowel recognition based on the auditory representation of American English vowels. *Journal of the Acoustical Society of America* (In Press).

Teele, D. W., Klein, J. O., and Rosner, B. A. 1980. Epidemiology of otitis media in children. *Annals of Otology, Rhinology, and Laryngology* Supplement 68, 89:5–6.

Ventry, I. M. 1980. Effects of conductive hearing loss: Fact or fiction. *Journal of Speech and Hearing Disorders* 45:143–156.

Zinkus, P. W., Gottlieb, M. I., and Schapiro, M. 1978. Development and psycho-educational sequelae of chronic otitis media. *American Journal of Diseases of Children* 132:1100–1104.

# 13

# Speech Perception in Children: Are There Effects of Otitis Media?

*Peter D. Eimas* and *Richard L. Clarkson*

## INTRODUCTION

It is becoming apparent that severe, recurrent otitis media (OM) during a child's early years may have profound negative effects on the acquisition of linguistic and academic skills. This realization, although of importance in and of itself, especially given the prevalence of OM among children in many societies, is of course only the initial step in the study of the disease and its sequelae. We need now to understand in depth how the disease functions to produce specific linguistic and academic deficiencies, and how these deficits may in turn produce further maladaptations to the demands of societies, particularly those that require relatively high levels of academic competence for successful and productive adult lives. Understanding requires that we unravel the causal chain between the immediate consequences of recurrent OM (for example, conductive hearing losses and the probable distortion of complex auditory signals including speech), and the later behavioral consequences (including for example, poor receptive abilities for speech and serious delays in the acquisition of language, reading, and other language-related academic competencies).

The present research on the perception of speech by children

This chapter is based in part on a doctoral dissertation by RLC under the direction of PDE. All of the research reported herein was supported by Grant HD 05331 from the National Institute of Child Health and Human Development to PDE. We are grateful to Dr. Joanne L. Miller for generously providing us with the stimuli for Experiment 2 and the first pilot study, and to Mary E. Cummings and Deborah Blicher for testing the children who participated in the two pilot studies.

with histories of OM was undertaken in the belief that it would serve to illuminate some of the earliest levels of association between the presence of the disease and later behavioral dysfunctions. Our view of at least a part of the underlying causal chain was influenced strongly by the earlier writings of Menyuk (1979). It seemed to us, as it did to Menyuk, quite reasonable to assume that some of the developmental delays might be attributable to alterations in the processes that underlie the perception of speech at the phonetic level—the level at which the speech signal is first given a categorical representation. Any disturbance in the processes providing a categorical representation of speech could, we believe, have further profound effects on the child's learning how the parental language maps the speech-relevant acoustic properties into the set of language specific phonemic categories. If this were indeed the case, it is relatively easy to imagine how deficiencies at this level of linguistic processing could have escalating consequences, and thereby provide at least one link in the causal chain between the repeated occurrence of OM and the broad range of developmental deficiencies that appear to be a consequence of this medical history. In any event, we were sufficiently intrigued by this hypothesis and its potential explanatory power, to initiate a series of studies into the speech processing abilities of young children who had had a history of severe, recurrent OM. What is extremely helpful for studies of this nature is the considerable body of knowledge concerning the perception of speech and its development at the level of phonetics. It is to a brief and selective review of this literature that we turn next so as to better rationalize the particular experiments that were undertaken.

## THE PERCEPTION OF SPEECH

The ultimate function of the mechanisms of speech perception is to provide the listener with the speaker's intended meaning, and it is this meaning that occupies and holds our attention. Indeed, it does so to such an extent that we are rarely aware of other mental representations that are derived from the acoustic signal and that mediate abstraction of the intended meaning. One of these representations is phonetic in nature, and it provides the listener with an ordered set of phonetic segments, roughly the consonants and vowels together with their syllabic combinations, that constitute the words of human languages. How this discrete representation is computed from a highly variable and nearly continuous signal has been a central concern of those who have studied the perception of speech for over 30 years (see Jusczyk in press; Liberman et al. 1967; and Pisoni 1978, for reviews of this literature).

One important conclusion of research on speech perception at the level of phonetics is that perception is categorical in nature. We tend to listen through the rather extensive variation that exists in the speech signal. This variation arises from a number of factors related to the act of articulation, including the effects of coarticulation, alterations in the rate of speech, age and sex differences among speakers, and the moment-to-moment differences in the processes of articulation that appear to be inherent in all acts of coordinated motor activity. What is thus heard are the phonetic categories that are intended by the speaker, despite the great complexity in the manner in which they are represented in the signal. This is not to say, however, that we cannot make judgments about nonsegmental aspects of speech, such as the speaker and the rate of speech for example; we obviously can. Rather it is simply that these sources of variation (and information) are not represented in the final phonetic percepts; these percepts, in other words, show constancy.

One source of evidence for the categorical nature of speech perception comes from experiments in which the acoustic variation from the momentary alterations in articulation is systematically examined. A good example of this research is found in the many studies concerned with perception of the information for voicing in syllable-initial stop consonants, which is also the concern of the present series of experiments, with one exception. Lisker and Abramson (1964, 1967) showed that an important source of information for the perceived distinctions among the voiced and voiceless stops is voice onset time or VOT. They defined VOT in acoustic terms as the time between the presence of acoustic energy representing the initial release of sound and the onset of quasi-periodicity in the signal that reflects the onset of vocal fold vibration or voicing. Relatively short delays in VOT signal the voiced stops, [b, d, g], whereas longer delays signal the voiceless stops [pʰ, tʰ, kʰ]. In addition, Lisker and Abramson (1964, 1967) found that there is considerable variation in VOT during the production of voiced and voiceless stops, but that there are also pronounced modal values. In subsequent perceptual experiments, Lisker and Abramson (1970; Abramson and Lisker 1970; 1973) showed that this variation in the production of voicing distinctions is perceived categorically. They constructed synthetic speech patterns that varied systematically in VOT, and presented them in a random manner for identification. Adult listeners assigned them to appropriate voicing categories with considerable consistency. Moreover, when pairs of stimuli varying in a specific difference in VOT, 10 or 20 msec, for example, were presented for purposes of discrimination, the resulting functions showed marked nonmonotonicities. There were peaks in the ability to discriminate VOT at the regions of the phonetic boundaries and near chance levels of discrimination for pairs of stimuli that lay within a phonetic category; our sensitivity to differences in VOT are, in other words, deeply constrained by the categories that are present in the sound system of our language, which of course may vary considerably across languages (Abramson and Lisker 1973, for example). This boundary effect has been taken as a strong indicant of categorical perception (e.g., Liberman et al. 1967; Wood 1976). Findings of this nature have also been obtained with different forms of acoustic information that are sufficient to signal many of the phonetic distinctions in a number of languages and thus have led investigators to believe that the categorical processing of speech is a necessary characteristic of this early stage of processing (see Repp 1984, for a comprehensive review).

The processes of categorization are actually more complicated than our discussion so far would lead one to believe. One reason for this is that there are many, often quite different, acoustic properties that are sufficient to signal most segmental distinctions, and these properties enter into perceptual trading relations during the course of perception (e.g., Best, Morrongiello, and Robson 1981; Fitch et al. 1980; Lisker et al. 1977; Miller and Eimas 1983; Summerfield and Haggard 1977; and see Repp 1982, for a review of this literature). Two cues enter into a perceptual trading relation if one acoustic property may substitute or compensate for another, within limits, of course. As a consequence of this equivalence, there is not a single range of values along some acoustic property that maps onto a phonetic category, but rather many ranges with many different category boundaries—these being determined by the values along a second (or third) acoustic property. The existence of trading relations means that listeners cannot achieve consistency in the categorization of speech by relying solely on a single acoustic property, as this property by itself does not provide a consistent mapping between signal and percept. Rather, it is only when all of the relevant acoustic properties are processed jointly and in relation to one another that consistency in mapping between the signal and the experienced phonetic category becomes possible, as does a beginning toward an explanation of the constancy in the perception of speech that we all experience.

The perception of voicing distinctions is no exception to this complexity in the categorization process. As Lisker et al. (1977) and Summerfield and Haggard (1977) have shown, VOT is in actuality a complex acoustic dimension, composed of a number of spectral and temporal properties that can serve as independent cues for the perception of voicing distinctions in syllable-initial stops. Two of these properties, the spectral information in the onset frequency of the first formant and the temporal information in the time between the release burst and the onset of periodicity in the signal (which we refer to hereinafter as VOT for purposes of simplicity in this discussion), have been shown to enter into a perceptual trading relation in adult listeners (Lisker et al. 1977; Miller and Eimas 1983; Summerfield and Haggard 1977), in young children and even in infants only three and four months of age (Miller and Eimas 1983). This form of processing speech would seem to be not only characteristic of speech perception, but also a consequence of our biological endowment. Whether this inherent ability to categorize speech and to form perceptual trading relations (cf. Eimas 1985; Miller and Eimas 1983) is affected by a history of recurrent OM was the focus of our first experiment.

## EXPERIMENT 1

In this experiment, we presented to children, with and without histories of OM, two series of synthetic speech sounds for identification and discrimination. In both series the stimuli varied in small steps of VOT (5 msec) and were heard by adult listeners as the syllable [da] when the VOT values were low and as the syllable [tʰa] when the VOT values were high. The difference between series was in the onset frequency of the first formant (F1), one series having values that were strong cues for voiced stops and the other having values that were strong cues for voiceless stops. Responses of interest within a given series were the consistency with which the sounds could be assigned to the voicing categories of English, voiced and voiceless as represented by the syllables [da] and [tʰa], respectively, the extent to which a small difference in VOT could be discriminated, and finally the extent to which discrimination was constrained by the categories to which the stimuli had been assigned. An additional concern was whether the two cues for voicing, VOT and the onset frequency of F1, would enter into a perceptual trading relation and thereby yield different boundary values along the two series. As with our other measures of perception, we were particularly interested in whether this phenomenon would be affected by a history of OM.

The subjects were 16 boys and girls, half of whom (Group E) had a history of severe, recurrent OM as well as sufficient linguistic delays to be placed in a special education program for children with developmental delays in speech and language. The remaining children (Group C) had medical histories that were nearly free of ear infections and had no known speech or language disabilities. The children in Group E had a mean age of 68 months and mean performance IQ of 104, neither of which differed significantly from the mean age of 72 months and mean IQ of 109 for the children in Group C.

With regard to the incidence of OM, Group E had an average of 3.4 infections per year up to the time of testing, for which their physicians prescribed decongestants and antibiotics at least three times per year and performed at least 1.5 myringotomies and 1.4 tubal insertions as part of the treatments of each child up to the time of our experiments. It should be noted that at the time of testing the results of the audiograms and tympanograms for the children in Group E were all within the range of normal functioning. The children in Group C averaged only .21 infections per year and these were rarely treated with drugs and never by more invasive procedures.

The stimuli were synthetic speech patterns originally constructed and used by Miller and Eimas (1983). There were, as noted, two series, each with 12 consonant-vowel patterns that varied in VOT by 5 msec steps from an initial value of +5 msec to a final value of +60 msec. The stimuli differed across the two series in terms of the onset frequency of F1, which was produced by varying the steepness of the slopes of the initial formant transitions. In one series the transitions were 25 msec in duration, whereas they were 85 msec in duration in the second series. Given that there is no energy at the F1 frequencies until voicing begins, the result of this difference in slope is that for each VOT value, except for the initial value of +5 msec, the onset frequency of the first formant was lower for each member of the series with the shallow transitions than for the corresponding stimuli with abrupt transitions. Low values of VOT and high first-formant onset frequencies are strong cues for voiced stops; conversely, high VOT values and low first-formant onset frequencies are strong cues for voiceless stops. Consequently, if these two sources of information for voicing enter into a trading relation, then the expectation is that the phonetic category boundary should have a lower value of VOT for the series with abrupt (25 msec) transition durations than for the series with shallow (85 msec) transitions. Moreover, if the discriminability of the stimuli is constrained by their categorical assignments, then the peak in the discriminability function should shift with a change in the abruptness of the formant transitions.

The stimuli were presented 20 times each for identification, with each child being instructed, in essence, to indicate whether a robot, which they were told was learning to talk, said "DA" or "TA." To obtain a measure of discriminability, a 2IAX procedure was used and the child had to indicate after hearing each pair of stimuli whether the two stimuli were the same or different ("even if only a little bit different"). The pairs of stimuli always differed by 20 msec of VOT, thereby yielding 8 possible pairs along each continuum (+5 paired with +25, +10 paired with +30, and so forth until +40 is paired with +60). Each pair of stimuli was presented 16 times when the two stimuli were different, and 16 times when the two stimuli were the same, with 8 same pairs for each of the two stimuli.

Examination of the identification functions, shown in Figure 1, reveals a number of interesting effects. First, both groups of children

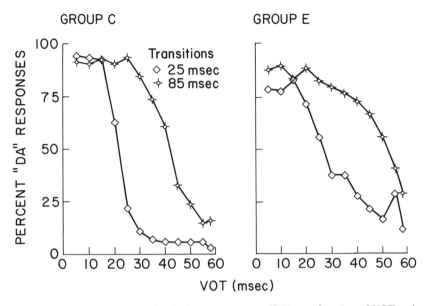

Figure 1. Mean percentages of voiced stop responses (DA) as a function of VOT and transition duration (25 or 85 msec). (Experiment 1)

were able to assign the stimuli to phonetic categories in a systematic manner: there was a progressive decrease in the percentage of "DA" responses as the value of VOT increased. Second, the consistency with which the stimuli were assigned to categories was considerably greater in Group C. This is evidenced by the more reliable assignment of endpoint stimuli to the appropriate categories by the children in Group C (92% vs. 82%; $p < .025$), and by the significantly steeper slopes in the identification functions of these same children ($-4.4$ vs. $-2.0$; $p < .001$). In addition, and of theoretical interest, is that both groups showed a highly reliable shift in the locus of the phonetic boundary ($p < .001$); the two sources of voicing information, in other words, entered into a perceptual trading relation, which did *not* differ in magnitude for the two groups ($p > .10$). Finally, the absolute VOT values of the boundary locations were greater by 9.1 msec on the average for the children in Group E ($p < .01$, in each instance). There are a number of possible reasons for this latter effect, including a poorer ability to process the temporal information per se by Group E or their assigning greater weight to the spectral information. A decision as to which explanation is correct, however, cannot be made on the basis of the available data.

The discrimination functions, which plot the discriminability of each pair in terms of a nonparametric estimate of d' (-ln eta; cf. Wood 1976) as a function of mean of the VOT values of the stimuli being discriminated, are shown in Figure 2. The estimate of discriminability

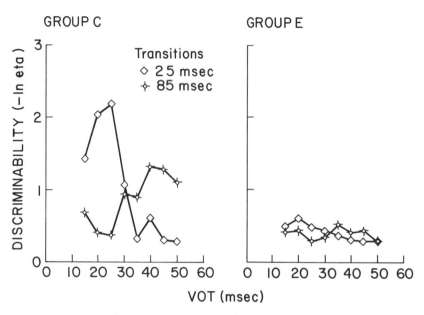

Figure 2. Mean discriminability scores as a function of VOT and transition duration (25 or 85 msec). The scores are plotted midway between the two VOT values being discriminated. (Experiment 1)

equals zero when performance is at chance and increases with increasing accuracy in discrimination and without contamination by bias to respond same (or different) more often.[1] Inspection of these functions reveals rather marked differences between the two groups. The children in Group E performed at a much lower overall level ($p < .001$), and, even more interesting, only the children in Group C showed evidence of a phonetic boundary effect ($p < .01$). That is, only these children showed reliable peaks in the discriminability functions at the region of the category boundaries. Further evidence of categorical-like perception comes from a comparison of the discriminability of the pairs of stimuli that form between-category discriminations (each stimulus is drawn from a different category as determined by the identification data) with the pairs that form within-category discriminations (both stimuli drawn from the same category of voicing). The between-category discriminations were significantly higher, as must be true if perception is categorical in nature, but only for the children in Group C ($p < .001$; see Table I).[2]

---

[1]The discriminability scores have an upper bound of 4.6 when the probabilities correct difference and correct same scores are both .99, the value assigned when the actual probabilities were 1.00.

[2]There is another measure of categorical perception, namely, the degree to which the discriminability scores can be predicted from the extreme assumption of categorical perception: discrimination of two stimuli is only possible to the extent to which differ-

Table I

Mean discriminability scores (-ln eta) as a function of group,
transition duration, and stimulus pair
(i.e., within-category vs. between-category discriminations). (Experiment 1)

| Group | Short Transitions | | Long Transitions | |
|---|---|---|---|---|
| | Within | Between | Within | Between |
| C | .40 | 2.27 | .69 | 1.19 |
| E | .41 | .65 | .38 | .24 |

In summary, the children with an extensive history of OM and an accompanying language delay were found to show marked differences in processing the information for voicing in syllable-initial stop consonants. They were much less consistent in assigning variants of VOT to phonetic categories, they required longer VOT intervals before perceiving a change in voicing, and they showed lowered levels of discrimination as well as no evidence of a category boundary effect. Perception, in essence, was less categorical in Group E. Both groups of children did, however, use the two sources of voicing information in the process of identification, and they did so in a manner that indicated the presence of a perceptual trading relation, which did not differ in magnitude between groups.

At issue now is how we are to account for these findings. There are two relatively simple, and not particularly interesting explanations, at least from the point of view of linguistic development. The first holds that the children in Group E are merely less able to process the somewhat unnatural and acoustically impoverished synthetic speech patterns. This occurs possibly because they suffer from subtle hearing losses that manifest their effects only when there is a loss of redundant information in the speech signal. Such a loss would have little consequence for perceiving speech in connected discourse, except perhaps in environments that were quite noisy and hence masked much of the critical information for linguistic decisions.

A second explanation posits that the children in Group E suffer from some general cognitive or attentional deficit and as a consequence are less able to perform any task that demands rather sustained cognitive activity. The origins of this loss, which again would probably have relatively little effect on the comprehension of

---

ential labels will be assigned to the stimuli (cf. Liberman et al. 1957). While this is often a useful measure, there are potential difficulties. These may occur in one case because predicted discrimination functions can be quite accurate not only when there is a marked peak in the discrimination functions and quite abrupt identification functions, as was the case for Group C, but also when the discrimination functions are without notable peaks and the identification functions are rather shallow, as was the case for Group E. As a consequence the goodness of fit between the predicted and obtained functions was about the same for both groups in Experiment 1, and thus not really an informative indicant of the perceptual process, i.e., the categorical nature of the perception.

speech under the normal conditions of linguistic communication, are not readily apparent, and any speculations regarding its development should best await confirming evidence. The next two experiments were designed to investigate these explanations.

## EXPERIMENT 2

In Experiment 2, we tested the hypothesis that the processing deficits of Group E are attributable to the use of acoustically impoverished synthetic speech patterns. Two groups of children, comparable in all respects to Groups E and C in Experiment 1, were presented with naturally produced, computer-edited patterns for identification and discrimination. The stimuli were constructed by carefully interchanging varying durations of the initial brief portions of the naturally produced words BATH and PATH, such that a series of seven stimuli varying in VOT were constructed. In essence, the initial burst and varying amounts of the following periodic acoustic information were excised from the word BATH and replaced by equivalent durations of aperiodic acoustic energy from the word PATH (that is, the initial burst and aspiration of the voiceless stop replaced the initial burst and voiced formant transitions of the voiced stop). In this manner, stimuli with VOT values of $+7$, $+15$, $+21$, $+32$, $+39$, $+48$, and $+59$ msec were constructed. (For more complete details, the reader is referred to Miller, Green, and Schermer 1984.) The stimuli were randomized and presented individually for identification as in Experiment 1. A 2IAX task was again used for obtaining discrimination functions. There were seven pairs of stimuli. In four of the pairs, the stimuli differed by approximately 26 msec of VOT ($+7$ vs. $+32$, $+15$ vs. $+39$, and so forth) and in the remaining pairs, the difference in VOT was approximately 34 msec ($+7$ vs. $+39$, $+15$ vs. $+48$, and $+21$ vs. $+59$). Each stimulus was identified 25 times as either BATH or PATH and each stimulus pair was presented 16 times when the two stimuli were different and 16 times when they were the same.

Of the eight children in each group, four in Group E and two in Group C had served as listeners in the first experiment. The characteristics of the children were very nearly the same as those described in Experiment 1. The children in Group E had a history of recurrent OM and were currently enrolled in a special program for children with language disabilities, whereas the children in Group C had had very few episodes of middle ear infections and no indication of any language disabilities. The mean age and performance IQ of the two groups did not differ statistically ($p > .10$, in each instance): the mean age was 66 and 68 months for Groups E and C, respectively, and the mean IQ was 110 and 109 for Groups E and C, respectively. The children did differ reliably with respect to the number of ear infections per year (4.0 for Group E vs. .53 for Group C), the number of decongestants and antibiotics prescribed per year (5.6 vs. .93), and the number of myringotomies and tubal insertions that had been performed up to the time of testing (2.83 vs. 0) ($p < .01$, in each case). It is worth noting again that the results of the audiograms and tympanograms for Group E were, at the time of testing, within the limits of normal functioning.

The results of the identification and discrimination tasks are shown in Figures 3 and 4, respectively. Inspection of these functions indicates that the differences between the two groups of children that were observed in Experiment 1 were not eliminated by the use of natural speech patterns. With respect to identification, the children in Group E again showed less consistency in identifying the endpoint stimuli (85% vs. 99%; $p < .01$), and the slopes of their functions were less steep ($-2.3$ vs. $-4.8$; $p < .01$). In addition, the locus of the category boundary was situated at a higher VOT value in Group E than in Group C (33.6 vs. 25.6 msec; $p < .01$).

The overall level of discrimination performance in Group C was markedly higher than that for Group E, and there was a more pronounced boundary effect in Group C. In other words, not only were the absolute discriminability scores higher in Group C but there was a larger difference when the discrimination scores for the within-

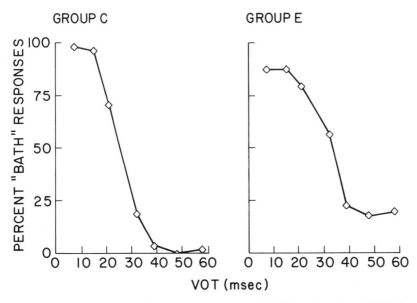

Figure 3. Mean percentages of voiced stop responses (BATH) as a function of VOT. The scores are plotted midway between the two VOT values being discriminated. (Experiment 2)

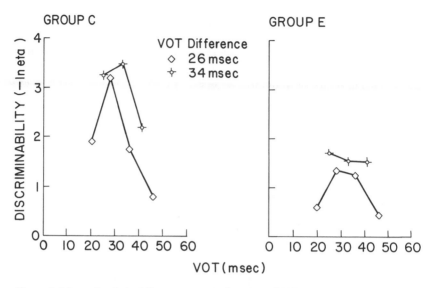

Figure 4. Mean discriminability scores as a function of VOT and difference in VOT between pairs of stimuli, 26 or 34 msec. The scores are plotted midway between the two VOT values being discriminated. (Experiment 2)

category pairs were subtracted from the scores for the between-category pairs ($p < .01$, for both measures). The latter effect could actually be evaluated only for the pairs of stimuli that differed by 26 msec of VOT as virtually all of the pairs differing by 34 msec were between-category pairs for all of the listeners. Despite the greater tendency for a category boundary effect in Group C, it is worth noting that the children in Group E showed a more pronounced category boundary effect in Experiment 2 than the same or comparable subjects had in the first experiment. It would seem that the additional information available in the natural speech did have some effect for the children in Group E, but not of sufficient magnitude to eliminate the processing deficits evidenced by the children in Experiment 1.

## EXPERIMENT 3

Experiment 3 tested the hypothesis that the differences obtained in Experiments 1 and 2 could be explained by some general attentional or cognitive deficit. This hypothesis yields the prediction that processing deficits should occur in any task that makes demands on the child similar to those in the first two experiments, regardless of the nature of the stimuli. We used the same tasks as in the first two experiments, identification and discrimination, but now with stimuli that were simple nonspeech auditory patterns that differed in intensity. There were seven patterns, as in Experiment 2, and each pattern consisted of the same, steady-state formant with a central frequency of 720 Hz and a bandwidth of 40 Hz. The intensity differences were created by reducing the intensity of each stimulus with reference to the next lowest stimulus of the series by 1.5 dB SPL. The difference was thus 9 dB SPL between the first and seventh stimuli. The seven stimuli were randomly presented 25 times each for identification, the children being asked to label each stimulus as LOUD or SOFT. A 2IAX procedure was again used to measure the discriminability of the pairs of stimuli that differed by 3, 4.5, or 9 dB SPL. The number of pairs was 5, 4, and 1, respectively. Each stimulus pair was presented 16 times when the two stimuli differed and 16 times when the stimuli were the same. The children from Experiment 2 again served as listeners.

The identification and discrimination functions are shown in Figures 5 and 6. Examination of these figures indicates very slight differences in performance between the two groups. With respect to identification, there were no reliable differences in the consistency with which the endpoint stimuli were identified (approximately 97% correct in both groups), in the slopes of the functions ($-6.4$ for Group E vs. $-5.7$ for Group C), or in the locus of the category boundary separating the listener's perception of loud and soft sounds ($-6.1$ dB for Group E vs. $-6.7$ dB for Group C) ($p > .10$ in each case).

An overall analysis of the mean level of discrimination, Groups by Intensity difference, revealed no reliable effect for Groups

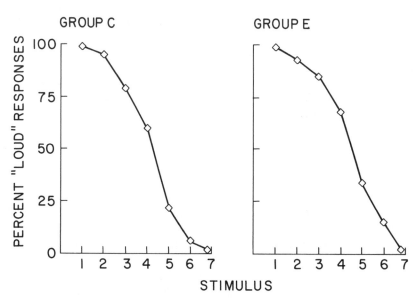

Figure 5. Mean percentages of LOUD responses as a function of intensity. (Experiment 3)

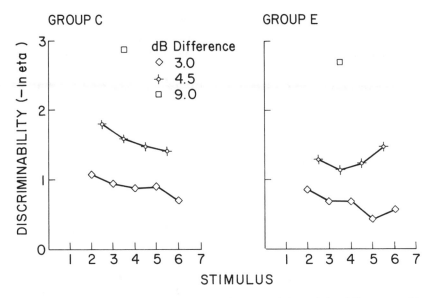

Figure 6. Mean discriminability scores as a function of dB and the difference in dB between stimuli. The scores are plotted midway between the two dB values being discriminated. (Experiment 3)

$(p > .10)$, and as expected a highly reliable effect for the differences in Intensity $(p < .01)$. Although there were no reliable interactions between Groups and Intensity, we did analyze the discriminability scores at each Intensity difference separately. There was a small, but reliable, difference for the pairs that differed by 3 dB that favored Group C $(p < .05)$, but no reliable differences for the remaining pairs. Although this difference in discriminability between the two groups may be due to a subtle loss in hearing inasmuch as it occurred only with the smallest Intensity difference, any explanation of the speech processing deficits solely on the bases of sensory deficiencies is not adequate, given the overall results of Experiment 3.

## DISCUSSION

If one takes these findings as evidence for a disturbance in the ability to process complex auditory patterns, whether restricted to the sounds of speech or not, then it becomes theoretically interesting and medically important to determine the extent to which this deficiency can be attributed to the specific effects of severe, recurrent OM and its associated conductive hearing loss, to the existence of a more general speech and language deficit, or to both. To begin to parcel out the contributions of these two possible causal agents, it is apparent that we must test additional children who are afflicted with similar language disabilities but without a history of otitis media, as well as children with histories of otitis media but no language disabilities (or at least language disabilities of a much less severe nature).

We are currently in the process of attempting to fill the cells of a factorial design in which the children in the four treatment combinations formed by the presence and absence of language disabilities and by the presence and absence of a history of recurrent OM are tested on their abilities to identify and discriminate differences in VOT when presented in the context of the natural speech patterns BATH and PATH. The work is still in progress and completion will be difficult, owing mostly to the fact that it is extremely hard to find sufficient numbers of children who not only meet the necessary criteria with regard to the major variables of interest, but who are also closely matched for such factors as education and economic status of their parents, amount of schooling, and an absence of any residual hearing loss beyond what might still be considered to reflect a normal range of hearing, i.e., no more than a 10 to 15 dB loss.

We have recently, however, completed two pilot studies in which children with histories of severe, recurrent OM, but no known accompanying language disorders, were compared to comparable control children without histories of recurrent OM or language disorders. In the first pilot study, we investigated the effects of contextual information in terms of the rate of speech (as specified by syllabic duration) and the lexical status of the stimuli on the perception of voicing information. There is now a considerable literature showing that rate of speech affects the categorization of the critical temporal information for phonetic distinctions. For example, when the rate of speech is relatively slow, a greater duration of VOT is required before there is a shift in the perceived voicing quality from that of a voiced to voiceless stop (see Miller 1981 for a review of this literature). In addition, there is considerable evidence showing that listeners have a strong disposition to perceive ambiguous values of VOT as exemplars of the voicing category that will yield a legitimate lexical item when combined with the rest of the acoustic pattern (e.g., Ganong 1976; Miller, Dexter, and Pickard 1984). Thus, for example, listeners will hear more voiced stops in a series of stimuli that vary in VOT and that are heard as either BEEF or PEEF, whereas they will hear more voiceless stops in a similar series in which the stimuli are heard as either BEACE or PEACE.

The stimuli were computer edited tokens of natural speech, used earlier by Miller et al. (1984). There were four series of 13 consonant-vowel-consonant stimuli, and the stimuli in each series varied in VOT from +9 to +61 msec. Two of the series consisted of short patterns, 210 msec in total duration, and two series consisted of longer patterns, 430 msec in duration. One short and one long series ended with the fricative /f/ and given the initial spectral information, each of the patterns was heard as the word BEEF or the nonsense syllable PEEF. The stimuli in the remaining series ended with the fricative /s/ and thus were heard as either the nonsense syllable BEACE or the word PEACE.

The stimuli were presented in blocks of ten stimuli, with each block consisting of stimuli from a single series, e.g., 430 msec patterns ending in /f/. Each of the stimuli within a single block had a different VOT value. The order of presentation of the VOT values was sequential, with half of the series having an ascending order and half a descending order. The starting values of each block varied randomly among the first three or final three stimuli of each series. Four blocks of stimuli from each of the four series were randomly ordered and presented to each child. The children had been given extensive training in identifying the endpoint stimuli and then were instructed to identify each of the patterns as they heard them. They were informed as to which stimulus was the first in each block of stimuli. Thus, the data could not be used to indicate the consistency with which endpoint and near-endpoint stimuli could be identified, nor could the data be used to estimate complete identification functions as there were too few data points for each stimulus in each series from each child. The measure of interest was the stimulus value that indicated a change from a voiced to voiceless stop or the converse. This was taken as the VOT value midway between the VOT value that signaled a change in perception and the VOT value immediately preceding a change. Our expectations, given the data of Miller et al. (1984), was that these values should be higher for the two series ending in /f/ than for the corresponding series ending in /s/ and that the cross-over values of VOT should be higher for the two series with the longer durations than for the corresponding shorter series.

There were 24 children, 11 in Group E and 13 in Group C. Their average age was 62.5 months, and did not differ across groups ($p > .10$). The children in Group E averaged 3.1 episodes of ear infections per year, whereas the children in Group C had less than .3 episodes per year ($p < .10$). There were also large reliable differences in the number of decongestants and antibiotics that were prescribed ($p < .01$). In addition, there were two children who received myringotomies and one who received tubal insertions on Group E. No child in Group C received either treatment.[3]

---

[3]The records of illness and treatments, and the presence of any known language disabilities or hearing losses were obtained from parental reports in the case of the children in the two pilot studies and not from medical records as was true for the children in the first three experiments. Thus, they may not be entirely accurate. We believe, however, that they do reflect, at the very least, quite different medical histories between

The boundary values in msec of VOT are shown in Table II as a function of the stimulus series and history of OM. What is most apparent is that there was very little difference between the two groups of children, and virtually no difference as a function of the rate of speech, that is, of the duration of the stimulus series. There was, however, a substantial effect of lexical status, which was confirmed by statistical analyses ($p < .01$). Thus, on the surface there was no effect of a history of OM. However, an analysis of the consistency with which the lexical status of the item altered the phonemic boundary showed a marginally significant effect of the child's history of OM. For each child, we computed how many times (zero, once, or twice) the two series ending in /f/ had higher VOT values than the corresponding series ending in /s/. A chi square analysis of these frequency data revealed that the children in Group C showed the predicted effect for both series more often than did the children in Group E ($.10 < p < .05$). While this effect is not very large, it does indicate that there may be quite subtle differences due solely to recurrent OM that will require very sensitive measures to detect. In any event, given the possible implications of such effects it would seem well worth the effort to continue the search for them, as well as to determine why the rate of articulation failed to alter the processes of categorization as it has in studies with adults (e.g., Miller 1981) and with children of about the same age (Miller and Eimas 1983).

Our second pilot study investigated the abilities of children to identify and discriminate the acoustic information that is sufficient to signal the difference between the consonants [r] and [l] in syllable initial position. The stimulus patterns, which were computer-generated, consonant-vowel sequences, varied in the starting frequency of the third formant from an initial value of 1700 Hz to a final value of 3060 Hz in eight steps of 170 Hz. The nine stimuli also differed in the duration of the initial steady state portion from 35 msec to 75 msec in 5 msec steps. All other acoustic parameters were held constant and were appropriate for perception of the syllables as [ra] (patterns with low third-formant starting frequencies and short initial steady-state portions) or as [la] (patterns with high third-formant onset frequencies and long steady-state portions).

The stimuli were presented as in our first three experiments for identification and discrimination. Each stimulus was presented 15 times for identification. Four pairs of stimuli, two forming within-

---

the two groups. Moreover, it is interesting that the actual incidence of the disease and various treatments are close to those of the children in the first three experiments. The one exception is the lower incidence of myringotomies and tubal insertions (treatments that probably would not be forgotten) for the children in the experimental groups of the pilot studies. Perhaps this reflects episodes of somewhat lesser intensity that might also have functioned to reduce the differences between Groups in these pilot studies.

Table II

Mean boundary values in msec of VOT (Pilot Experiment 1).

| | Syllable Duration | | | |
| | 430 msec Final Consonant | | 210 msec Final Consonant | |
| | /f/ | /s/ | /f/ | /s/ |
|---|---|---|---|---|
| Group C | 30.7 | 24.9 | 29.3 | 25.0 |
| Group E | 30.8 | 24.5 | 27.5 | 24.5 |

category and two forming between-category discriminations, were presented for discrimination using a 2IAX procedure as in previous experiments. Each pair was presented 16 times when the stimuli were different and 16 times when the stimuli were identical.

There were again two groups of children with an average age of 59 months; the difference between groups was less than two months and not reliable ($p > .10$). The children in Group E had an average of 4.1 ear infections per year prior to testing, whereas the children in Group C averaged about .2 infections per year ($p < .01$). Two of the children in Group E had undergone myringotomies and one had been treated by means of tubal insertions. The number of prescriptions for decongestants and antibiotics per year was again more than four times as high in Group E as compared to Group C ($p < .01$).

The results of the second pilot study are shown in Table III. For both measures of identification, the percentage of correct identifications of the endpoint stimuli and the slopes of the identification functions, the children in Group C did better than the children in Group E. However, only in the case of identifying the endpoint stimuli was the difference statistically reliable ($p < .01$). The four measures of discriminability, i.e., overall performance, within-category discriminability, between-category discriminability, and the difference between the latter two measures, all favored the children in Group C. The differences, however, did not reach the .05 level significance, although in three instances the probabilities were less than .10, these being the overall level of discriminability, the between-category level of discrimination, and the difference between the within- and between-category levels of discrimination.

## Final Comments

We began our research on the assumption that the presence of severe, recurrent OM during the early years of childhood could have quite specific effects on the processes that enable listeners to transform the acoustic signal that is speech into a discrete phonetic representation. It seemed to us (cf. Menyuk 1979) that repeated,

Table III

Mean identification and discrimination performance on the [ra]–[la] speech patterns. (Pilot Experiment 2).

| | Identification | | | Discrimination | | |
|---|---|---|---|---|---|---|
| | Endpoint Stimuli | Slopes | Overall Category | Within-Category | Between-Category | Difference |
| Group C | 99% | −4.19 | 2.56[a] | 48 | 2.08 | 1.59 |
| Group E | 93% | −3.82 | 1.51 | .23 | 1.28 | 1.05 |
| $p$ | <.01 | >.10 | <.10 | >.10 | <.10 | <.10 |

[a]This discriminability scores are values of -ln eta

intermittent hearing losses that are often quite severe and quite prolonged could make it exceedingly difficult for the child to learn just how the parental language maps very fine acoustic differences onto different, language-specific categories. These consequences could well be further exacerbated by the inconsistency with which the infections occur in the ears of the child—it is not always both ears that are infected, nor is it always the same ear when a single ear is infected. It is not difficult to speculate on a causal chain of events that begins with describing the conductive hearing losses that produce deficits in abstracting a phonetic representation and continues with these deficits producing further difficulties in acquiring the phonological rules and lexical entries and with these difficulties producing in turn the higher-level linguistic and academic delays that appear to be associated so frequently with the presence of recurrent OM.

The ultimate scientific worth of this speculation rests, of course, on future research that must be not only wide ranging but highly programmatic. Nevertheless, the results of our own research into what we believe is the initial link in the relation between severe, recurrent OM with its concomitant conductive hearing losses and later behavioral deficits are encouraging. We found that a history of OM even in the absence of language deficits and residual conductive hearing losses, can produce subtle deficits in the abilities of children to categorize the sounds of speech and in their ability to use at least one form of contextual information, namely, lexical status, in deriving this level of representation. When a history of OM is combined with what may well be an independent disposition for speech and language delays, the processes underlying the categorization of speech appear to be quite seriously affected. It is interesting to note at this juncture that deficits in the processing of speech at the phonetic level are associated with such general dysfunctions as a delay in the development of linguistic competence (e.g., Tallal 1980) and dyslexia (e.g., Liberman 1982; Lieberman et al. 1985; Mann and Liberman 1982). What we must determine, as noted earlier, is the extent to which this presumably genetic disposition for linguistic and academic deficits interacts with a history of OM. It would not be surprising to us if the presence of both conditions jointly had a greater negative consequence for linguistic and academic development than did the sum of their individual contributions, and it is just this possibility that we are in the process of investigating within the domain of phonetic perception.

Of course, the study of speech perception at the level of phonetics is but one of a large number of specific linguistic functions that are in need of investigation in children with histories of OM with or without other concomitant linguistic and learning disabilities as well as in children without any of these afflictions. Thus, for example, we need carefully controlled studies on the manner in which the lexicon is accessed and how the information that is represented and stored in the mental dictionaries of children is used in the process of comprehension. Perhaps as we begin to discover the nature of linguistic processing in children and its course of development, together with the nature of the particular linguistic and academic deficits that are associated with various medical and genetic histories, we will begin to understand more fully the causal links between the initial state of the child and the final levels of competence. With this understanding it may then be possible to develop effective remedial measures for linguistically-based dysfunctions and perhaps even the means for their prevention.

## REFERENCES

Abramson, A. S., and Lisker, L. 1970. Discriminability along the voicing continuum: Cross-language tests. In *Proceedings of the Sixth International Congress of Phonetic Sciences, Prague, 1967*; Prague: Academia.

Abramson, A. S., and Lisker, L. 1973. Voice-timing perception in Spanish work-initial stops. *Journal of Phonetics* 1:1–8.

Best, C. T., Morrongiello, B., and Robson, R. 1981. Perceptual equivalence of acoustic cues in speech and nonspeech perception. *Perception & Psychophysics* 29:191–211.

Eimas, P. D. 1985. The equivalence of cues in the perception of speech by infants. *Infant Behavior & Development* 8:125–138.

Fitch, H. L., Halwes, T., Erickson, D. M., and Liberman, A. M. 1980. Perceptual equivalence of two acoustic cues for stop-consonant manner. *Perception & Psychophysics* 27:343–350.

Ganong, W. F. III 1980. Phonetic categorization in auditory word perception. *Journal of Experimental Psychology: Human Perception and Performance* 6:110–125.

Jusczyk, P. W. In press. A review of speech perception research. In L. Kaufman, J. Thomas and K. Boff (eds.). *Handbook of Perception and Performance.* New York: Wiley.

Liberman, A. M., Cooper, F. S., Shankweiler, D. S., and Studdert-Kennedy, M. 1967. Perception of the speech code. *Psychological Review* 74:431–461.

Liberman, A. M., Harris, K. S., Hoffman, H. S., and Griffith, B. C. 1957. The discrimination of speech sounds within and across phoneme boundaries. *Journal of Experimental Psychology* 54:358–368.

Liberman, I. Y. 1982. A language oriented view of reading and its disabilities. In *Status Report on Speech Perception, SR-70.* New Haven, CT: Haskins Laboratories.

Lieberman, P., Meskill, R. H., Chatillon, M., and Schupack, H. 1985. Phonetic speech perception deficits in dyslexia. *Journal of Speech and Hearing Research* 281:480–486.

Lisker, L., and Abramson, A. S. 1964. A cross-language study of voicing in initial stops: Acoustical measurements. *Word* 20:384–422.

Lisker, L., and Abramson, A. S. 1967. Some effects of context on voice onset time in English stops. *Language and Speech* 10:1–28.

Lisker, L., and Abramson, A. S. 1970. The voicing dimension: Some experiments in comparative phonetics. In *Proceedings of the Sixth International Congress of Phonetic Sciences, Prague, 1967.* Prague: Academia.

Lisker, L., Liberman, A. M., Erickson, D. M., Dechovitz, D., and Mandler, R. 1977. On pushing the voice-onset-time (VOT) boundary about. *Language and Speech* 20:209–216.

Mann, V. A., and Liberman, I. Y. 1982. Phonological awareness and verbal short-term memory: Can they prevent early reading problems. In *Status Report on Speech Perception, SR-70.* New Haven, CT: Haskins Laboratories.

Menyuk, P. 1979. Development in children with chronic otitis media: Design factors in the assessment of language. *Annals of Otology, Rhinology, and Laryngology, Supplement* 88:78–87.

Miller, J. L., 1981. Effects of speaking rate on segmental distinctions. In P. D. Eimas and J. L. Miller (eds.). *Perspectives on the Study of Speech.* Hillsdale, N.J.: Lawrence Erlbaum Associates.

Miller, J. L., Dexter, E. R., and Pickard, K. A. 1984. Influence of speaking rate and lexical status on word identification. *Journal of the Acoustical Society of America* 76:S89.

Miller, J. L., and Eimas, P. D. 1983. Studies on the categorization of speech by infants. *Cognition* 13:135–165.

Miller, J. L., Green, K., and Schermer, T. M. 1984. A distinction between the effects of sentential speaking rate and semantic congruity on word identification. *Perception & Psychophysics* 36:329–337.

Pisoni, D. B. 1978. Speech perception. In W. K. Estes (ed.). *Handbook of Learning and Cognitive Processes, Vol. 6.* Hillsdale, NJ: Lawrence Erlbaum Associates.

Repp, B. H. 1982. Phonetic trading relations and context effects: New experimental evidence for a speech mode of perception. *Psychological Bulletin* 92:81–110.

Repp, B. H. 1984. Categorical perception: Issues, methods, findings. In N. J. Lass (ed.). *Speech and Language: Advances in Basic Research and Practice, Vol. 10.* New York: Academic Press.

Summerfield, Q., and Haggard, M. P. 1977. On the dissociation of spectral and temporal cues to the voicing distinction in initial stop consonants. *Journal of the Acoustical Society of America* 62:435–448.

Tallal, P. 1980. Language disabilities in children: A perceptual or linguistic deficit? *Journal of Pediatric Psychology* 5:127–140.

Wood, C. C. 1976. Discriminability, response bias, and phoneme categories in discrimination of voice onset time. *Journal of the Acoustical Society of America* 60:1381–1389.

# Prevention, Intervention and Treatment of Otitis Media and Its Sequelae

# 14

# Otitis Media: The Surgical Approach

*LaVonne Bergstrom*

## INTRODUCTION

Surgery is important in the management of chronic otitis media and its complications. The less generally well known complications include masses of tympanosclerosis in the middle ear, ossicular discontinuity, facial palsy, acute mastoiditis associated with post-auricular subperiosteal abscess; zygomatic abscess, petrositis with Gradenigo's syndrome; Bezold's abscess, and thrombophlebitis of the lateral dural venous sinus. These entities are operable. Surgery is not appropriate for fibro-cystic otitis media, adhesive otitis media or sensorineural hearing loss. Cultures and sensitivities facilitate the selection of intravenous antibiotics for administration preoperatively, intraoperatively and postoperatively. Neurosurgical collaboration is required in some instances.

Diagnosis in these entities depends heavily on physical examination, including a neurologic and vestibular examination, and on various imaging studies. In some of these entities reconstructive surgery may be futile or even hazardous.

## PHYSICAL EXAMINATION AND OTOLOGIC MEDICAL TREATMENT

The otologic surgeon must be skilled in history-taking and physical examination of the patient who appears to have chronic otitis media. He or she will use the operating microscope in the clinic to get the optimum examination of the ears, will do a careful examination of the upper air and food passages, the skull, neck, function of the facial nerve, motility of the eyes, and the vestibular system. Tuning forks can be useful in checking the audiogram. The patient's mental status might also need to be assessed. It is the surgeon's responsibility to determine the patient's general health and his or her use of medications, tobacco and alcohol. This points up the fact that chronic otitis media is a lifelong disease. Patients may seek consultation in their seventh or eighth decade of life for worsening hearing caused by otitis media (Paparella, Brady, and Hoel 1969) (Figure 1).

Foul pus draining from the ear may occur in entities other than otitis media. In young children or retarded adults a foreign body may be found in the external ear canal. External otitis occurs in both children and adults, and may show a moderate amount of drainage and tenderness of the ear when the otic speculum is inserted. Infected cancers of the middle ear and external canal occur generally in adults, but young children who have undiagnosed histiocytosis X may drain right through the mastoid or via the ear canal.

All draining ears should be cleaned with suction and if necessary with alligator forceps debridement. Young children or retarded or autistic individuals may require sedation, anesthetic block of the external canal, and restraint. The canal must be cleaned so that the entire tympanic membrane and the walls of the ear canal can be seen. This is important so that small perforations, areas of granulation,

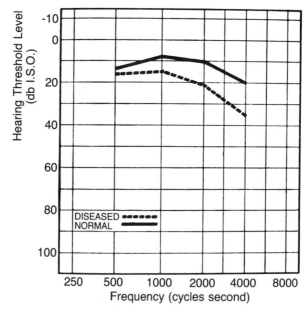

Figure 1. Mean hearing levels seen in 32 patients who had otitis media in one ear (dashed line), and no disease in the other (solid line). (From Paparella, M. M., Brady, D. R., and Hoel, R. 1970. Sensorineural hearing loss in chronic otitis media and mastoiditis. *Transactions of the American Academy of Ophthalmology and Otolaryngology* 74:108–115. Used with permission.)

previously placed middle ear ventilating tubes, retraction pockets of the tympanic membrane or the crust overlying an attic cholesteatoma can be seen and tympanic membrane mobility assessed. Aural polyps or masses suspicious of tumor should be biopsied. Ideally this is done before audiometry, unless sedation might dull the young child's responses to auditory stimuli.

Cholesteatoma and external otitis may have similar appearance and odor, since both are infected with *Pseudomonas aeruginosa* (Harker and Koontz 1977) (Table I). In the latter instance the tympanic membrane is usually intact. Cholesteatoma presents as a somewhat dirty-appearing, foul smelling, purulent, white mass of keratin presenting through a perforation in the pars tensa of the membrane or as a keratin-filled sac presenting in the pars flaccida of the drum (Figure 2) or even through an erosion of the bony scutum just above the pars flaccida. The squamous epithelium of the sac may invade under the middle ear mucosa (Figure 3). Cholesteatoma, also called keratoma, produces osteolytic enzymes which degrade the collagen molecule (Abramson and Huang 1977). More recent work shows that keratoma also exerts pressure which contributes to bone erosion.(Macri and Chole 1985) These properties account for erosion through the bony tegmen of the epitympanic space into the middle cranial fossa, through the posterior plate of the mastoid into the posterior fossa or laterally to form a subperiosteal abscess (Figure 4). The bone of the fallopian canal which covers the facial nerve and the ossicles may be eroded (Figure 5).

Table I

Bacteriology of Cholesteatoma*

| Aerobic Organisms | Anaerobic Organisms |
|---|---|
| Pseudomonas aeruginosa | Bacteroides |
| P. flurescens | B. fragilis |
| Proteus species | B. melaningoenicus |
| E. coli | Not specified |
| Klebsiella-Enterobacter-Serratia | Peptococcus-Peptostreptococcus species |
| Streptococcus | Propionibacterium acnes |
| Beta hemolytic | Fusobacterium |
| Alpha or gamma hemolytic | F. russii |
| Faecalis | F. nucleatum |
| | Not specified |
| | Bifidobacterium species |
| Achromobacter alcaligenes | Clostridium |
| Staphylococcus aureus | C. bifermentans |
| S. epidermidis | C. tertium |
| CDC group F | C. sordelli |
| | Eubacterium species |

*From Harker, L and F. P. Koontz. 1977. *Transactions of the American Academy of Ophthalmology and Otolaryngology* 84:683–686.

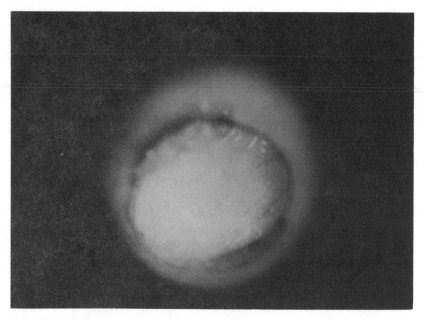

Figure 2. Large middle ear cholesteatoma filling the ear canal, having grown out of a perforation in the tympanic membrane. (From Goodhill, Victor 1900. *Ear: Diseases, Deafness and Dizziness.* Harper and Row. Used with permission.)

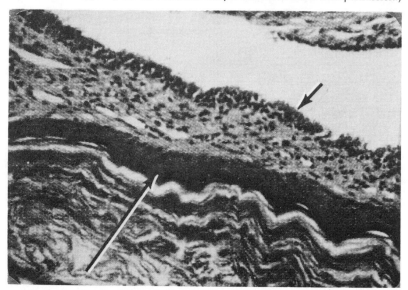

Figure 3. Photomicrograph of an autopsied middle ear showing one of the unique qualities of cholesteatoma. The short arrow shows the respiratory epithelium of the mucosa. The long arrow indicates the squamous epithelium of the cholesteatoma sac which has infiltrated under the mucosa. Between the two epithelia is fibrous granulation tissue. (From I. Friedman. 1974. *Pathology of the Ear.* Oxford: Blackwell Scientific Publications Ltd. Used with permission.)

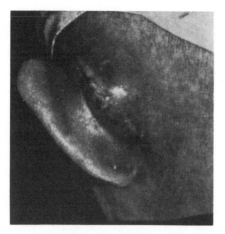

Figure 4. Postauricular swelling due to a subperiosteal mastoid abscess resulting from acute otitis media (from Becker et al. 1969. *The Atlas of Otorhinolaryngology and Bronchoesophagology*. Philadelphia. W. B. Saunders. Used with permission.)

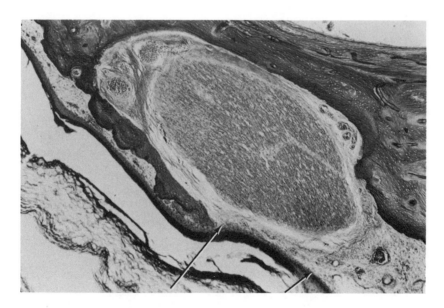

Figure 5. Partial erosion by cholesteatoma of the bone of the fallopian canal covering the facial nerve as indicated by the arrows. (Nager, G. T. 1972. *In* Glorig, A. and Gerwin, K. *Otitis Media: Proceedings of the National Conference*, Dallas. Springfield, IL: Charles C Thomas. Used with permission.)

If the stapes footplate is breached the cholesteatoma has access to the perilymph-containing vestibule (Figure 6). The potential sequelae of these processes are suppurative labyrinthitis, otitic meningitis (Figure 7), and epidural, cerebellar or intra-cerebral abscess. More commonly the bone over the horizontal semicircular canal may be thinned, sometimes leaving only the endosteal bone. Patients in whom this occurs may have vertigo at times.

## SURGICAL PRINCIPLES AND TECHNIQUES

Surgery of the ear should restore function to normal as much as possible; unfortunately this is not always possible. Two general principles guide otologic surgery. The first, and paramount, is removal of disease; the second, restoring or preserving hearing or reconstruction of anatomy. A brief description of the complications of otitis media has been presented early in this paper to make clear their potential for a disastrous or lethal outcome.

However, when the surgeon is called in early in the child's course of otitis media relatively simple measures may restore function and allow the anatomy of the middle ear to return to normal. These procedures are myringotomy in acute purulent otitis media, well timed

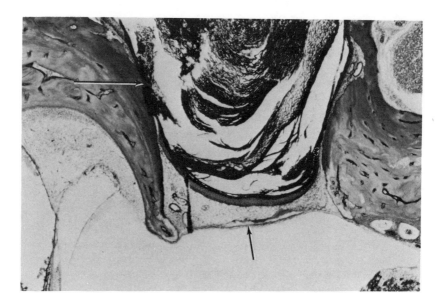

Figure 6. Cholesteatoma (long arrow) in the oval window in contact with the stapes footplate (short arrow). (Nager, G. T., 1972. *In* Glorig, A. and Gerwin, K. *Otitis Media: Proceedings of the National Conference, Dallas.* Springfield, IL: Charles C Thomas. Used with permission.)

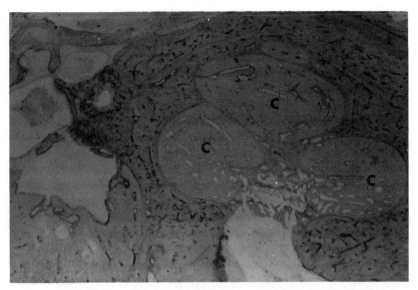

Figure 7. Neo-osteogenesis in the cochlea (C) as an endstage finding after suppurative labyrinthitis and meningitis. (Black, F. O., Bergstrom, L., Downs, M., and Hemenway, W. 1971. *Congenital Deafness*. Boulder, Colorado: Associated University Press. Used with permission.)

so as to evacuate all of the pus from the ear, provide a sufficient collection of pus for bacteriologic studies and relieve the child's agony which is caused by a bulging ear drum. The other procedure, done all too seldom nowadays, is simple mastoidectomy. Mastoiditis may follow even performance of a crescent-shaped myringotomy in the inferior ear drum and may become chronic because ulceration, granulation tissue, and bone necrosis become established. Host factors, local and anatomic factors make children vulnerable to cholesteatoma (Tables II, III, IV). This process can be reversed by a thorough, simple

Table II

Cholesteatoma in Children: Host Factors

Heredity
Congenital malformations
Cleft palate
  Eustachian tube malfunctions
Immuno-incompetence
Energetic growth of epithelium and connective tissue
High esterase in subepithelial layer of childhood cholesteatoma
Ease of obstruction of Eustachian tube
Frequent URI's and otitis media
Vitamin A deficiency

Table III

Cholesteatoma in Children: Local Factors

Inhibition between two layers of mucosa
Epithelial migration
Adhesions
Enzymes
Negative middle ear pressure
Low middle ear oxygen tension
High middle ear carbon dioxide tension
Open injury (e.g., tympanic membrane perforation)
? isolation from lymphatic access
Pressure

mastoidectomy which leaves tympanic membrane, ossicles, and bony ear canal wall intact (Rambo 1972). All cell tracts are exenterated; as many as seven tracts may need to be followed (Kohut and Singleton 1969). Failure to do so will result in chronicity and abscess formation. Many of the anatomic tracts communicate directly with the central nervous system (Allam 1969) (Figure 8).

The most frequently performed operation in the United States is myringotomy and placement of middle ear ventilating tympanostomy tubes after meticulous removal of the fluid in the middle ear. The type of fluid found can be classified as mucoid (glue ear), mucopurulent, purulent, or serous. The latter is relatively infrequent in children. Mucoid material in the ear is very tenacious and thick. The degree of conductive hearing loss in secretory, purulent or serous otitis is quite variable, but generally returns to normal after myringotomy alone or with tubes, as long as abnormalities of the tympanic membrane, ossicles, or middle ear space have not developed. A randomized, controlled prospective study of otitis-prone young children by Gebhart in 1981 showed that tympanostomy tubes significantly decreased the frequency of bouts of otitis media while the tubes were in place as compared with intervals after the tubes had extruded from

Table IV

Cholesteatoma in Children: Anatomic Factors

Degree of mastoid pneumatization
Aeration channels
Attic mesenteries
Persistent mesenchyme
Deficient annular ligament
Annular ligament displaced
Chorda tympani lateral to posterosuperior bony external auditory canal
Shelf of bone extending medially from notch of Rivinus
Deformed incus

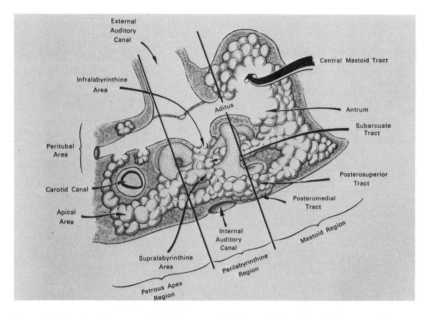

Figure 8. The air cell tracts of a fully pneumatized mastoid system. This suggests areas
into which acute mastoiditis or cholesteatoma could spread. (Allam, A. 1969.
Pneumatization of the temporal bone. *Annals of Otology, Rhinology and Laryngology* 78:49–64. Used with permission.)

the tympanic membrane or clogged up and before the condition was
discovered and successfully treated, often with repeat tympanostomy
tube placement. Complications may occur, for example postoperative
infection, premature clogging or extrusion of tubes, persistent tympanic membrane perforation at the myringotomy site, myringo-
sclerosis, or an atrophic area of drum at the place where the tube was,
and, rarely, keratoma of the tympanic membrane or middle ear.
Infection and premature extrusion are the most frequent.

Unfortunately secretory and serous fluid may linger in the
middle ear after an episode of acute purulent otitis media. The acute
episode was detected because the child was symptomatic, but vigilance after the acute attack may lessen. Followup doctor's visits or
audiometric and tympanometric testing appointments may not be kept
for economic reasons, or because the parents were not informed of
their importance. Young children and babies do not have the vocabulary to report stuffy or clogged ears and poor hearing, and poor
hearing may make it difficult for them to acquire the necessary vocabulary. It may be some months before the asymptomatic child is seen by
the doctor because "he is slow to talk" or "inattentive." Physicians may
be somewhat inattentive to this complaint also in the sense that
antibiotics may be prescribed, but not an audiogram.

Once a child has needed surgical treatment for middle ear effusion the surgeon and the primary physician should follow the child. If the child previously had competent audiometric and acoustic bridge testing, so that sensorineural hearing has been found to be normal, physical examination and tympanometry should constitute adequate followup. However, the physician needs to be certain that his or her testing instruments are kept in calibration.

Another complication of secretory and serous otitis media is seromucinous mastoiditis, believed to be the cause of idiopathic hemotympanum and associated with cholesterol cysts. The effusion is brownish. The condition may be cured by mastoidectomy.

In certain babies and young children the presence of otitis media with effusion should be presumed present until proved to be absent. Even if the initial examination is normal, vigilance should continue. Infants at risk include those who spent the first weeks of life in a neonatal intensive care unit and those who have craniofacial malformations, especially cleft palate, and those children whose families have a strong history of otitis media. In the process of this followup an occasional congenitally deaf baby might also be detected early.

Hearing testing in all babies and young children requires special technology and a high degree of expertise in those doing the testing. This type of expertise is not to be found in a primary physician's office nor in the usual general otolaryngologist's suite. Screening for speech and language delay using instruments designed for that purpose may identify a child who then requires evaluation and treatment by a speech specialist skilled in developmental assessment. Such a specialist possesses techniques appropriate to the young child, so that the at-risk child's first speech and language evaluation should not wait until the first or second grade in school. Effective intervention can be begun much earlier.

Tympanoplasty for otitis media perforata can be done in a preschool child who can cooperate in postoperative care. This makes the ear "safer," and often results in an intact tympanic membrane and normal hearing if Eustachian tube function is adequate and if there is no other pathology such as middle ear tympanosclerosis fixing the ossicles or blocking natural aeration of the middle ear. If fluid is found in the middle ear a tympanostomy tube may be placed. If cholesteatoma surrounds the ossicles the prognosis for normal hearing is guarded at best and total cholesteatoma removal has priority over reconstruction at the first sitting. At a "second look" six to twelve months later reconstruction may be tried if there is no evidence of recurrent or residual cholesteatoma, granulation tissue, or bone erosion not noted at the first ear exploration.

Unfortunately even very young children may be found to

have extensive cholesteatoma in a well pneumatized mastoid and require a radical mastoidectomy (Table V). The presence of such extensive pathology may not be believed because of the child's young age and because primary physicians are often unaware of this entity. A case illustrates this.

A three-year-old hispanic child was hospitalized on the pediatric service because of foul ear discharge. Culture showed predominantly *Pseudomonas* species. She was treated with ototoxic drugs by the house staff for three weeks until an experienced attending physician recognized that her problem was more complex and sought consultation. Examination showed a dry perforation in one ear and in the other a large middle ear, epitympanic and mastoid cholesteatoma. Audiogram showed a 60 dB conductive hearing loss in one ear and a 35 dB deficit in the other. Temporal bone x-ray studies were compatible with the physical findings. At surgery the entire mastoid, middle ear, and even the middle ear orifice of the Eustachian tube contained cholesteatoma and granulation tissue. Adherent cholesteatoma could not be removed from the stapes footplate. For this and other reasons a radical mastoidectomy was done. She continues to have an intermittently wet mastoid cavity in spite of a variety of local treatments with suction, cautery, drops, otic powders, and occasionally systemic antibiotics. She wears binaural hearing aids sporadically in the opposite ear and occasionally in the operated ear. This case illustrates well the severe pathology, auditory defects, and less-than-satisfactory postoperative results in these cases, compounded by lack of any consistency in wearing hearing aids, even in school.

Subperiosteal abscess of the mastoid is recognizable by erythema, edema, and tenderness and in more advanced cases by massive swelling over the mastoid process which causes the ear to lop over. Treatment is prompt mastoidectomy as soon as the child's temperature is controlled and antibiotics are given either empirically or based on a Gram stain. If severe pain, "picket fence" fever, headache, and marked mastoid tenderness is present lateral dural venous sinus thrombophlebitis is present. Mastoidectomy, including opening of the sinus and

Table V

| Age Distribution of 562 Cases of Cholesteatoma* | |
| --- | --- |
| Age in Years | Total |
| 0–9 | 35 |
| 10–19 | 78 |
| 20–59 | 399 |
| 60–79 | 50 |

*From Friedmann, I., 1974, *Pathology of the Ear*, Oxford: Blackwell Scientific Publications Ltd. Used with permission.

evacuating the infected clot is required. If not treated, otitic hydrocephalus and death may occur.

Mastoiditis may spread to the zygomatic air cells, producing a swelling which may be confused with acute parotid swelling (see Figure 9). An inflamed, immobile, or perforated drum with otorrhea and radiographic studies confirm the diagnosis.

Bezold's abscess presents as an ill-defined mass deep in the neck. It can be differentiated from a primary neck abscess, infected branchial cleft cyst, or parapharyngeal abscess by physical examination that includes the ear. Newer imaging studies can be quite useful in this entity, which occurs generally in young children.

Gradenigo's syndrome of petrous apicitis rarely occurs in persons in the pediatric age group except in those instances where a congenital cholesteatoma of the temporal bone erodes into the petrous apex. Symptoms include diplopia, retro-orbital pain, and ear discharge. The diplopia is due to monocular paresis of the abducens nerve which is close to the infected area.

In all of these instances surgical exenteration of the involved mastoid air cells is mandatory. Antibiotic treatment is also essential, and at times neurosurgical consultation is prudent.

For completeness one other type of otitis media should be mentioned. It occurs primarily in persons living in Third World countries, as well as underdeveloped areas in our own country. It is

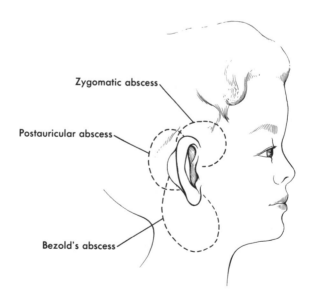

Figure 9. Diagram of three areas of the mastoid air cell system where abscess may occur as a complication of acute otitis media. (Saunders, W. H., Paparella, M. M., and Miglets, A. W. 1980. *Atlas of Ear Surgery*, ed. 3. St. Louis: The C. V. Mosby Co. Used with permission.)

tuberculous otitis, characterized by a thin, foul-smelling drainage and often multiple eardrum perforations. Ordinary cultures do not reveal the pathogen, and the usual antibiotics have little effect on this entity. Destruction of ossicles is often extensive. It may be eradicated by appropriate antituberculosis medications. Surgery after the infection has been controlled may be helpful (Schuknecht, 1974).

## CONCLUSION

The surgeon has multiple roles: the early diagnostician of ear disease that would benefit from surgery, the ear surgeon also interested in rehabilitation of hearing, facial paralysis, and other problems due to otitis media, and the otologist seeking consultation whenever it is in the best interest of the patient. If necessary the ear surgeon performs radical surgery to remove irreversible, life-threatening disease. Of all these roles the most satisfying is restoring an ear and a patient to normal function.

## REFERENCES

Abramson, M., and Huang, C. C., 1977. Localization of collagenase in human middle ear cholesteatoma. *Laryngoscope* 87:771–791.

Allam, A. 1969. Pneumatization of the temporal bone. *Annals of Otology, Rhinology and Laryngology* 78:49–64.

Gebhart, D. E. 1981. Tympanostomy tubes in the otitis prone child. *Laryngoscope* 91:849–864.

Kohut, R. I., and Singleton, G. T. 1969. Avenues of central spread in chronic ear disease. *Southern Medical Journal* 62:802–805.

Macri, J. R., and Chole, R. C. 1985. Bone erosion in experimental cholesteatoma—the effects of implanted barriers. *Otolaryngology—Head and Neck Surgery* 93:3–17.

Paparella, M. M., Brady, D. R., and Hoel, R. 1969. Sensori-neural hearing loss in chronic otitis media and mastoiditis. *Transactions of the American Academy of Ophthalmology and Otolaryngology* 74:108–115.

Rambo, J. H. T. 1972. Surgical treatment of chronic otitis. *In* A. Glorig and K. S. Gerwin (eds.). *Otitis Media: Proceedings of the National Conference.* Springfield: Charles C Thomas.

Schuknecht, H. F. 1974. *Pathology of the Ear.* Cambridge: Harvard University Press.

# 15

# Prevention and Medical Treatment of Otitis Media

*G. Scott Giebink*

The morbidity of childhood otitis media in the United States is impressive. At least 70 percent of children experience one or more episodes of otitis media by age five years, and 35 percent have at least three otitis media episodes during the first three years of life. Moreover, 5 to 10 percent of children develop chronic otitis media with effusion (OME) following an otitis media episode.

The impact of childhood otitis media on national health care expenditures is equally impressive. Based on the age-related incidence of otitis media and assuming a health care cost of $80 for each acute otitis media episode and a cost of $650 for each surgical treatment of chronic OME, the annual cost of medical treatment is approximately $446 million, and the annual cost of surgical treatment is approximately $182 million for total health care expenditures of nearly $630 million.

During the symposium on which this book is based, Dr. Klein defined the otitis media types. In the discussion following the presentation of papers, the term "acute otitis media" is used to describe a new middle ear effusion accompanied by signs of acute inflammation, including tympanic membrane erythema and constitutional symptoms, such as otalgia, fever, or signs of upper respiratory infection. The term "otitis media with effusion" is used to describe a middle ear effusion that is diagnosed in the absence of constitutional signs of illness but often with mild hearing loss. Effusions are chronic when they persist continuously for at least eight weeks.

We have learned that otitis media often has its onset during early infancy and peaks in prevalence during the second six months of life. Many children experience persisting middle ear pathology, and some children develop chronic otitis media, which is defined as irreversible middle ear pathology. To understand medical prevention and intervention strategies, it is important to begin with an understanding of otitis media pathogenesis.

In 1977 an interdisciplinary team of investigators began a collaboration at the University of Minnesota to study the pathogenesis of otitis media. During the first five years of this research program, nearly 1,000 children with chronic OME were enrolled at the time of tympanostomy placement for ventilation of the middle ear cavity (Giebink, Le, and Paparella 1982; Giebink et al. 1982). In addition, nearly 200 children and young and older adults were enrolled in a study of middle ear tissue pathology at the time of exploratory or reconstructive middle ear surgery for treatment of chronic otitis media. By starting our discussion of pathogenesis with the sequelae and complications of otitis media, it will become apparent which outcomes must be prevented by effective intervention strategies.

Table I illustrates middle ear tissue pathology described in 169 consecutively operated ears with chronic otitis media. Types of middle ear pathology observed included middle ear granulation tissue, mucosal thickening, cholesteatoma, ossicular erosion, tympanosclerosis, cholesterin granuloma, and ossicular fixation and erosion. Granulation tissue was observed more frequently in children and young adults, whereas ossicular erosion was more frequent in middle aged and older adults. Cholesteatoma decreased in prevalence with increasing age. Tympanosclerosis appeared to become more prevalent as the disease progressed. Another pathological entity recently described is "silent otitis media." Histopathological studies of temporal bones in infants and young children dying of unrelated conditions have demonstrated pathological evidence of otitis media in children who never experienced clinical otitis media.

Table I

Chronic Otitis Media Pathology

| Type of middle ear pathology | Prevalence (%) of pathology in the following age groups | | | |
|---|---|---|---|---|
| | 5–14 yrs. (n = 49) | 15–24 yrs. (n = 41) | 25–44 yrs. (n = 31) | 45–64 yrs. (n = 48) |
| Granulation tissue | 51.0 | 51.2 | 35.5 | 39.6 |
| Mucosal thickening | 44.9 | 31.7 | 25.8 | 45.8 |
| Cholesteatoma | 38.8 | 29.3 | 38.7 | 16.7 |
| Ossicular erosion | 26.5 | 26.8 | 51.6 | 33.3 |
| Tympanosclerosis | 8.2 | 9.8 | 3.2 | 27.1 |
| Cholesterin granuloma | 6.1 | 2.4 | 3.2 | 8.3 |
| Ossicular fixation | 8.2 | 12.2 | 3.2 | 10.4 |

Studies in animal models and episodic observations of humans with otitis media indicate that the otitis media occurs along a continuum, beginning with symptomatic or asymptomatic middle ear effusion, usually of either a purulent or serous quality, leading to enhanced middle ear secretion with the development of mucoid effusion, and eventually resulting in permanent tissue pathology, as described above (Giebink and Quie 1978; Giebink, Meyerhoff, and Cantekin 1986). To understand the disease process and rationale for various medical interventions, it is important to understand etiologic factors in the pathogenesis of this disease.

Figure 1 illustrates the interaction of the two principal etiologic factors. Events leading to middle ear inflammation include viral and bacterial infection of the upper respiratory tract and functional or mechanical dysfunction of the eustachian tube. Current evidence suggests that the most common cause of acquired eustachian tube dysfunction is upper respiratory viral infection. Clinical studies in children have shown that upper respiratory infection is associated with eustachian tube dysfunction and negative middle ear pressure. Moreover, controlled studies of influenza virus infection in chinchillas have demonstrated a close relationship between the onset of viral infection, morphologic damage to the eustachian tube, negative middle ear pressure, and, in the presence of pneumococcal colonization of the upper respiratory tract, the development of acute purulent otitis media. Thus, viral and bacterial infection of the upper respiratory tract and associated eustachian tube dysfunction are the principal etiologic factors in the development of middle ear inflammation and effusion.

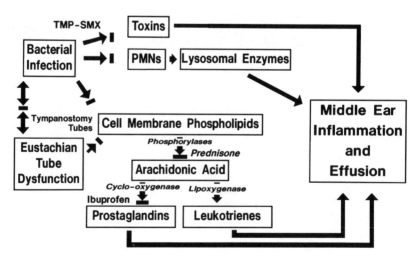

Figure 1. Intervention strategies in chronic otitis media with effusion.

As illustrated in the figure, the additive effects of eustachian tube dysfunction and middle ear infection lead to the release of inflammatory mediators in the middle ear space. Bacterial toxins may accumulate, and recent evidence suggests that bacterial toxins may actually pass through the round window membrane from the middle ear space to the perilymphatic space of the cochlea. There is evidence that these toxins can damage hair cells in the basal turn of the cochlea, which is the region of high frequency hearing, thereby explaining the occasional development of high frequency sensorineural hearing loss in persons with acute otitis media.

Complement proteins are activated in middle ear effusion with the consequent influx of polymorphonuclear leukocytes, which release their lysosomal enzymes into the middle ear and tissue spaces, resulting in enhanced capillary transudation and edema. Stimulation of cell membranes activates the phospholipid, arachidonic acid, in the presence of phospholipase, an enzyme present in extracellular fluids. Arachidonic acid is metabolized by the enzyme lipoxygenase to several inflammatory mediators, including the leukotrienes. Arachidonic acid is also metabolized by the enzyme cyclooxygenase to several prostaglandin metabolites. Leukotrienes and prostaglandins mediate inflammation by acting directly on vascular endothelium, phagocytic cells, platelets, and other cells. Many of these inflammatory events also appear to be triggered by subcellular components of bacteria, which may persist in middle ear tissues after bacterial multiplication has been controlled by antimicrobial treatment or host defense mechanisms. Thus, effective prevention and intervention strategies need to address inflammatory mediators triggered by viable bacterial cells and subcellular components.

As illustrated in the figure, the etiologic and pathogenic factors, which contribute to the development of middle ear inflammation, can theoretically be blocked by one or more interventions. In the treatment of acute purulent otitis media, antimicrobial drugs given to eradicate invading bacteria are the mainstay of therapeutic intervention. In chronic otitis media with effusion, tympanostomy tube insertion ventilates the middle ear cavity, thereby, theoretically blocking the additive effect of upper respiratory tract infection and eustachian tube dysfunction. Moreover, interference with eustachian tube obstruction might theoretically reduce cell membrane trauma and consequent release of arachidonic acid metabolites. Corticosteroid drugs stabilize cell membranes and are known to prevent phospholipase-mediated release of arachidonic acid. Corticosteroid drugs, such as oral prednisone, would thereby interfere with the lipoxygenase and cyclooxygenase breakdown of arachidonic acid metabolites. In contrast, nonsteroidal anti-inflammatory drugs, such as acetylsalicylic acid or ibuprofen, appear to block predominantly the cyclooxygenase metabolism of arachidonic acid, reducing the formation of prostaglandin metabolites; these drugs are not thought to have a significant effect of lipoxygenase metabolism of arachidonic acid.

To better understand pathogenic mechanisms and to study several intervention strategies for otitis media, we initiated a prospective, randomized clinical trial in 1982. Children one to eight years of age who had OME that had persisted for at least eight weeks were randomized to receive the antibiotic trimethoprim-sulfamethoxazole for four weeks; the nonsteroidal anti-inflammatory drug, ibuprofen, for two weeks; the corticosteroid, prednisone, for two weeks; or no treatment. Subjects were examined three and six weeks before randomization to document the persistence of OME. Analysis of these data indicated that OME lasting more than four weeks before enrollment, bilateral OME, and attendance by the child in a day care setting were factors which increased the risk of chronic OME. After chronic OME had been confirmed, subjects were randomized to medical intervention. Treatment failure was defined as persistence of OME after treatment, and these patients were referred for tympanostomy tube ventilation of the middle ear cavity. All subjects were examined at least monthly for 12 months after randomization, and hearing thresholds were determined at the conclusion of the study period.

A total of 449 children were enrolled in the study, and 80 had chronic OME which persisted during the six weeks of initial observation. An additional 26 percent of subjects developed symptomatic otitis media during this period and were dropped from the study. Of the 80 patients with chronic OME, 76 consented to randomization. Randomized subjects had a mean age of 43 months, a mean age at the first otitis media episode of 10.8 months, an average of eight prior otitis media episodes before enrollment, and an average of 9.4 weeks of continuous OME before randomization; 59 percent were male, and 95 percent were white. All were in the middle socioeconomic class.

Preliminary analysis of these data suggests that none of the medical intervention strategies caused OME resolution as rapidly as tympanostomy tube insertion, nor did any of the medical interventions delay as significantly the reoccurrence of OME after initial resolution. We anticipate that the results of this study, when completely analyzed, will provide important information as to the relative contribution of different arachidonic acid metabolites to the pathogenesis of OME.

In addition to the clinical trial described above, our research group addressed the question of medical intervention in an animal model. After producing acute purulent pneumococcal otitis media by direct middle ear inoculation in chinchillas, penicillin treatment with or without the corticosteroid drug, hydrocortisone, or ibuprofen was initiated. Biochemical and histopathological examination of middle ear effusion and tissues, respectively, indicated that combined penicillin and corticosteroid treatment resulted in the lowest prevalence of middle ear pathology. Penicillin treatment alone also led to prompt resolution of effusion and inflammation. Penicillin combined with ibuprofen treatment, however, led to somewhat more severe tissue pathology despite low levels of prostaglandin mediators; these results suggest that leukotriene metabolites not blocked by the nonsteroidal anti-inflammatory drug were important contributors to middle ear inflammation.

Although the results of these clinical and experimental studies of otitis media pathogenesis do not provide guidelines at the present time for treating OME with anti-inflammatory drugs, the studies have indicated the important effect of medical and surgical management on the disease state. Therefore, in studying speech, language, and cognitive development in children with otitis media, it is important to measure the impact of medical and surgical intervention on the disease state.

## REFERENCES

Giebink, G. S., and Quie, P. G. 1978. Otitis media: The spectrum of middle ear inflammation. *Annual Review of Medicine* 29:285–306.

Giebink, G. S., Juhn, S. K., Weber, M. L., and Le, C. T. 1982. The bacteriology and cytology of chronic otitis media with effusion. *Pediatric Infectious Diseases* 1:98–103.

Giebink, G. S., Le, C. T., and Paparella, M. D. 1982. Epidemiology of otitis media with effusion in children. *Archives of Otolaryngology* 108:563–566.

Giebink, G. S., Meyerhoff, W. I., and Cantekin, E. I. 1986 in press. Animal models of otitis media. *In* M. Sande and O. Zak (eds.). *Animal Models in the Evaluation of Chemotherapy of Infectious Diseases.* London: Academic Press.

# 16

# Remediation of Hearing, Speech, and Language Deficits Resulting from Otitis Media

*Julia M. Davis*

There are two major unanswered questions regarding the nonmedical treatment of otitis media: Is remediation indicated for children with repeated occurrence of middle ear disease? If so, what type of remediation is required? These questions are still unanswered after at least 10 years of intensive study by representatives of several professional groups largely because there are few established facts about the effects of otitis media on the psychosocial, linguistic, and cognitive development of young children. Although there are many published studies on these topics, their results are inconsistent and inconclusive. It is possible to cite studies that support opposite views about whether or not deficits in speech development, language learning, and cognitive functioning result from otitis media (Holm and Kunze 1969; Owrid 1970; Kaplan et al. 1973; Lewis 1976; Zinkus, Gottlieb, and Shapiro 1978; Friel-Patti et al. 1982). Authors who agree that middle ear disease results in negative effects on children's development often disagree about whether the effects are temporary or permanent. It is difficult to interpret the disparate results of the published studies because of methodological differences among them. Furthermore, the nature of the disease itself and the complexities involved in measuring the developmental areas of interest contribute to our lack of understanding of this common childhood disease.

In contrast, the literature regarding nonmedical treatment of the effects of otitis media is largely nonexistent. A survey of 250 articles about this disease resulted in finding only two that mentioned remediation of communication or educational problems, except in passing. One of these referred the reader to an in-house publication of the Toledo, Ohio public schools (Garrard and Clark 1985) and the other suggested the need for remediation by outlining some possible components that might be included (Downs, Jafek, and Wood 1981).

This scarcity of information about management of the sequelae of otitis media is not surprising when we consider that so little is really known about the specific effects of the disease. Nevertheless, there is enough known about the general nature of the disease to allow the development of a few guidelines for determining both the need for remediation and its most appropriate form. We know, for example, that otitis media is most prevalent in very young children, especially those of preschool age. We also know that, for those children who experience recurrent otitis media characterized by several episodes a year, the onset of the disease usually occurs between the ages of five and seven months. Furthermore, children who experience early onset of otitis media tend to have more recurrences than those who have their initial episode later in life. We know also that the disease is often accompanied by mild hearing loss, which averages about 25–30 dB. Finally, we know that some, but not all, children who experience repeated bouts of middle ear disease suffer delays in the development of speech and language skills which may or may not result in other learning problems. Therefore, we can assume that otitis media carries with it a risk of developmental problems. The fact that these do not always occur indicates that the middle ear disease probably interacts with other factors in a child's life to produce the problems we sometimes see. These factors are poorly understood and may be quite numerous and varied.

## Deficits Associated with Otitis Media

Close examination of the studies that report lasting deficits as a result of otitis media indicates that the effects most commonly reported fall into five general areas.

### HEARING LOSS

First, at the time the disease is active there is likely to be a mild hearing loss of around 25 dB (Dobie and Berlin 1979). The hearing loss is not permanent, however, and tends to vary with the stage of the disease. When evaluated several years after the most active disease period, most children no longer exhibit hearing loss. Although 25 dB is considered to be a mild loss of hearing, it represents a serious reduction of hearing sensitivity for a young child who is first learning language. The relationship between the intensity of sound and the perception of loudness is such that a reduction of 10 dB in intensity results in a signal that is perceived to be only half as loud as it sounded before. Thus, a 10 dB loss of hearing would result in perceiving sound as one-half as loud as normal, a 20 dB loss would cause sound to seem one-fourth as loud, and a 30 dB loss would cause sound to be perceived as one-eighth as loud as usual. Considered in these terms, the 25 dB loss is not as mild and benign as it originally seems. Listening with such a hearing loss is difficult and requires concentration, a skill that the average infant does not possess, at least not for long periods of time nor for sounds that are present more or less constantly in the environment.

AUDITORY PROCESSING PROBLEMS

The second effect of recurrent otitis media is a reduction in the ability to process auditory information normally. Older children who have histories of early middle ear disease sometimes perform poorly on tasks involving auditory sequencing and memory, listening in noise, and perception of speech in noise and in quiet (Kessler and Randolph 1979; Zinkus and Gottlieb 1980; Hoffman-Lawless, Keith, and Cotton 1981). If these deficits are present, a child may experience great difficulty in the usual classroom situation, where the signal-to-noise ratio is often as poor as 0 dB and seldom better than +10 dB. Regardless of whether or not hearing loss persists, some children with early onset of otitis media exhibit auditory processing difficulties for as long as 10 years after the active stage of the disease has passed.

LANGUAGE DELAY

The third area in which delays are reported is language learning, especially the learning of vocabulary and morphology. Problems in these areas appear to be related to the reduction in language stimulation that results from diminished hearing. Because many of the bound morphemes of the English language (such as 's, -ing, and -ed) are low in intensity and high in frequency, even a mild hearing loss renders them inaudible. The learning of vocabulary and grammatical rules by young children depends upon repeated exposure to spoken language. When exposure is reduced significantly, by hearing loss or any other type of deprivation, the learning of language may be delayed. Indeed, children with histories of otitis media have been shown to be delayed in developing both lexical and grammatical knowledge (Holm and Kunze 1969; Lewis 1976; Rapin 1979; Friel-Patti et al. 1982).

EDUCATIONAL DEFICITS

The fourth effect of otitis media follows naturally from the preceding one. Academic achievement may be reduced, especially in subject areas that are most language dependent, such as reading and language arts (Ling 1972; Zinkus et al. 1978; Freeman and Parkins 1979; Rapin 1979). The development of reading skills requires mastery of an auditory-verbal code that can be represented in visual form. Therefore, any reduction of knowledge about the underlying code will affect adversely the ability to use the code as a basis for learning new language skills, such as reading. A reading deficit interferes with the learning of most school subject matter.

DELAYED SPEECH DEVELOPMENT

Finally, otitis media has been shown to affect the development of articulation skills in young children. It is logical to assume that a child who does not hear speech normally may have difficulty learning to produce speech sounds accurately. Needleman (1977) has shown that children who have histories of recurrent otitis media develop speech sounds at a slower rate than children who have no history of middle ear disease early in life. Their acquisition of speech sounds follows a normal developmental sequence, however.

In every instance, the deficits associated with otitis media are the same as those associated with permanent hearing loss. The fact that some children who experience fluctuating hearing loss exhibit these characteristics suggests strongly that it is the reduction in hearing sensitivity that places a child with otitis media at risk. The fact that many children who experience otitis media do not show speech, language, or educational deficits suggests that factors other than fluctuating hearing loss may be involved as well.

Because hearing loss is a critical factor in predicting the effects of otitis media on development, it is important to know how much hearing loss a child suffers during episodes of middle ear disease and how long it persists. Unfortunately, this is the least well-documented aspect of otitis media in young children. Nevertheless, hearing impairment must be the focal point of any remediation strategy for children with middle ear disease.

## GUIDELINES FOR DETERMINING THE NEED FOR REMEDIATION

There are five major factors involved in the decision to initiate non-medical treatment programs for children with otitis media. They are:

Duration of episodes
Frequency of occurence
Presence of hearing loss
Questionable progress in the development of speech and language
   skills
Presence of other risk factors

To use these five guidelines appropriately, we will need to develop ways of monitoring the conditions of importance. Infants and young children are most often seen by family practitioners or pediatricians during their first episodes of middle ear disease. Therefore, the initial decision that a child is at risk for developmental problems must be made by these physicians. To do so, they will need measures that are easy to administer within their busy practices. Measures of the duration and frequency of episodes can be obtained easily from medical records. Generally speaking, if any single episode continues longer than two months, remediation should be recommended. Children who experience extended episodes are more likely to have recurrences of the disease and to suffer a loss of hearing for a significant period of time. In addition, if episodes occur at a rate of four or more times per year, the remediation program described below should be instituted.

Because the adverse effects of otitis media appear to result from hearing impairment, the presence of hearing loss during episodes of the disease should be monitored carefully. Tests of hearing should be performed at the time of the initial episode and periodically thereafter, because audiological data constitute the best indicators of the need for remediation. If hearing loss is present at any time, the remediation strategies described below should be instituted. It is unlikely, however, that most primary care physicians will have the equipment or personnel to carry out hearing testing in their offices, so referral resources will be essential to appropriate use of this guideline.

Referral to audiologists who have the training and expertise to test the hearing of young children will also facilitate evaluation of speech and language skills at an early age, although it is no easy task to obtain valid measures of these abilities in very young children. The use of parental survey instruments that ask about listening behavior and responses to communication efforts by parents and siblings could yield important information about children under the age of 2 or 3, whereas the use of standardized measures of speech and language will be most helpful for older children. The language evaluation should include measures of both receptive and expressive communication skills.

Until recently we have tended to focus our attention on the presence of otitis media alone rather than on any additional conditions that may place a child at risk for learning problems. There are two reasons this factor has received less attention: we are unsure which risk factors are most relevant and estimates of many of these factors require subjective judgments with which we are often uncomfortable. Even so, it seems safe to assume that overall cognitive skills, quality of the linguistic environment, general health, parenting skill, parental expectations, and the communicative demands placed on children might interact significantly with the presence of fluctuating hearing loss to influence children's development. If one or more of these factors is less than optimal, the effects of temporary hearing loss may be exacerbated. Therefore, it is important that we attempt to estimate whether or not additional risk factors are present.

Once a child is diagnosed as being at risk for developmental delays, a treatment program should be initiated at once.

## REMEDIATION MODEL

Given the fact that the onset of otitis media usually occurs early in life and that the immediate effects of the disease are likely to be quite subtle, it is not surprising that remediation programs are seldom introduced before several years have passed. The most appropriate treatment program for this early childhood condition has two stages, prevention and remediation.

### PREVENTION

This stage of treatment involves educating primary care physicians and parents regarding the possible effects of otitis media and ways of minimizing the adverse effects of reduced language stimulation caused by hearing loss. If physicians can be persuaded to inform parents of the necessity of monitoring their children's behavior carefully and seeking periodic evaluation of hearing and speech and language skills, speech-language pathologists and audiologists then can train parents to provide optimal auditory and language stimulation in the home. It is a relatively simple matter to adjust communication patterns used with infants and toddlers to maximize their use of auditory input. Engaging in activities in which the parent reads, sings, or talks close to the child's ear can overcome the effects of a mild loss of hearing. Systematic stimulation with language such as is involved in reading, reciting nursery rhymes, naming body parts, or engaging in other verbal games is good for all children, but essential for those with hearing impairments. Parents should be encouraged to provide as many verbal experiences as possible, including the use of recorded music, play with siblings, and provision of enrichment experiences (trips to the park, zoo, a neighbor's house, and so on) accompanied by verbal descriptions of what is seen or heard. The more exposure to spoken language the child has, the less likely it is that there will be language delay.

If parents can provide an optimal auditory and linguistic environment in the home, further intervention may be unnecessary. If we assume that the problems associated with otitis media result from the presence of hearing impairment, and we are able to circumvent the hearing loss by manipulating the communication environment to the child's advantage, there should then be few, if any, negative effects of the middle ear disease.

REMEDIATION

There is considerable evidence that when negative effects of otitis media occur, they are present long after the recurrences of the disease have ceased and hearing loss is no longer present. If early intervention in the form of preventive measures has not been provided, it may be necessary to carry out remediation programs that are designed to address the deficits experienced by a given child. There are four possible components to these programs: use of amplification, auditory training, speech-language therapy, and academic tutoring.

*Amplification* The decision to use amplification should be based on the degree of hearing impairment, its duration, and the status of the middle and outer ears. Generally speaking, I do not recommend the use of personal hearing aids unless the child has a bilateral hearing loss of long standing. Hearing aids are expensive and many families can scarcely afford to purchase them if they are to be used only sporadically or for a short period of time. If, however, the hearing loss cannot be resolved quickly, it may be necessary to insist on their use. Children appear to benefit little from the use of a hearing aid when the hearing loss is a mild, unilateral one. Of course, the ear must be free of drainage if an earmold is to be used.

Personal amplification in the form of a hearing aid is not the only form of amplification that might be considered. There are a number of different kinds of classroom amplification systems that can be employed with hearing impaired children, including FM, infra-red, and loop systems. The advantage to these is that they can be the property of the school system and only used by children on an as-needed basis. The disadvantage is that many of these systems require the child to have a personal hearing aid. Also, in most cases the amplification unit is a more powerful one than is required for a mild or moderate hearing loss and is therefore inappropriate for the child's use.

A unique approach to providing amplification in the classroom has been taken by a school district in Illinois. Entitled the MARRS Project (Mainstream Amplification Resource Room Study) (Sarff 1979), this program equipped classrooms with loudspeaker and microphone systems that amplified the teacher's voice and delivered it via sound field to the classroom as a whole. There are several major advantages to such a system for children with mild to moderate, fluctuating hearing losses. First, the amplification is always present; it is not necessary to know when the child experiences hearing loss in order to provide the needed boost in the signal. Second, the signal-to-noise ratio in the classroom is improved for everyone. Third, there is no stigma attached, because no child is singled out for attention. Finally, the system is less expensive than other amplification devices.

*Auditory Training*   Whether the child uses amplification or not, training in the use of the auditory system should be implemented. Children who have histories of otitis media sometimes show problems with the ability to discriminate speech in noise and to blend sounds auditorily. The auditory skills of localization, auditory memory, and auditory comprehension are also sometimes affected. Remediation programs should give children the opportunity to practice these and other auditory skills. Association of familiar and new vocabulary with its auditory representation will enhance the child's ability to perceive these words in a classroom or social situation. There are several auditory training programs that can be used with this population. One of the best is the Auditory Skills Instructional Program developed by personnel in the Los Angeles County School System (1979). One advantage of this program is that it can be carried out by teachers, parents, or other individuals who have had little or no formal training in such activities.

*Speech and Language Therapy*   The particular speech and language therapy procedures used with children who have had histories of otitis media must be based on an assessment of the individual child's use of these skills. If articulation problems are present, conventional articulation therapy, in which the affected sounds of the language are targeted for practice in a developmental order, is appropriate. Special procedures involving tactile stimulation or emphasis on the visual aspects of speech sounds are not usually necessary.

Language therapy should involve exposure to the unstressed function words of the language, word endings, vocabulary, and rules of grammar that appear to be a problem to the individual child. The pragmatic use of language in social and educational situations should be evaluated, and, if necessary, targeted in remediation. In any event, the oral communication problems of this population of children are not likely to be severe unless additional handicapping conditions are present.

*Academic Instruction*   If assessment reveals significant educational problems, academic tutoring should be considered. Children who no longer exhibit hearing impairment are not usually eligible for educational services from teachers of the hearing impaired. They are eligible, however, for services from learning disabilities specialists, speech-language pathologists, and other school personnel who have had training and experience in the management of language problems in educational settings. Services from reading specialists and tutors in the language arts are usually appropriate.

## SUMMARY

If the remediation program described above could be made available to all children who meet the guidelines for initiating treatment, it is possible that most of the negative effects associated with otitis media could be eliminated. Even if preventive measures are not instituted in time to avoid all problems, the prognosis is good, especially for those children whose hearing losses are no longer present and who have no other serious handicapping conditions. The combination of auditory training, speech and language therapy, and academic tutoring should result in a reduction of the severity of the problems experienced. Whether these children will ever reach their true potential is unknown. By the time they are enrolled in a remediation program, their problems are usually long standing; communication habits are not easily changed once they have been in use for a number of years. It seems essential, therefore, that we emphasize the preventive aspects of remediation, doing whatever is necessary to orient primary-care physicians and parents to the potential communication and related problems associated with recurrent otitis media. In particular audiologists and speech-language pathologists must be ready to offer assistance in preventing deficits and, if necessary, provide effective programs to remediate those problems we are unable to prevent.

## REFERENCES

Dobie, R., and Berlin, C. 1979. Influence of otitis media on hearing and development. *Annals of Otology, Rhinology and Laryngology* (suppl. 60), 88:54–63.

Downs, M., Jafek, B., and Wood, R. 1981. Comprehensive treatment of children with recurrent serous otitis media. *Otolaryngology, Head and Neck Surgery* 89:658–665.

Freeman, B., and Parkins, C. 1979. The prevalence of middle ear disease among learning impaired children. Paper presented at the annual Convention of the American Speech and Hearing Association, Chicago.

Friel-Patti, S., Finitzo-Hieber, T., Conti, G., and Brown, K. 1982. Language delay in infants associated with middle ear disease and mild, fluctuating hearing impairment. *Pediatric Infectious Diseases* 2:104–109.

Garrard, K., and Clark, B. 1985. Otitis Media: The role of speech-language pathologist. *Asha* 27: 35–39.

Hoffman-Lawless, K., Keith, R., and Cotton, R. 1981. Auditory processing abilities in children with previous middle ear effusion. *Annals of Otology, Rhinology and Laryngology* 90:543–545.

Holm, V., and Kunze, L. 1969. Effect of chronic otitis media on language and speech development. *Pediatrics* 43:833–839.

Kaplan, G., Fleshman, J., Bender, T., Baum, C., and Clark, P. 1973. Long-term effects of otitis media: A ten-year cohort study of Alaskan Eskimo children. *Pediatrics* 52:577–585.

Kessler, M., and Randolph, K. 1979. The effects of early middle ear disease on the auditory abilities of third grade children. *Journal of the Academy of Rehabilitative Audiology* 12:6–20.

Lewis, N. 1976. Otitis media and linguistic incompetence. *Archives of Otolaryngology* 102:387–390.

Ling, D. 1972. Rehabilitation of cases with deafness secondary to otitis media. *In* A. Glorig and K. Gerwin (eds.) *Otitis Media.* Springfield, IL: Charles C Thomas.

Los Angeles Public Schools. 1979. *Auditory Skills Instructional Planning System.* North Hollywood, CA: Foreworks.

Needleman, H. 1977. Effects of hearing loss from early recurrent otitis media on speech and language development. *In* B. Jaffe (ed.) *Hearing Loss in Children.* Baltimore: University Park Press.

Owrid, H. 1970. Hearing impairment and verbal attainment in primary school children. *Educational Research* 12:209–214.

Rapin, I. 1979. Conductive hearing loss: Effects on children's language and scholastic skills. A review of the literature. *Annals of Otology, Rhinology and Laryngology,* 88 (suppl. 60):3–12.

Sarff, Lewis. 1979. (Director of Research, Wabash and Ohio Valley Special School District, Norris City, IL 62869), personal communication.

Zinkus, P., and Gottlieb, M. 1980. Patterns of perceptual and academic deficits related to early chronic otitis media. *Pediatrics* 66:246–253.

Zinkus, P., Gottlieb, M., and Shapiro, M. 1978. Developmental and psychoeducational sequelae of chronic otitis media. *American Journal of Diseases of Children* 132:1100–1104.

# 17

# Otitis Media: A Model for Long Term Effects with Implications for Intervention

*Lynne Feagans*

## INTRODUCTION

This chapter is an attempt to draw implications for intervention from the diverse and sometimes conflicting literature on the long term effects of otitis media with effusion. After reviewing the literature, I will propose a model that represents one way that otitis media and its resulting fluctuating hearing loss can lead to long term developmental sequelae. Implications for intervention will stem from the model and its supporting evidence; the target group for intervention will be the preschool population with increased risk for the disease and its subsequent developmental effects.

Before presenting the evidence for long term effects, it is important to understand first the nature of this disease and the scope of the problem. Although these points have been discussed in other chapters, a short review is helpful here in order to understand why intervention strategies are necessary, even though there is no definitive evidence for the long-term effects of this disease.

### THE NATURE OF THE DISEASE

Physicians and parents have long been concerned about the effects of otitis media with effusion (middle ear disease). It is the second most frequent reason parents take their children to physicians and the single most frequent diagnosis made by pediatricians (Shurin et al. 1979; Teele, Klein, and Rosner 1984). In 1982 it was estimated that

*192*

two billion dollars a year were spent in health care for this disease alone (Feigin 1982). Thus, it should garner the attention of health professionals on the basis of morbidity rates alone. Recent studies have indicated that otitis media may be much more prevalent than first suspected. Estimates have indicated that from 30 to 50 percent of children experience otitis media in the preschool years, but even these estimates are based on acute episodes that rely on parents taking their children to physicians for treatment of symptoms. Studies of children's ears examined on a regular basis, whether signs of illness were present or not, have indicated that up to 75 percent of children under the age of five experience episodes of otitis media and that between 50 percent and 75 percent of these episodes are silent ones, without fever or other symptoms (Marchant et al. 1984; Schwartz et al. 1981). Thus, it appears that the morbidity rates were initially too low and that the true incidence may indeed pose an even greater problem for physicians and other professionals interested in the long term health of children.

Although the advent of penicillin-type antibiotics reduced the chances of the bacterial infection resulting in mastoiditis and other dangerous secondary infections, treatment for the fluid (effusion) that often remains behind the tympanic membrane for days or months after the acute infection has subsided is still unsatisfactory. A variety of therapies have been employed to reduce the effusion, including antibiotic regimens, antihistamine therapies, decongestants, and myringotomy (insertion of tiny drainage tubes into the eardrum itself). In general, the results of studies on these therapies have been quite disappointing (Dusdieker et al. 1985; van Buchem, Dunk, and van't Hof 1981), although this volume does report some promising data on myringotomy.

Speech and hearing specialists have been concerned about lingering effusion from acute otitis media because it is highly correlated with a mild to moderate hearing loss, usually between a 10 and 30 dB loss within the speech frequencies (Fria, Cantekin, and Eichler 1985). At first this loss was considered to cause only short-term problems for the young child, since a permanent hearing loss from otitis media is relatively rare. Recent evidence has begun to accumulate that indicates that the intermittent hearing loss associated with otitis media may have long-term effects on the language and cognitive development of the child, especially because the hearing loss usually occurs during the language formative years.

Otitis media with effusion is most frequent in the first two years of life and, with maturation, the incidence decreases (Shurin et al. 1979). It is, therefore, most frequent during the time that children are acquiring many important cognitive skills, including language.

At present we know relatively little about how the course of the disease may initially affect the child. The child with persistent otitis media is likely to have periods of prolonged mild hearing loss and then other periods when he/she can hear normally. This intermittent hearing loss has not been well understood since children with permanent hearing loss do not experience these inconsistencies of speech input. Menyuk (1980) has postulated that the mild fluctuating hearing loss can cause problems in language acquisition because the child is continually using a different input base from which to infer the rules of the language, including phonological, semantic, and syntactic rules.

CHILDREN AT RISK FOR OTITIS MEDIA

There are a variety of factors that influence a child's susceptibility to this disease. A discussion of these factors can help us identify which groups of children may need intervention, as well as what kind of intervention is needed.

A variety of studies show an association between otitis media and socioeconomic status. A study of 407 Canadian Indians shows a striking relationship between middle ear pathology and social ratings based on observations of housing conditions, house-keeping, income, and family functioning (Cambon, Galbraith, and Kong 1965). Active ear disease was found in 6 percent of children with a socioeconomic rating of good or fair contrasted with 35 percent of children with a poor rating. Although others have also found this relationship, there are other factors associated with socioeconomic status that also could be related to otitis media. Living in crowded conditions, in apartments, or in cities has placed children at higher risk of otitis media than living in a rural area or in a single-family dwelling (Pukander, Spila, and Karma 1984). Children with a large number of siblings are also at greater risk. All of these factors are more prevalent in low-income homes. Breast feeding has been thought to have a protective influence for the child, although some believe this may be only an artifact since bottle feeding does increase the risk of otitis media. Studies have indicated that bottle feeding, especially when the bottle is propped up so the child is in a recumbent feeding position (Beauregard 1971), may cause milk to collect in the back of the throat which, in turn, is a breeding ground for infection.

Especially important for the intervention strategy proposed here is the consistent finding that children in day-care are at much greater risk for otitis media than children who stay at home. A large-scale epidemiological study in Denmark using 938 children in two birth cohorts were followed for three years (Fiellau-Nikolajsen 1979). It was found that children in day-care were three times more likely to have abnormal tympanograms than children who were at home. Children in family day-care were at intermediate risk. Tympanometry is used as another way to show abnormal eardrum functioning. It measures the compliance of the eardrum and is highly correlated with a mild hearing loss. Other studies using a variety of other techniques have also confirmed this relationship between day-care and otitis media (Haskins and Kotch in press; Vinther, Brahe-Pedersen, and Elbrond 1984).

Other factors that are associated with otitis media are the sex of the child, with boys being more likely to contract the disease than girls; racial differences, with whites more likely than blacks to be affected; and premature infants more likely than other infants to contract otitis media (Berman, Balkany, and Simmons 1978). If parents or siblings have a history of otitis media, the target child is at increased risk. Last, there is increasing evidence that children with learning and behavioral problems are at much greater risk of having otitis media in early childhood. This risk has led some to postulate a causal relationship, discussed in the next section, between otitis media and learning and behavior.

OTITIS MEDIA AND LATER DEVELOPMENTAL PROBLEMS

Only in the last fifteen years has evidence begun to accumulate about the relationship between otitis media and later language and learning problems. Primarily the information about this relationship comes from a series of retrospective studies. These studies examined the medical records of children with already-known academic, behavioral, or learning problems. Thus, they have generally been a select pool of clinic-referred children with some form of academic or behavioral problems. Many of these studies showed that children with these problems have a greater incidence in early childhood of otitis media compared to children who do not have these problems.

Although more and more studies are being published about the possible long-term effects of this disease, most parents and physicians are unaware of these consequences. For instance, in a recent medical update in *Woman's Day Magazine* (Stern 1986), the headline of the article indicated that it would discuss how to prevent serious consequences of otitis media. One might think this was an article to alert parents of the possible long-term developmental effects, but it was not. It was geared to alerting parents to the acute signs of otitis media which, if not attended to, can cause perforation of the eardrum and possible scarring which, in turn, can cause permanent hearing loss. This advice from a popular magazine was understandable given the frequency of the disease as well as the intense pain that often accompanies the acute episode, pain that cannot always be communicated to the parent by the child and even if identified by the child, not localized to the ear. Many parents know the anguish of staying up all night with a child in pain from an ear infection. From the parents' and physicians' points of view, the reduction in fever and pain with an antibiotic regimen belies the long-term developmental effects of the hearing loss. Most parents are unaware of the hearing loss and most children do not show any aberrant behavior for which parents seek help. It is only after prolonged periods of hearing loss and often when the child is much older and is no longer experiencing bouts of otitis media that parents report problems.

EVIDENCE ABOUT LONG-TERM EFFECTS

Although it is clear that otits media is a frequent medical problem for children, it is not clear what the long-term effects of the disease actually are. Thus, it is important to review some of the evidence before a strategy for intervention is proposed.

One of the first studies to indicate a relationship between otitis media and later problems was a report by Holm and Kunze (1969). They studied 16 children who had a history of chronic otitis media and compared them with a group of children who were matched on age, sex, and race. They found that the high otitis media group had significantly lower scores on vocabulary and language tests. Howie (1979) studied two groups of children who were matched on the same factors plus an important additional one—socioeconomic status (SES). The high otitis children were again found to have lower IQ scores and poorer reading and language scores.

Further studies examined the preschool health records of children who had been diagnosed as having reading or learning problems. Zinkus and his associates (Zinkus and Gottlieb 1980; Zinkus, Gottlieb, and Shapiro 1978) carried out a series of studies using two groups of children in elementary school who were referred to a clinic for academic underachievement. One group had a history of otitis media in the first three years of life and had had myringotomies as a result of the ear infections. The other group was matched with the high otitis group on a variety of demographic variables but had no history of otitis media. The findings from these studies indicate that the otitis media group had significantly more verbal and academic deficits than the low otitis group. Other retrospective studies that specifically studied children with learning disabilities have found that these children had a higher incidence of otitis media (Freeman and Parkins 1979; Masters and Marsh 1978).

While most of the studies have focused on the relationship between otitis media and some form of verbal deficiency, a few studies have found a relationship between otitis media and behavioral and attention deficits. Hersher (1978) studied a group of 22 hyperactive children and 772 normal children. The groups were matched on background factors, but the hyperactive group had a significantly higher percentage of children (54 percent) who had more than six episodes of otitis media in comparison to the normal group (15 percent). Other types of behavioral problems have been reported also. In the Dunedin sample ($n$ = 951) (McGee, Silva, and Stewart 1982), children who were followed from birth and later identified as having behavioral problems by parents and teachers were examined. These 90 identified children had significantly more otitis media and this relationship was even stronger when the hyperactive children only were used ($n$ = 30). In another study from this same sample (Silva et al. 1982), children with bilateral otitis media, matched to children with no otitis media on background characteristics, were observed to have shorter attention spans and were reported to be more restless, fidgety, and destructive. In addition, lower scores were found in speech, language, and intelligence for those children with bilateral otitis media.

A growing number of studies have shown a relationship between otitis media and later developmental problems. Yet the causal link can be established only through a longitudinal prospective study of otitis media. Such a study will be summarized in this chapter as a prelude to the intervention strategies proposed.

NOTES OF CAUTION

Although more and more literature is pointing to the long-term effects of otitis media, it is not the case that all children are affected. At this point we do not have, from retrospective studies, confirming evidence of the percentage of children who have long term problems and the few prospective studies available indicate that it is only children with many and prolonged infections in the preschool years who are seriously affected by this disease.

In one of the most recent comprehensive studies of otitis media (Fischler, Todd, and Feldman 1985), 167 healthy Apache children aged six to eight years were divided into four mutually exclusive otitis media groups. Careful documentation of the disease was implemented from infancy onward. Tests of language and intelligence were administered to the children. No differences were found among the groups on the developmental outcome measures. Another recent study reported similar no-difference findings on global language and IQ measures in a longitudinal study of day-care children (Roberts et al. in press).

I did not find studies about whether otitis media might covary with other disease processes. It may be that general illness in early childhood, and not otitis media per se, is really the causal mechanism of some later developmental problems. There are still many aspects of this relationship that we are not confident about. Several authors have written critical reviews of otitis media literature (Paradise 1981; Ventry

1980). They discuss the many flaws in the retrospective design and they challenge researchers to present more convincing prospective evidence. Given the evidence presented thus far, I will next present an argument for a relationship between otitis media and later developmental problems in a vulnerable population of children.

## A MODEL OF THE EFFECT OF OTITIS MEDIA

In the study reported here a model was developed by which otitis media could have an effect on later functioning. This model was my best-guess scenario of the most serious long-term effects, given the literature on language acquisition and the retrospective studies just reported (Feagans et al. 1985). The hypotheses about which language and developmental processes might be affected have been imbedded in a model of the long-term effects (see Figure 1). It is clear from numerous studies that although language development may be hindered by a number of factors including brain injury, severe environmental deprivation, and certain physical handicaps, a review of the literature indicates how robust the language system is. Many major insults to the young child have only a temporary effect on the acquisition of language (Lenneberg 1967). My conceptualization of the link between otitis media and later language functioning, then, was seen as an indirect one. It appeared to me that there might be one or more mediating variables that could result in the long-term global language deficits reported in the retrospective studies.

I would argue that continued bouts of otitis media over the early preschool years may create initial language delays, but the critical effect of otitis media that produces longer term developmental delays is reduced attention to the environment, language in particular, caused by an intermittent hearing loss. Children may more easily recover their basic language skill in syntax, semantics, and phonology after bouts of otitis media become less frequent in the later preschool years, but the habit of not attending to language may remain after hearing has returned to normal. This habit may have been created because listening and understanding takes greater effort for children with a hearing loss. This could be especially true in group situations where background noise can make processing of language difficult for children with a mild hearing loss. This may be the case particularly in the day-care setting where we know otitis media is more frequent.

Attention problems may have a subtle but important impact on language processes that require sustained attention. More basic language processes like syntax and semantics may not be as affected as discourse and narrative skills. These skills require processing of language beyond the sentence level in stories and in conversations.

## EFFECTS OF OTITIS MEDIA

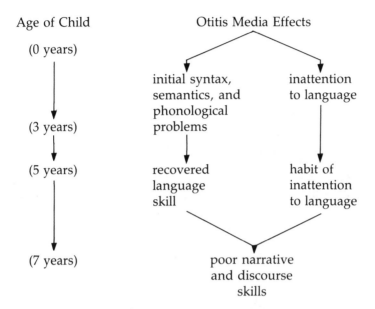

Figure 1.

EVIDENCE FOR THE MODEL

Obviously there may be other processes implicated in the causal relationship; we chose one to examine. We also had a population to study which was at risk for otitis media. It was a population of 44 children who had been followed from birth, were from low SES backgrounds, and were attending day-care centers from three months of age until they began public school at age five. A detailed description of this population can be found elsewhere (Ramey and Campbell 1979).

The children in this study were part of a large longitudinal study of children from low socioeconomic backgrounds. One of the studies associated with the project followed the language development of the children and another was aimed at documenting the health of the children on a daily basis, with special interest in otitis media. Physicians examined the children whenever there were any signs of illness. They used pneumatic otoscopy to assess the movement and the nature of the eardrum if otitis media was suspected. Details of the procedures and reliability can be found elsewhere (Roberts et al. in press). In general, children were examined every ten days to two weeks as long as they had fluid behind the eardrum. Tympanometry was employed during the study and as children grew older hearing testing was conducted.

In order to test the model, a regression model was set up to predict a global expressive language measure as well as a narrative language measure at five and seven years of age. A backward elimination procedure was used to examine the viability of both the full and final models. Given the rather modest sample of 44 children, we restricted ourselves to six predictor variables.

*Predictor measures*    Three variables collected on the children at the time they were 0 to 3 years of age were selected. These variables have been shown to predict later academic and intellectual status. There were: (1) the mother's IQ (WAIS) at the time of the child's birth; (2) the Caldwell HOME (1970) (18 months) which is a measure of the home environment as rated by an interviewer who goes into the home; and (3) the mother's education as measured by the last grade she completed.

Two otitis media variables were used, i.e., the frequency and duration of otitis media in the first three years of life. Both of these measures were included because theoretically they may index different processes through which language and attention may be affected. The duration of otitis media with effusion may index length of hearing loss while frequency may index more effectively the fluctuating nature of the hearing loss. For instance, one child may have had only two episodes of otitis, each lasting 270 days. Another child might have had nine episodes each lasting 60 days. Although each child had the same duration in days, their hearing experiences could be quite different with respect to the fluctuation between normal and impaired hearing.

Finally, we chose a sixth variable which was a concurrent measure of the language outcome variables, the WPPSI IQ at five years of age. This measure was used in order to examine whether the measure of otitis media could account for additional variance above that accounted for by a powerful concurrently measured test of developmental status—IQ. These six measures were used as the predictors in the regression model.

*Outcome measures*    A narrative task was administered to all children at kindergarten entry and in the middle of second grade. Two measures were derived from this task to measure overall language development as well as narrative skill specifically. The task involved having the children listen to six stories ranging from easy to difficult. Children were required to demonstrate understanding by acting out the stories using props. Children were read the stories over again until they could act out each story without error. Once overall comprehension was assured, children were asked to paraphrase the stories. First, a global measure of language development called the mean length of utterance (MLU) was scored from the paraphrases at kindergarten and second grade. MLU is the mean number of words per utterance in each paraphrase and indicates general language development. It was predicted that otitis media would not be related to this variable at five and seven years of age.

Second, the quality of the paraphrase was scored at kindergarten by counting the number of critical elements included in the paraphrase (a possible score of twelve for each story). These critical elements included each different actor, action, or object in the story. A more detailed description of the scoring can be found in Feagans and Farran (1981). By second grade a different scoring system was employed because the children could remember and paraphrase much longer stories. The number of critical propositions used in each paraphrase was used as the measure of interest. There were ten propositions in each story. For further details of this scoring system see Feagans and Short (1984). Scoring systems at both kindergarten and second grade were devised to capture the essence of a good paraphrase. It was hypothesized that otitis media would contribute only to the prediction of the paraphrase measure at five and seven years of age. In order to form more stable measures, all scores were averaged across the six stories.

*Post-hoc measures*    Another set of measures was examined after the fact as a validation of the regression outcomes and an exploration of inattention as a mediating variable. These measures were taken at school entry. Project children were observed on two consecutive days in their kindergarten classroom with the behavioral observational system called The Schedule of Classroom Activity Norms (SCAN). This system was a time-sampling technique in which the children's behavior was coded every five seconds into one of fourteen categories of mutually-exclusive task-oriented and social behavior (Feagans and McKinney 1981). Each child was observed for twenty minutes on two consecutive days during academic activities. Thus, each child had 480 five-second intervals of data. For the purposes of this paper only the categories that measured inattention were used (see below). These three categories were summed together for each child to form an off-task measure of classroom behavior.

1.  Distractibility: The attention of the child is diverted from the task to task-irrelevant stimuli. Example: A child looks up from his/her task and stares out the window.
2.  Non-participation (passive waiting): Child is withdrawing from classroom activity, daydreaming, pouting, or visibly detaching himself from his on-going task. Example: The child stands on the periphery of a group activity, watching the activity, but not participating in it.
3.  Non-constructive self-directed activity: The eye fixation of the child is on his/her own manipulation of objects, cloth-

ing, or body parts irrelevant to his/her classroom work, or the child is using task-related materials in an inappropriate manner. Example: The child is banging a pencil on a desk and watching the pencil while the teacher is lecturing.

Results from the backward elimination procedure at kindergarten indicate that the full model did not predict MLU and none of the variables were significant in the final model. The full model did predict the paraphrase quality ($R^2 = .47$) with both the WPPSI and the frequency of otitis media as significant predictors in the final model. The results of the regressions at second grade were similar to kindergarten. A fuller description of these results can be found elsewhere (Feagans et al. 1985).

By inspecting the regression line produced by these three significant variables, it is clear that a linear relationship does not exist among the frequency of otitis media, IQ, and the paraphrase variable. It appears that there is little relationship among the variables at low frequencies of otitis media and a strong relationship at a later point. Although there are several statistical techniques that can be employed to examine break points in a regression line, these techniques were not useful or appropriate with the small number of subjects in this study. Visual inspection supports the fact that an association is observed in children who had beyond eight episodes of otitis media (13 children).

In order to better understand this effect and to better validate the hypothesis, we analyzed other data collected on the kindergarten children that could index their inattention in school. We compared the thirteen high otitis media children (nine or more episodes) to the thirty-one other children (eight or fewer episodes) on the SCAN off-task categories summed together. The high otitis group produced significantly more inattention/distractibility in comparison to the other group, thus supporting the model's prediction.

DISCUSSION OF THE MODEL

The results of this exploratory prospective study indicate that the frequency and duration of otitis media in the first three years of life account for variance in language functioning at five and seven years of age in addition to variance accounted for by a measure of IQ given at the same time as the language measure. In addition, findings suggest that attentional processes may be the possible mediating variable between otitis media and later language deficits.

These results support findings of previous retrospective studies (Holm and Kunze 1969; Zinkus and Gottlieb 1980) with some limitations. First, this study can be shown only to substantiate the relationship between otitis media and later discourse or narrative skill. Although this skill is an important one for school success (Feagans and Short 1984), the more basic language measure, MLU, was not related to otitis media. Secondly, even though our regressions were significant, visual inspection revealed a threshold effect. Therefore, our results indicate that there is a relationship between otitis media and later narrative skills only when there are many episodes of otitis media in the first three years of life. Thirdly, these studies are limited to children in day-care settings where the incidence of otitis media is known to be quite high (Haskins and Kotch in press). Only one child in our sample did not have an episode of otitis media in the first three years of life. This incidence may be the highest ever reported in an otitis media study. And although we have good reliability of the measurement of the disease, other studies of this nature are needed to document the notion that this is typical of a day-care population. Fourth, the population used in this study is already at risk for retardation due to sociocultural factors. Therefore, it may be that only a vulnerable population like this one would show the later effects of otitis media. Other populations with more environmental supports may counter the possible negative effect of mild fluctuating hearing loss and thus show no later language or attentional effects.

Taking these qualifications into account, the results are still interesting, especially since they suggest that attentional problems may be found in children with high incidence of otitis media in early childhood. The differences between the high otitis media group and the other children are not just a difference of statistical significance, but appear to be meaningful for classroom learning. The high otitis media group had double the number of five-second intervals in which they were found off-task, as compared to the other children. Other studies have shown that off-task behavior may lead to lower achievement and other negative classroom outcomes (Feagans and McKinney 1981).

## INTERVENTION STRATEGIES

As can be seen from the chapter by Julia Davis in this volume, there is almost nothing in the literature to guide the development of a program for children at risk for otitis media. Because of the dearth of information, the strategies suggested here, along with the previous information about the risk groups for otitis media, come from the model and the study just described.

Since the review of the literature and the present study indicate a high incidence of otitis media in young children and give supporting evidence for long term effects, day-care centers should be places for early intervention. As we reported, there was only one child in our day-care who did not have at least one bout of otitis media in the first three years of life. A model for intervention in day-care is presented in Figure 2.

DAY-CARE MONITORING AND INTERVENTION
FOR OTITIS MEDIA

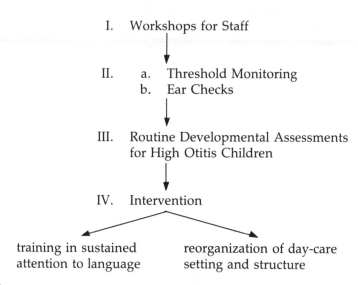

I.    Workshops for Staff

II.   a.  Threshold Monitoring
      b.  Ear Checks

III.  Routine Developmental Assessments
      for High Otitis Children

IV.   Intervention

training in sustained              reorganization of day-care
attention to language              setting and structure

Figure 2.


This model contains four components. First, workshops should be set up for day-care staff and teachers to inform them of the prevalence of otitis media in day-care as well as of the possible short- and long-term effects of the disease. Educating the adults who care for young children should make the staff more sensitive to the needs of the children.

Second, day-care centers should provide routine hearing-threshold monitoring of young children. Although difficult below the age of two, routine threshold monitoring can be done by trained day-care workers or by health paraprofessionals. Nurse practitioners who have been trained to use the pneumatic otoscope can perform routine examination of ears. A combination of these procedures would allow the monitoring of hearing as well as the identification of silent episodes of otitis media. This second component would be cost-effective if communities, parents, and physicians were willing to cooperate in such monitoring.

The third component of intervention should be a routine evaluation, using a battery of cognitive, attention and language measures, for those children who have had continual bouts of otitis media. Although a threshold of incidence of otitis media for later developmental effects has not been established, the study reported here indicates that three bouts a year is a high incidence. Those children with three or more incidents should be assessed periodically and if decrements in performance on tests begin to appear, then referral for more extensive testing could be made.

Along with the testing would be a fourth component. This component includes the intervention itself. There are two sub-components of this intervention strategy. Although both are aimed at all children, they are especially geared to the otitis-prone child.

The first part of the intervention itself places emphasis on training the child to sustain attention to language. Specifically, this might include opportunities for sustained one-to-one interaction with an adult. Joan Tough (1982) has indicated how important this activity is for normal language development and that this kind of interaction may be difficult for otitis-prone children in the noisy, somewhat chaotic atmosphere of some day-care settings. Tough has presented a frame-work for extending the meaning relationships in the children's language. By providing contexts in which children might talk about complex relationships, including explanations and predictions, her framework has worked well for day-care teachers to engage in extended dialogues with children about complex phenomena. In addition she has suggestions about how the teacher can adjust her speech to match that of the child while still encouraging the child to talk at length about complex phenomena. Such a framework has worked well in day-care settings and could be modified for otitis-prone children.

Joint book reading, in which an adult reads to a child, while helping him/her understand the theme and the structure of the text, has also been found to be an important prerequisite for reading and school success. Again, this kind of activity can help the otitis-prone child develop attention skills that are necessary for later language processing of narratives and other language tasks required in school (Goelman, Oberg, and Smith 1984). Marion Blank (1982) has set up procedures to help learning disabled children acquire those aspects of language necessary for success in classroom interaction and for understanding narrative text. Her question-asking-answering paradigm can foster sustained attention to language in young children.

The second part of the intervention is the easier one to suggest, but may be the most difficult to implement. The auditory structure of the day-care setting has an effect on all children, but the otitis-prone child may be especially vulnerable to some of the noise characteristics. These can be modified for all children without affecting the large unaffected group adversely.

Teachers can schedule smaller groups, seating the otitis-prone child closer to the teacher. Rooms in the day-care center can have more rugs and other acoustical features that reduce the ambient noise that is so often overwhelming in the day-care setting. Teachers can try to reduce the noise level by a number of techniques if they realize how detrimental it is to children with a slight hearing loss.

There can also be a special place for the tutorial sessions suggested in the previous intervention component. This might be a hallway, a teacher's room, or even outside if the weather is nice. Teachers who observe that otitis-prone children are not listening or are distracted from the task should try to arrange for a more conducive environment, including more small group interaction or even one-to-one interaction with the teacher when possible. It is important to remember that even when the child is hearing well, he/she may have established a habit of not listening which can contribute to the restricted input.

All these measures can be instituted if priorities are set by those who see the real need to institute such practices. Although the focus of invervention is day-care, these same procedures can be used in any setting where children spend much of their waking time.

## CONCLUSION

Otitis media with effusion is a serious health problem for infants and young children. Although the acute period of this disease presents the most clear symptoms, it may be the long term effects of the slight hearing loss accompanying the disease that pose the greatest threat to children. Evidence for the long-term effects is still equivocal but the mounting evidence in certain risk groups, including low-income and day-care groups, should garner the attention of professionals and policymakers alike who are concerned about the health and development of children. Fairly simple procedures outlined at the end of this chapter might be instituted in day-care settings, pediatric and family practice groups, and community school programs. By beginning at least some of these practices for young children, we may prevent some of the developmental problems we see in many otitis-prone children. Even without definitive studies, intervention for these children should be begun now.

## REFERENCES

Beauregard, W. G. 1971. Positional otitis media. *Journal of Pediatrics* 79:294.

Berman, S. A., Balkany, T. J., and Simmons, M. A. 1978. Otitis media in the neonatal intensive care unit. *Pediatrics* 62(2):198–201.

Blank, M. 1982. Language and school failure: Some speculations about the relationship between oral and written language. *In* L. Feagans and D. C. Farran (eds.), *The Language of Children Reared in Poverty.* New York: Academic Press.

Caldwell, B. M. 1970. *Instruction Manual for Infants (Home Observation for Measurement of the Environment).* Little Rock, AR.

Cambon, K., Galbraith, J., and Kong, C. 1965. Middle ear disease in Indians of the Mount Currie reservation, British Columbia. *Canadian Medical Association Journal* 93:1301.

Dusdieker, L. B., Smith, G., Booth, B. M., Woodhead, J. C., and Milavetz, G. 1985. The long-term outcome of nonsupportive otitis media with effusion. *Clinical Pediatrics* 24(4):181–186.

Feagans, L., and Farran, D. C. 1981. How demonstrated comprehension can get muddled in production. *Developmental Psychology* 17:718–727.

Feagans, L., and McKinney, J. D. 1981. The pattern of exceptionality across domains in learning disabled children. *Journal of Applied Developmental Psychology* 1:313–328.

Feagans, L., and Short, E. J. 1984. Developmental differences in the comprehension and production of narratives by reading disabled and normally achieving children. *Child Development* 55:1727–1736.

Feagans, L., Sanyal, M., Henderson, F., Collier, A., and Appelbaum, M. 1985. *Middle ear disease in early childhood and later language skills.* Paper presented at the Society for Research in Child Development, April, 1985.

Feigin, R. D. 1982. Otitis media: Closing the information gap. *The New England Journal of Medicine* 306:1417–1418.

Fiellau-Nikolajsen, M. 1979. Tympanometry in 3-year-old children: Type of care as an epidemiological factor in secretory otitis media and tubal dysfunction in unselected populations of 3-year-old children. *Otolaryngology* 41:193–205.

Fischler, R. S., Todd, W., and Feldman, C. M. 1985. Otitis media and language performance in a cohort of Apache Indian children. *American Journal of Diseases of Children* 139:355–360.

Freeman, B. A., and Parkins, C. 1979. The prevalence of middle ear disease among learning impaired children. *Clinical Pediatrics* 18(4):205–212.

Fria, J. J., Cantekin, E. I., and Eichler, J. A. (1985). Hearing acuity of children with otitis media with effusion. *Archives of Otolaryngology* 111:10–16.

Goelman, H., Oberg, A., and Smith, F. 1984. *Awakening to Literacy.* London: Heinemann Educational books.

Haskins, R., and Kotch, J. in press. Day care and illness: Evidence, costs, and public policy. *Pediatrics.*

Hersher, L. 1978. Minimal brain dysfunction and otitis media. *Perceptual and Motor Skills* 47:723–726.

Holm, V. A. and Kunze, L. K. 1969. Effect of chronic otitis media on language and speech development. *Pediatrics* 43:833–839.

Howie, V. M. 1979. Developmental sequelae of chronic otitis media: The effect of early onset of otitis media on educational achievement. *International Journal of Pediatric Otorhinolaryngology* 1:151–155.

Lenneberg, E. H. 1967. *Biological Foundations of Language.* New York: John Wiley & Sons, Inc.

Marchant, C. D., Shurin, P. A., Turczyk, V. A., Wasikowski, D. E., Tutihasi, M. A., and Kinney, S. E. 1984. Course and outcome of otitis media in early infancy: A prospective study. *The Journal of Pediatrics* 104:826–831.

Masters, L., and Marsh, II., G. E. 1978. Middle ear pathology as a factor in learning disabilities. *Journal of Learning Disabilities* 11:103–106.

McGee, R., Silva, P. A., and Stewart, I. A. 1982. Behaviour problems and otitis media with effusion: A report from the Dunedin Multidisciplinary Child Development Study. *New England Medical Journal* 95:655–657.

Menyuk, P. 1980. Effects of persistent otitis media on language development. *Recent Advances in Otitis Media with Effusion* 89 (3, Pt. 2).

Paradise, J. L. 1981. Otitis media during early development: How hazardous to development? A critical review of the evidence. *Pediatrics* 68:869–873.

Pukander, J., Spila, M., and Karma, P. 1984. Occurrence of risk factors in acute otitis media. *In* D. J. Lim (ed.). *Recent Advances in Otitis Media with Effusion.* Philadelphia: B. C. Decker.

Ramey, C. T., and Campbell, F. A. 1979. Early childhood education for psychosocially disadvantaged children: The effects on psychological processes. *American Journal of Mental Deficiency* 83:645–648.

Roberts, J. E., Sanyal, M. A., Burchinal. M. R., Collier, A. M., Ramey, C. T., and Henderson, F. W. In press. Otitis media in early childhood and its relationship to later verbal and academic performance. *Pediatrics.*

Schwartz, R. H., Stool, S. E., Rodriguez, W. J., and Grundfast, K. M. 1981. Acute otitis media: Toward a more precise definition. *Clinical Pediatrics* 20(9):549–554.

Shurin, P. A., Pelton, S. I., Donner, A., and Klein, J. O. 1979. Persistence of middle-ear effusion after acute otitis media in children. *The New England Journal of Medicine* 300:1121–1123.

Silva, P. A., Kirkland, C., Simpson, A., Stewart, I. A., and Williams, S. M. 1982. Some developmental and behavioral problems associated with bilateral otitis media with effusion. *Journal of Learning Disabilities* 15:417–421.

Stern, L. 1986. Childhood ear infections: How to prevent real damage. *Woman's Day* 49(6):23–24.

Teele, D. W., Klein, J. O., and Rosner, B. A. 1984. *Otitis media with effusion during the first three years of life and development of speech and language.* Paper presented by the Greater Boston Otitis Media Study Group, supported by Contract Number NO1 A1 5252 from the National Institute of Allergy and Infectious Diseases.

Tough, J. 1982. Language, poverty, and disadvantage in school. *In* L. Feagans and D. C. Farran (eds.). *The Language of Children Reared in Poverty.* New York: Academic Press.

van Buchem, F. L., Dunk, J. H. M., and van't Hof, M. A. 1981. Therapy of acute otitis media: Myringotomy, antibiotics, or neither? A double-blind study in children. *Lancet* 2:883–887.

Ventry, I. M. 1980. Effects of conductive hearing loss: Fact or fiction. *Journal of Speech and Hearing Disorders* XLV:143–156.

Vinther, B., Brahe-Pedersen, Chr., and Elbrond, O. 1984. Otitis media in childhood: Sociomedical aspects with special reference to day care conditions. *Clinical Otolaryngology* 9:3–8.

Zinkus, P. W., and Gottlieb, M. I. 1980. Patterns of perceptual and academic deficits related to early chronic otitis media. *Pediatrics* 66:246–253.

Zinkus, P. W., Gottlieb, M. I., and Shapiro, M. 1978. Developmental and psychoeducational sequelae of chronic otitis media. *American Journal of Diseases of Children* 132:1100–1104.

# An Analysis of the State of the Science/Art.
# What Do We Need to Know?

# 18

# Cognitive Development in Children with Recurrent Otitis Media: Where Do We Stand?

*James J. Jenkins*

When Dr. Kavanagh opened the conference that is reported in this volume, he reminded us of some of the questions that would arise: Which populations are at risk for recurrent otitis media? Should we intervene medically in the course of otitis media and, if so, when and how? Finally, he raised the major question of the conference— What is the relation between otitis media and the cognitive development of the child? Specifically, what is the relationship between recurrent otitis media and the incidence and extent of language disabilities and learning difficulties?

In the course of the conference we addressed all of these questions, but we were especially concerned with the last one. For the most part we have been occupied with an even narrower focus: *What is the effect of otitis media with effusion (OME) on the child's hearing, and what is the effect of any such conductive hearing loss on that child's cognitive development?* Time and again we turned to two questions: How does otitis media affect hearing in the short term and in the long term, and what is the effect of early fluctuating hearing loss on the nature and course of development?

The participants noted in passing, as I shall here, that otitis media may affect the child through mediating influences other than hearing loss, or via other sequelae of the total experience. For example, the child who is frequently ill may be different from the normal child by that fact alone, without respect to the source of the illness. Also, it is possible that the vestibular system may be involved in some forms of otitis media and that involvement may produce problems with balance and vision. In addition, the treatment of otitis media may produce sequelae through the child's reaction to antimicrobial agents, or the consequences of tube implantation, or the experience of being anaesthetized. Finally, the child may develop a different attitude toward doctors, clinics, treatments, medicines, etc., as a result of early experience associated with the disorder. In short, there may be many consequences of otitis media that we have neglected. But, of course, no conference can cover everything, and, with that apology, we must press on to what the conference participants *did* choose to talk about.

In the course of the conference I heard a number of comments about our lack of information. I began to keep a running account of the sentences that I heard. What follows is a partial list, in no particular order, of some of the things that we confessed we do not know in sufficient detail to answer the questions posed in this conference:

We do not know enough about the consequences of mild to moderate hearing losses.

We do not know much about the consequences of unilateral hearing losses.

We do not know in detail what counts as a "supporting environment" for the development of speech and language in the hearing-impaired child (although we have some strong ideas).

We do not know enough about how to measure cognitive development in an analytic manner, i.e., in the sense of knowing how to measure the "important" aspects of information processing.

We lack testing paradigms that measure, in analytic and fine-grained detail, either speech perception or speech production.

We are not sure what the best measures are to estimate severity in otitis media: frequency, persistence of fluid, or severity of attacks.

We do not have enough information about the relations between pure-tone audiometry, tympanometry, reflectance audiometry, speech discrimination tests, and hearing in noise.

The list could be extended, but it is only a confession of the usual situation in applied science; we never seem to know enough about any problematic situation that we face. A more constructive approach to commenting on the conference is to ask where we are with respect to the major issues developed in the conference.

In the subsequent remarks I will focus on the following questions:

1. What are the relevant facts about otitis media that allow us to bring it under better scrutiny as a predictor of developmental problems?

2. What is the nature and degree of hearing loss associated with otitis media with effusion?

3. What is the relation between mild and moderate fluctuating hearing loss and several aspects of cognitive development?

4. Given our current knowledge, what steps should be taken in our research to give us a more complete picture of the relationships mentioned above?

5. What can we do in clinical practice now to prevent and treat problems in cognitive development in children with recurrent otitis media with effusion?

## RELEVANT FACTS ABOUT THE DISORDER

Many disorders of childhood are extremely difficult to study because of their low incidence in the population. For example, the Sudden Infant Death Syndrome, although it is a frightening spectre for parents, is extremely difficult to study in a prospective manner because of its very low rate of occurrence (about 1 case in 30,000 births). One would have to follow an enormous number of children (at incredible cost) to ensure finding even a few cases in one's sample. In contrast, (unfortunately for many children) the incidence of otitis media is very high. Klein reported that more than two-thirds of the 2,565 children in the prospective Boston study had at least one episode of acute otitis media by the age of three years and more than one-third of the children had at least three episodes by age three. Researchers will obviously not lack for subjects and the research need not search for justification given this rate of the disorder.

Even this high rate of observed cases can be increased by proper selection of the population. Investigators have reported sex differences (males at greater risk than females), race differences (American Indians and Eskimos at higher risk than the White American population; Black Americans at lower risk), familial differences (higher risk if a sibling has had recurrent otitis media), and experience differences (breast-fed children are at lower risk than bottle-fed children, and children in day-care centers at higher risk than children reared at home). Further, in the individual case, early onset (prior to six months of age) of the first instance of otitis media is predictive of recurrent bouts of the disease. (Todd suggested that a major predisposing factor was a genetically "different" eustachian tube which encourages infection.) In addition, certain clinical categories such as children with cleft palate or Down syndrome are known to be subject to very high rates of otitis media. Thus, it is relatively easy to identify a population of children who will have a high rate of otitis media and a high probability of repeated episodes. Prospective studies are obviously feasible, although a variety of questions about adequate controls remains.

Another finding of potentially great importance is that the persistence of effusion (and resulting mild to moderate hearing loss) is much longer than the persistence of the acute phase of the infection. Thus, while parents and the physician may have done all that was needed to reduce the infection, fever, and pain, the presence of fluid in the middle ear may be observed for many weeks. The impressive figures in Klein's report suggest that the "half-life" of effusion is about one month; that is, about half of the children may have detectable effusion three to four weeks after the acute phase of the disease is treated. This fact, coupled with a high frequency of recurrence, suggests that many children may suffer from reduced hearing for a substantial portion of their early years.

## OTITIS MEDIA AND HEARING DISABILITY

It is surprising that we do not have more data on the temporal course and degree of hearing loss associated with OME. At the same time perhaps there is little need for such data because there is general consensus that otitis media is associated with conductive hearing loss and in some cases with sensorineural loss as a result of invasion of toxins and inflammatory mediators through the round-window membrane. In addition, current information concerning the persistence of effusion following the acute phase of otitis media leads to the reasonable belief that there is fluctuating hearing loss over a long period. Because otitis media is recurrent in many cases, there is good reason to believe that at least some children must suffer a mild to moderate hearing loss over a significant portion of their early lives. The full extent of this hearing loss is not precisely determined, nor, I suspect, is it widely appreciated by the physicians, audiologists, and therapists who deal with these children.

If one uses the child with permanent sensorineural loss as a model of what to expect in the cases of persisting variable loss, there is serious cause for concern. Matkin points out that the magnitude of expressive and receptive language delay in children with permanent loss is directly correlated with the magnitude of the hearing loss. Although there are several difficulties in comparing these two groups of children, the implication that the children with recurrent OME are at risk for speech and language problems because of their hearing loss is clear.

Because hearing impairments have widespread effects beyond the specific acquisition of the speech-sound system of a language, there is ample reason to examine the acquisition of linguistic, social, and cognitive skills by these children as well. The form, the content and the use of language by these children may be aberrant and that, in turn, may adversely affect the child's social interactions, acquisition of information about the world, expression of emotions, and behavior in a host of situations, especially academic performance and achievement.

## HEARING LOSS AND COGNITIVE DEVELOPMENT

One important emphasis in this conference that would have been missing some years ago was the concentration on the early years, from birth to three years. The more we learn about cognitive and perceptual development, the more we are inclined to attribute importance to these very early years. In the last few decades there has been a rash of studies pointing to the first year of life as an important, active, learning period. Because this period coincides with the peak in episodes of otitis media, there is great concern with examining the relationship of hearing loss and subsequent cognitive development.

Unfortunately, not all studies of the cognitive development of children with hearing deficits can be considered to be studies of the consequences of the hearing deficit itself. Matkin pointed out that at least one third of all cases of bilateral hearing loss (due to sensorineural impairment) have additional handicapping conditions which may confound the results of these studies and render the conclusions suspect with respect to the causal role of hearing loss. Matkin argued that we need a list of important variables that must be controlled before we can expect the field to generate studies of sufficient quality to be interpretable. Further, for the studies to be useful to the field, they must be reported in sufficient detail to allow for appropriate interpretations of the data. Matkin reported that in most studies, even those published in refereed journals, there is not enough information about characteristics of the subject sample to enable us to place the results in a meaningful matrix.

How severe must a hearing loss be to be an important factor in cognitive development? At present we cannot say. Strange suggested that the terms used by the audiologists (mild, moderate, severe) may be misleading descriptors with respect to the impact that the hearing disorder might have during the period that the child is developing a language-specific phonemic system. Although an adult who already knows the language can comprehend speech even with a considerable hearing loss, part of that achievement is due to the redundancy of language as a system. This enables the experienced language user to decode the message "from the top down" even though the listener has relatively impoverished information from the auditory input. On the other hand, when one is acquiring the system, such impoverished or degraded information may simply be insufficient to support the comprehension of the message or to furnish data that will enable the child to abstract the phonological system.

If one studies the figures presented in Matkin's chapter, it is clear that even a mild hearing loss can render the quietest speech sounds below threshold and unintelligible. If, during the first years of life, children are abstracting the speech patterns of importance to their native language, the degraded or distorted signal may lead to abnormal patterns. With a fluctuating hearing loss, such children may receive inconsistent and inadequate information, or may have to devote so much attention to the decoding process itself that there is little capacity left over for higher-order cognitive operations. If children are, in fact, doing something different or expending more resources on lower levels of speech perception, we may see deficits in other processes at a later period. Thus, Strange speculates that the first year might be crucial to the development of the phonemic system and that difficulties during that period might later lead to difficulties in the acquisition of markers for syntactic structures important to linguistic development. A delay at that level might, in turn, generate difficulties continually when the child is learning to read, and as the child lags behind and the culture requires the acquisition of new linguistic and cognitive tasks.

Menyuk pointed out that this does not necessarily mean that there is a "critical period" for speech and language acquisition in the strict sense but rather that delays may accumulate and have future consequences. Gelman argued that there is little evidence for "critical periods" in human cognitive development of any sort. She also urged us to consider the extent to which the child structures and manipulates the preschool world, thus raising the possibility that hearing-impaired children may create "different worlds" for themselves which may lead to different kinds of learning (some of which might be advantageous and some disadvantageous.)

Davis reinforced the point that language learning is a continuous process that goes on over a period of many years and that the children who are hearing-impaired are continually playing "catch-up." Even though language learning may not be strictly sequential, learning does build on previous learning and deficits will have further implications at later points. Instead of "critical periods" it seems that we would do well to talk about "optimal periods" or sequences of development that are appropriate in our time, in our culture, and under the medical, educational, and social circumstances in which we find ourselves.

## FUTURE RESEARCH DIRECTIONS

With regard to research, we are in a position that occurs so often that I have a little slogan for it: "We need to know what we need to know before we can find out what we need to know." To put this in a less tangled linguistic form, we must have a clear enough picture of the situation to be able to define critical issues before we can mount research leading to a clarification and understanding of those issues. To a certain extent, I believe that this conference has provided some of that kind of clarification of issues. We are in a better position now to set forth some of the general research needs and even some of the specific research problems that need to be investigated than we were before this conference.

One impressive finding that was highlighted by this conference is the presence and persistence of effusion in the absence of the acute symptomatology that is usually associated with otitis media. It is apparent that we have no real base rate data for effusion. As Shurin and Klein pointed out, we cannot know the base rate of this "silent" effusion unless we specifically look for it as part of well-baby examinations, as part of specific studies of children at risk, and as part of the follow-up of children who have had episodes of otitis media. This information is needed and can be obtained. It is a matter of getting the right people to obtain it.

A second obvious need is for information relating effusion to hearing status. We simply do not know enough at the present time about the relation of the findings of otoscopy and tympanometry to measures of hearing loss. Although the data are troublesome to obtain, a study with extensive and repeated measurements of effusion and hearing loss is clearly possible; it simply needs to be funded and performed. Such a detailed study could furnish the fine-grained information concerning effusion in a small sample of children to complement the data asked for in the large-scale base rate studies suggested above. At the same time the specific relation between effusion and audiological data could be worked out in more detail. As Matkin and Bess emphasized several times, we are not going to advance our understanding of the effects of otitis media on development without good information on the nature, degree, and persistence of the hearing loss of the children involved. Without such data, we are still just supposing what might be the case.

Of course, there are formidable problems in the examination of young children. As often was observed during the conference, it is difficult to examine an infant's ears properly; it is difficult to employ pneumatic otoscopy with small children and sometimes painful for the child; and it is difficult to assess the hearing and speech discrimination of infants and children. Nevertheless, recent developments in technique and technology are making these examinations more feasible. Several behavioral techniques for assessing hearing thresholds of infants and small children have been developed and can be performed in a relatively short time in a computer-assisted procedure in the clinic.

With these techniques a trained technician can conduct a rather rapid appraisal of the infant's capacity for free-field binaural detection of acoustic stimuli. While such techniques are coarse, they can provide important data concerning functional hearing.

One of the major research needs that became apparent in the discussions concerned observational research in the home. Menyuk mentioned watching for changes in the parents' behavior as the child goes into and out of an otitis media episode. In addition, the Boston study will examine different patterns of parent-child interaction in a "teaching" situation. But many of the naturalistic observations reported at this conference suggested a number of specifics to be studied in the child's usual settings. Feagans is curious about the child's performance in the presence of speech noise. Her work suggests that in some cases children who are communicatively adequate in a one-to-one situation may not be able to function satisfactorily in an open classroom or in the presence of other voices. All of us know that a standard complaint of aging adults is that they have great difficulties in understanding speech in social groups although they may still have normal audiograms. Apparently, the same is true of some children whose hearing status is marginal.

These studies are only a beginning, however. For instance, throughout the conference we heard that improvement in balance and motor control are reported after tubes are inserted. Behavior problems are said to disappear and the child "becomes a different person." These assertions can be investigated with relatively straightforward observational schedules and simple tests. Beyond that, with careful preparation we could examine the extent to which children with otitis media do, in fact, create a different environment or shape the world to fit their restricted auditory capacity.

Another important question is, do children with recurrent otitis media have the same attentional patterns as children who do not have repeated episodes? Again, Feagans' research suggests that these children may have learned, as a result of their unreliable reception histories, *not to attend to acoustic stimuli.* Gelman wondered whether these children might find it difficult to engage in *any* learning activity, regardless of modality of stimulation, during the acute phase of the infection. Matkin and Friel-Patti told us that parents describe children with otitis media as lethargic, irritable, and unresponsive. One reaction to this situation could be greatly reduced interaction with other family members as they try to cope with the sick child. As Davis pointed out, keeping the child quiet, isolated and non-interacting may be exactly the wrong thing to do relative to the child's cognitive development. And, of course, the problem may be compounded in a family where the parents are employed outside the home, both in terms of care for the child and in terms of the parent's reaction to being forced to take time off from work and career. It is clear that we need to gather firm data before we can decide whether these are important variables which affect the development of these children.

MISSED RESEARCH OPPORTUNITIES

It is easy to feel that there are many problems that we cannot solve because we do not have definitive measures, but there are many cases where the techniques are within our grasp but we do not yet have the desired information. I am impressed by the fact that we have missed opportunities to obtain much of this information. Part of our failure is attributable to a lack of resources and part is probably a failure to realize that such data were needed. But in any case we are missing opportunities.

As mentioned above, it is often asserted that a child who undergoes tympanostomy tube insertion "acts like a different person." Why do we lack careful data to verify and explicate that statement? We know in advance that the operation to place the tubes is going to be done. We could very well put observers in the child's day-care setting, in the home, or in the preschool. We could obtain behavioral data about the child both before and after the surgical procedure. We have a variety of behavioral schedules to choose from; we know how to train observers; we *can* conduct this study, but we have not. Such studies are expensive, of course, and they are socially intrusive, but they can be performed. (In our department there is a child-abuse clinic that sends trained graduate students into the homes of child abusers for relatively long periods of time. This is viewed as an important prerequisite for and adjunct to successful behavioral therapy. If we can enter the home under those drastic conditions, we can do so under much more benign circumstances.)

I was surprised that we have so little information on the hearing of children before, during, and after medical therapy. Todd collected that information as a standard protocol in his Arizona study, but it is not normal procedure. In the more typical case a particular therapeutic procedure is begun and the hearing is not checked after the acute phase of the disorder is cleared.

On the same grounds, I would argue that we ought to have many studies of the relation of tympanometry to speech discrimination and to audiometric profiles, yet such data are relatively rare. We have the techniques and the cases are available; we simply have not taken advantage of the opportunities to gather the data.

STUDIES ON SMALL SAMPLES

Of course we cannot have an unlimited number of large-scale, global studies such as the ones reported by Klein and Menyuk, Todd,

Friel-Patti, and others. These studies, precisely because they are global and relating very large numbers of variables, cannot do all of the analytic research that the participants in this conference have expressed a need for. I think we are seriously in need of "little studies" that examine in fine detail the points where we need critical information. As Gelman suggested early in the conference, we need to be looking for special interactions.

I think that Eimas' work is to be praised here. Recall that he studied children with and without a history of extensive otitis media. While there are always ways to criticize the sampling and while one can always cavil, Eimas has set before us an impressive interaction. He showed that the clinical population was like the normal population with respect to loudness discrimination but *in the same testing situation* was unlike them in speech discrimination. Further, he found that as the speech was degraded, the differences between the clinical cases and the normal children increased. To conduct such studies of children requires a great investment of time (for both investigators and children) and special apparatus in the laboratory. It is not easy to incorporate this testing into a global study with many variables, but it is wholly appropriate to conduct such studies as projects in themselves, always remembering to look for interactions of the kind that are specifically of interest to our concerns.

In passing, I must put in a word for "flawed studies." I am not in favor of doing "sloppy work" but certainly we must not wait until we can run perfect studies before we do any research. All of us at the conference know of studies that were flawed, but were also informative and pointed the way to more adequate research. We know that all studies except laboratory exercises are flawed in some respect. The brutal fact is that clinical work is always subject to great limitations. Just because a study is not perfect does not mean that we cannot learn something from it; history refutes that claim. But if we do not run any study, it is certain that we will not learn anything.

## CLINICAL PRACTICE

As Davis and Matkin urged, when we are confronted with a child who may be at risk (with, say, persistent effusion and the anticipation of repeated bouts of otitis media), it is simply good practice to instill good speaking habits in the parents and to "inoculate" them psychologically against their attributing "stubbornness" and "willful inattention" to the child who may be suffering from a fluctuating hearing loss. These procedures cannot in themselves do damage and there is the possibility that they may do a great deal of good.

Clinic handouts of instructional materials and programs of

parent education are important responsibilities that must be recognized. By sensitizing parents (without frightening them), we can recruit them as observers to detect the symptoms that indicate that a child is not hearing well. They can then direct the therapist's attention to the potential problem. Without such sensitization, misinterpretation is both possible and likely. As Giebink suggests, this is the kind of material that should be included in the "Guidelines for Child Health Screening" published by the American Academy of Pediatrics.

## A FINAL WORD

This conference has achieved an impressive consensus. The participants in the main agreed that recurrent otitis media with effusion represents a hazard to the cognitive development of children, even though the complete details have yet to be worked out.

The mediating variable that was discussed here was that of hearing loss. Recurrent otitis media with effusion can result in a fluctuating hearing loss which in some cases interferes with children's hearing for a major portion of their early lives. Research on the development of speech perception and production marks these early years as those in which children normally abstract and identify the phonemes of their native language. The acoustic information for many of these classes of speech sounds may well be unavailable for children with mild to moderate hearing losses. There is a strong suggestion that a lag in early development has ramifications for the later stages of language development as well. It seems highly likely that language delay has further consequences for the cognitive development of the child. A variety of additional possible sequelae were suggested, ranging from a general pattern of auditory inattention to maladaptive social behavior.

Research is currently underway on major aspects of the disorder. Causes and correlates of otitis media and its detection, prevention, and treatment are being explored on the medical front. The consequences of fluctuating hearing loss are being explored by audiologists, speech pathologists, and psychologists. In almost every domain, there is a need for further, more detailed information which is within the reach of current research technologies. This conference's participants urged that research be pursued both at the level of large global studies trying to bring the major variables into relation with each other and at the level of small studies examining specific effects of the disorder and determining the relations of various measures of physical examinations and hearing functions.

# Index

*(Numbers in italics indicate material in figures or tables.)*

# Name Index

*(Only the names of authors whose work is discussed in some detail are included in this index.)*